Published by Avenue Media Solutions

© Neil Thompson 2022

All Rights Reserved

It is refreshing to come across an HR book that bridges the gap perfectly between the academic theory and the practicality of 'how to do it'. Dr Neil Thompson takes us on a humanistic journey that genuinely captures the human dimension of people management. This is an extremely helpful manual full of important and practical information about promoting well-being to achieve the best outcome for various everyday people management issues. The easy-to-understand inclusive language of this book calls to anyone interested in people management, meaning this is a perfect book for students, HR leaders, and practitioners. I know I will be recommending this to my university students. Go read it now, it is a breath of fresh air. **Rayhan Abdullah Zakaria Lecturer and Researcher, University of Chester Business School**

Mostly people do not leave a job, they leave a boss. This is challenging for organizations as they want to create workplaces that are psychologically safe, inviting, inspiring and stimulating. They will want to enhance a leadership culture that fosters trust as the ultimate platform for growth of individuals, teams, and customer relationships. This manual is a great gift for leaders and their organizations. It helps us understand the often complex, emotionally loaded dynamics of working with people, particularly when we are confronted with change of all kinds. Neil has brought together deep knowledge and embodied experience in an impressive manual for this decade of transitions. He shows us the way forward! **Jakob van Wielink, The School for Transition, the Netherlands and Portland Institute for Loss and Transition.**

This manual takes account of the need to ensure that people are at the centre of the organization. Recovering from the pandemic there has never been a timelier reminder of the need to ensure that leading, supporting and developing staff are critical aspects of creating the right organizational culture to grow and develop. Written with sensitivity, the manual brings together essential learning and underpinning theoretical knowledge and frameworks to support readers with essential learning in the art of promoting staff and their well-being. I urge everyone who is in a leadership role to invest in this publication.
Lee Pardy-McLaughlin, Principal Social Worker, Stoke City Council

This practice manual is an essential handbook for managers and leaders who want to develop the full potential of their people. It not only covers the fundamental issues of human resource management, but also highlights important topics that organizations sometimes find difficult to address, such as empowerment, stress management, mental health, equality, diversity, inclusion, the promotion of well-being at work (and more). All of these are crucial for best practice. This book covers the essential elements necessary to make individuals feel valued and develop a sense of belonging, making the organization a highly desirable place to work.
Dr Rozana Huq, Organizational Behaviourist, Author, Leadership Educator, RHM LEADERSHIP, www.rhmleadership.com

The Managing People Practice Manual

By

Neil Thompson

With a Foreword by Alan Winters

Contents

Welcome	2
About Avenue Media Solutions	3
About the author	4
Foreword by Alan Winters, Co-founder/COO, Vigoroom	5
Introduction	7
Part One: The Fundamentals of People Management	**17**
Chapter 1: Equality, Diversity and Inclusion	18
Chapter 2: Communication	28
Chapter 3: Supervision	37
Chapter 4: Recruitment, Selection and Workforce Planning	48
Chapter 5: Induction	57
Chapter 6: Workload Management	67
Chapter 7: Appraisal and Performance Management	77
Chapter 8: Staff Departures	87
Chapter 9: Disciplinary Matters	96
Chapter 10: Dealing with Grievances	106
Part Two: Achieving Best Outcomes	**116**
Chapter 11: Leadership	117
Chapter 12: Managing Change	128
Chapter 13: Industrial Relations	138
Chapter 14: Team Development	149
Chapter 15: Motivating Staff	160
Chapter 16: Staff Retention	169
Chapter 17: Career Planning	179
Chapter 18: Mentoring and Coaching	188
Chapter 19: Training and Development	197
Chapter 20: Making Work Meaningful: Meeting Spiritual Needs	207
Part Three: Promoting Well-being	**216**
Chapter 21: Dealing with Stress	217
Chapter 22: Health and Safety	227
Chapter 23: Sickness Absence	236
Chapter 24: Bullying and Harassment	245
Chapter 25: Dealing with Conflict	254
Chapter 26: Handling Aggression	263
Chapter 27: Loss, Grief and Trauma	272
Chapter 28: Mental Health Problems	282
Chapter 29: Drug and Alcohol Abuse	291
Chapter 30: Inclusion	300
References	309

Welcome

... to *The Managing People Practice Manual*. This manual has been developed as an important resource for anyone involved in a role that includes managing people. It has long been recognized that an organization's most important resource is its human resource – that is, its people. Put another way, an organization's success depends on its people – who they are, how they are treated and how effective those people in management and leadership positions are. This manual has been written to help make a real difference in terms of how people are managed and led. In technical terms, it is here to help you and your organization get the best return on your investment in people. Or, in more human terms, this manual will help the people you manage and lead to not only survive, but also to thrive – to flourish as fully as possible.

Much of the manual was originally published in book form as *People Management* (Palgrave Macmillan, 2013). This version retains the blend of theory and practice, but with greater emphasis on the practice guidance offered. It is also considerably expanded and updated.

About Avenue Media Solution

Avenue Media Solutions offers a range of learning resources:

- Books and practice manuals
    - The Problem Solver's Practice Manual
    - The Values-based Practice Manual
    - The Spirituality and Religion Practice Manual
- Training manuals
    - Promoting Equality, Valuing Diversity
    - Developing Leadership
    - Reflective Supervision
- E-learning courses
    - Making Appraisal Work
    - Effective Meetings
    - How to Lead a Team under Immense Pressure

The two linking threads across our work are **people** and **communication**. Throughout our work we recognize the significance of the human element of people's working lives and the central role of communication. So, if it is a matter of personal and professional development, our focus is on helping you achieve the best results at value-for-money prices.

Our products and services are available from: **www.humansolutions.org.uk**

About the author

Dr Neil Thompson is an independent writer, educator and adviser. Very many people have come to see Neil as a guide and mentor, not only on their learning journey, but also on their whole outlook on life, people, problems and potential. With an impeccable academic pedigree, an outstanding publications record and a wealth of direct experience of making a positive difference in a number of ways, he stands out as a source of invaluable wisdom and guidance.

He has held full or honorary professorships at five UK universities and is currently a visiting professor at the Open University. He has well over 40 years' experience in the helping professions as a practitioner, manager, educator and consultant

He has over 40 books to his name. These include:

Promoting Equality (Bloomsbury, 4th edn, 2018)
Effective Communication (Bloomsbury, 3rd edn, 2018)
The Managing Stress Practice Manual (Avenue Media Solutions, 2019)
The Problem Solver's Practice Manual (Avenue Media Solutions, 2020)
The Values-based Practice Manual (with Bernard Moss, Avenue Media Solutions, 2020)
People Skills (Bloomsbury, 5th edn, 2021)
Anti-racism for Beginners (Avenue Media Solutions, 2021)
The Critically Reflective Practitioner (with Sue Thompson, Bloomsbury, 3rd edn, 2023)

He has qualifications in social work, management (MBA), training and development, mediation and dispute resolution, as well as a first-class honours degree in Social Sciences, a doctorate (PhD) and a higher doctorate (DLitt). Neil is a Fellow of the Chartered Institute of Personnel and Development and the Royal Society of Arts, elected to the latter on the basis of his contribution to workplace learning. He was the founding editor of the *British Journal of Occupational Learning*.

He is also the Vice President of Vigoroom UK, a sophisticated employee wellness platform geared towards improving productivity, engagement and more user-friendly workplaces (www.vigoroom.co.uk).

His website, with his acclaimed *Manifesto for Making a Difference*, is at www.NeilThompson.info. He is active on social media – see https://linktr.ee/drneilthompson.

Foreword

I first met Dr Neil Thompson several years ago after researching possible new expert contributors for my corporate wellness platform, Vigoroom. We were looking to add to our team of experts to provide new content for mental and emotional health. This was an area of heightened concern for our corporate clients, whose employees were experiencing dramatically escalated rates of clinical depression and anxiety disorder during the COVID pandemic. Although we were a relatively new player in the crowded wellness space, we had gone through this "search process" several times previously and had a sense of the type of person – strong credentials, smart, good communicator, personable – who fit best with us. It was immediately clear that Neil met all of our core criteria.

As I got to know Neil better, something else more important happened. Almost every conversation with Neil led me to periods of self-reflection, questioning assumptions, rethinking goals and objectives, and even considering new ways of looking at and talking about the role and purpose of our company. During my career as a creative and business executive in the media, broadcasting and technology fields (and later as an entrepreneur), I had crossed paths with many brilliant, dynamic people. But the experience with Neil and his impact on me was an unusual and exhilarating experience.

Thinking more about this, I realized that Neil continually brings an insightful and fresh perspective, and presents it in a thoughtful, warm manner. He takes the complex and makes it easy to understand and digest. And this has made a big impact on me.

With *The Managing People Practice Manual*, Neil offers a unique and comprehensive vantage point into the world of workplace wellness. It's built on his lengthy academic and professional foundation in social work. Social work is where the core values are the dignity of the individual, the importance of interpersonal relationships, and well-being. As Neil described it to me recently, it's amazing how the dynamics of individuals and groups within an organization reflect the principles of social work.

This is different than a human resources or 'people management' perspective. Neil's entry point into workplace wellness is that when it comes to human resources, by focusing on the *human*, we make people more *resourceful*.

The Managing People Practice Manual is an essential guide for anyone who manages people. You will appreciate the easy-to-digest structure that Dr Thompson uses for each topical area – the organizational theory, the issues that come up in practice, and questions/exercises the reader should entertain. It is comprehensive in scope. It is broad-based theoretically, drawing on psychology, sociology and organizational theory. The thirty chapters each cover an important aspect of people management - from equity, diversity and inclusion to team development to managing conflict. If you're looking for a 'go to' resource for the broad array of issues that arise in the workplace – this book is for you.

The last few years have resulted in a more complex and changing workplace. We have seen the impact of the worldwide COVID pandemic, the shift of a large portion of the workforce from home based to office based, and a fundamental change in how people view and experience work within the scope of their broader lives. These are changes that are not temporary. And forward-thinking leaders will need to draw on many tools to keep their organizations on track and growing. New features in the employer-employee dynamic mean that organizations will require a firm foundation in working productively with employees.

This is why *The Managing People Practice Manual* is so essential right now. Neil shares critical insights and important action steps to create an environment where people feel positive about coming to work each day, are put in a position to deliver their best performance and contribute to the attraction/retention of valuable human talent.

Alan Winters, MBA, Co-Founder/COO, Vigoroom

Introduction

The overall aim of the manual is to provide a substantial introduction to the knowledge, skills and values managers need to draw on in order to get the best out of their staff. It is intended that it will appeal primarily to students of management, leadership and human resources and practising managers and human resource professionals.

The specific objectives are:

- To demonstrate the central role of managing people for all managers, leaders and human resource professionals
- To introduce readers to key elements of people management
- To provide a foundation of knowledge that will act as a gateway to the further development of knowledge, skills and confidence in this area.

The manual parallels my highly successful *People Skills* book (Bloomsbury, 5th edn, 2021) in terms of structure, style and level. There are also links to be drawn to my *The Problem Solver's Practice Manual* (Avenue Media Solutions, 2020) which offers 101 problem-solving tools of benefit in managing people.

There is a significant irony relating to the existing literature. This is because much of it is very dry and technical and, despite its focus on *people,* so much of it fails to capture a truly human dimension. It lacks the human warmth, vitality and passion that are needed if we are to do justice to the complexities involved in working with people. My approach has therefore been to combine not only theory and practice, but also head and heart and, in doing so, to be experienced as *authentic*, as genuinely human, rather than cold and clinical.

I also believe the length of the manual is significant, in so far as it fills a gap between the quite short 'how to do it' type books that have little or no theoretical content and the major textbooks that provide far more detail than most people are looking for.

The manual's consistent and coherent message is that effective people management plays a central role as an underpinning of organizational success. It draws on wide multidisciplinary roots (including elements of psychology, sociology, social policy, philosophy and anthropology, as well as specific management and human resource theories) and the skilful integration of theory, research and practice.

It is to be hoped that the insights it offers will provide a firm foundation for continuing to develop your knowledge and understanding of the complexities of helping people achieve optimal outcomes across a wide variety of work settings. People really are at the heart of organizational success, and so there is considerable benefit for all parties to be gained from developing a more sophisticated understanding of human resource management. This manual can play a key role in promoting that fuller understanding.

There are various reasons for developing this manual. For some time now, it has been a mainstay of human resource practice to assume that people are an organization's most important resource: its human resource. There is substantial evidence to suggest that the people aspect of an organization is indeed a fundamental aspect of that organization's success or otherwise (Turner, 2002). Stewart (2010) makes the point that management is all about people. In effect, he argues, it comes down to the simple fact that if you are nice to people, they will usually be nice back to you. He describes this as a timeless precept that is largely tautological. In other words, it pretty much goes without saying that if you do not treat people well, you will significantly reduce the chances of achieving optimal outcomes. This fundamental point is central to what this manual is all about. There is, however, a considerable irony in the fact that, while people clearly are important to organizations, the language that is used to refer to employees is often of a dehumanizing nature. The very term, 'human resource', for example, has been criticized for neglecting the fact that people are people first – that is, glossing over the human part of the phrase and hearing only the reference to 'resources', there to be used and exploited (Bolton and Houlihan, 2007b). As Allcorn points out: 'the workplace is saturated with our humanity' (2005, p. 21). In this regard, the UK Arbitration and Conciliation Advisory Service offer helpful comment:

> It is often said that people are every organisation's most important asset. This is perfectly true, but people are not like other assets. As well as being very valuable in their own right – in terms of performance skills and creativity – it is individual employees who bind every other aspect of working life together.
>
> (ACAS, 2015)

People managers (whether line managers or human resources professionals) would therefore be very wise to take on board the need to ensure that this vitally important resource – the organization's people – is managed effectively, paying due attention to the implications of the fact that this is a *human* resource, and not one that can simply be moved about and manipulated at will without major detrimental consequences for all concerned.

More recently, the term 'human capital' has been used to refer to people in the workplace as well and that, too, can be seen as a dehumanizing term, in so far as the emphasis is on the objective measurement of what the workforce is worth as a form of organizational capital (Becker, Huselid and Ulrich, 2001), with little or no reference to the subjective dimension of human experience, relatively little emphasis on the fact that the better we treat people, the more value they will be to the organization. A fundamental underpinning of this manual is the idea that, if we are to get the best out of people, if we are to help employees to achieve their best, then we need to move away from dehumanizing language (and practices) and have a much fuller sense of the humanity of the people who populate organizations (Bolton and Houlihan, 2007b). It is important to distinguish between getting the *best* out of people (that is, facilitating their achievement of optimal results and development) and getting the *most* out of them – that is, trying to drain every last drop of work and energy from them (Thompson, 2016a).

One of the implications of this is that we need to pay attention to the well-being of the people who populate our organizations. The notion of workplace well-being has become something of a fashionable idea in recent years, but we need to recognize that it is more than a fad, that there is a genuine need to take seriously the idea that if an organization does not invest in staff care, then it will not be able to fulfil its potential. As Robertson and Tinline comment:

> Psychological well-being [PWB] is the platform for low rates of sickness absence, optimal levels of employee turnover and high productivity. It is worth emphasising that the general reaction of employees to a PWB initiative is likely to be positive – because the aim is to make them feel good at work. This is very different from some other types of initiatives that are designed to improve organisational performance and which often elicit more guarded, or even actively negative reactions. This is another facet of the benefits associated with pursuing a PWB approach.
>
> (2008, p. 48)

This is part of what is involved in recognizing that people are a human resource and not just a resource per se. It entails recognizing that employees have well-being needs (the need to be treated with dignity, for example), and if we ignore those needs, not only will we fail to get the best out of them, but we could also create major problems (stress, conflict, sickness absence and so on). This is not to say that staff need to be pampered or 'wrapped in cotton wool', but it does mean that we need to clear about what needs to be done to ensure that staff are empowered to do their best, with no unnecessary obstacles brought about by a failure to see them as people first and a resource second. We will return to this point below.

This manual is also important in terms of the messages it gives for wider society, in the sense that we need to recognize the importance of work in people's lives (Cheese, 2021; Jaffe, 2-21. Work is a key factor underpinning not only the economy, but also the quality of life of our citizens. There are therefore wider social goals that can be achieved with a fuller understanding of the challenges of people management in contemporary organizations (this is consistent with the idea of corporate social responsibility – Crane *et al.*, 2009).

Organizational toxicity

Certain organizations can be very positive places to work, with the people who work there enjoying great job satisfaction and benefiting from being validated as human beings. It is not uncommon for people to report that a particular period of employment was extremely enjoyable, rewarding and enriching. However, unfortunately, this is not always the case. For many people, work is something just to be endured, and the organization they work within is seen in not particularly positive terms. Sadly, for some other people, work is a major detrimental feature of their life. This could be because of: stress; bullying or harassment; conflict; discrimination and related matters; or a combination of any of these. The result can be that someone's life is made a misery because of their negative experiences of working life. Sometimes this is temporary, but at other times bad experiences at work can lead to long-term problems – for example, someone who is perpetually anxious and unconfident as a result of having been bullied.

But perhaps what is worst of all is when organizations become so harmful that they regularly bring pain, distress, suffering and even trauma because of very destructive processes that are going on within them. Such organizations are often described as 'toxic', as if the environment there poisons people. Walton provides a helpful insight into this:

> a toxic organisation is defined as one within which behaviours which poison, are disruptive, destructive, exploitive, dysfunctional and abusive are pervasive and tolerated. Instances of this would include workplace bullying and harassment in its various forms, deception and fraudulent dealings, the forced imposition of unrealistic workloads and the fostering of disruptive internal competition resulting in bitter and destructive 'turf' battles. In such environments feuding between different departments and functions is likely to lead to a 'blame' culture, embedded patterns of misinformation and misrepresentation, together with the condoning of overly competitive interpersonal behaviour.
>
> (2008, pp. 9–10)

This passage presents in a nutshell the importance of good people management, as the harmful processes described here can feature very strongly in working life if the people managers in that particular organization are not taking their responsibilities seriously. Precisely what those responsibilities are will be an important feature of each of the chapters that follow. If we are not 'tuned in' to what is required of us and/or not making the positive difference expected of us, then the net result could easily be that we are contributing, albeit unwittingly, to a toxic organization.

A key part of avoiding the development of a toxic organization is the recognition of the importance of trust. Without a bedrock of trust people managers will struggle to get people 'on board' and help them achieve their best. The good practices that help to build up trust will be precisely the same ones that will help to prevent a culture of toxicity from developing.

Johnson argues that:

> many employers and employees feel that trust has gone: packed its bags one day and left town for good. If that's true – and many think it is – then what's in the gaping chasm that trust left behind when it walked out the door? Is there something else in this post-industrial, knowledge-driven age that is a superior product to trust that can keep us in mindless corporate ecstasy forever? The simple short answer to that is No.
>
> (2004, p. 9)

Trust is particularly important as the basis of the respect and credibility people managers need to be able to influence staff in a positive direction. This will therefore feature in many of the chapters of the manual, although it could potentially be discussed in every single one, such is its importance.

One further important point to note is that organizations can become toxic because the people managers within that organization 'lose the plot'. That is, they can get so immersed in day-to-day pressures, tasks and hassles that they lose sight of the bigger picture. They forget about the importance of the human dimension of working life and the need to take such matters very seriously. The result is that the human factors are neglected because people who should have retained a strategic overview of the people issues have allowed themselves to get bogged down in the minutiae of operational matters. They have failed to retain a firm grip on critically reflective practice and have therefore not been thinking through the consequences of their actions. They have thereby been contributing to a culture characterized by what comes to be seen as having no real commitment to the human dimension of human resources. Critically reflective people managers can very much be part of the solution, but people managers who have 'lost the plot' can be very much part of the problem.

The employer–employee relationship

Central to this manual is the recognition that people management is not simply a technical matter of following procedures. It requires the ability to form meaningful and effective working relationships with staff and other people managers. This involves being able to manage some of the inevitable tensions that arise between the interests of the organization and those of staff. Colling and Terry point out that employees:

> have an abiding interest in cooperating to ensure the viability and success of the firm and thereby their employment, but they will guard against arbitrary or excessive demands placed upon them. In Edwards' term (1986), therefore, the employment relationship is characterized by 'structured antagonism'. There is an underlying conflict of interest between employers and workers but it is not always apparent. Contingent pressures may act on the parties to induce high levels of cooperation but tensions may remain beneath the surface and emerge during moments of crisis or change. An ability to understand and anticipate changes in the character and perception of employment relations is thus an important requirement of those involved in them.
>
> (2010a, p. 8)

These tensions need not be destructive. Indeed, it is the hallmark of high-quality people management that we are able to create win-win situations by trying to ensure, as far as possible, that the needs of both the organization and of staff are met. Sometimes this is relatively straightforward, while at others it can be very challenging indeed. However, if we are able to do our jobs effectively in each of the areas covered in this manual, we will be in a significantly stronger position to: (i) prevent any such tensions from becoming problematic; and (ii) deal with them successfully whenever they do lead to problems.

Strategic human resources

The human resource element of organization life is often referred to these days as a strategic enterprise (Turner, 2002). It is important to ask ourselves what that means. Strategy is the overall plan of an organization to achieve its goals, and so, from that point of view, it can be seen that no organization is going to be successful in achieving its goals if it neglects the needs of the people working in that organization and does not take account of such basic factors as how many people are needed, with what skills, what knowledge, what experience and so on. But, beyond these basic elements of HR, there is also the question of how fundamental a role people play in the way in which an organization moves towards its goals.

An important distinction in terms of strategy is that between planned and emergent (Whittington *et al.*, 2020). The traditional idea is that strategy is planned, that the senior figures in an organization sit down and develop an explicit strategy identifying their vision of where they want to be and what steps they need to take to get there. However, Porter (2004) has argued that strategy in reality is not quite so clear cut, that it is more a case of emergent strategy – that is, while an organization goes about its business, its overall sense of direction and its purpose change and evolve over time. This latter version of strategy also relies on having the people issues correctly balanced. We can see, then, that whichever way we look at strategy, it would be a mistake not to include the people element within it. For example, a strategy that relates purely to financial or technological matters, or other such concerns in an organization, without also incorporating the human element is likely to be a very weak and vulnerable strategy. It has to be recognized that all enterprise is a human enterprise, in the sense that, whatever other aspects of strategy we are looking at, there will be a human dimension to it. For example, the financial side of things will depend on having the right people who are able to deal with the finances appropriately and do what is necessary to generate the income needed. If we look at the technological side of strategy, then technology is of little use unless there are sufficient people with the appropriate knowledge, skills and experience to be able to use that technology to optimal effect.

Similarly, where technical, financial or other problems arise, they will often originate from the human dimension of the workplace. In this regard, the comments of Argyris are insightful: 'Time and time again, we found examples where the basis for many so-called organizational or technical problems were actually rooted in the feelings people held' (1999, p. 213). The common view that people issues are, or should be, subordinate to other organizational concerns can therefore be seen to be highly problematic. Consequently, what we need to do is to make people less invisible in organizational strategy. Much of the problem stems from the traditional reliance in management and organizational theory on the systems approach (Senge, 2006). A key feature of this manual is that the emphasis is on people theory, not systems theory, as a longstanding criticism of systems theory is its tendency to dehumanize people, to neglect the human element in the way systems work. While the holistic nature of systems theory is to be welcomed, its neglect of human agency and decision making makes it problematic as a basis for understanding human resources management.

The Staying CALM approach
To emphasize the human element of working life, I am going to be focusing on what I shall refer to as the Staying CALM approach. This is a mnemonic used to refer to what I regard as four key elements of effective people management:

- *Connection*. This refers to the importance of people linking together and to the fact that people cannot be understood in isolation. We need to understand how people interact and the dynamic nature of the human element of organizational life. Much of the theory base underpinning management and human resources is individualistic (the technical term for this is 'atomism' – as opposed to holism). The emphasis of connection then is on a more sociological approach (Thompson, 2017a), on the way in which people form a broader whole, the way people interact to produce new situations. Communication is, of course, central to organizational life (and organizational success), and this is very much a matter of 'connection' (Thompson, 2018a).
- *Authenticity*. This is a question of genuineness. Much of the traditional management literature gives the impression that management is a process of manipulating people into doing what we want them to do. This is hardly compatible with our more human, people-oriented approach. What is needed, then, is a recognition that if we want to help people achieve their best, if we want to get the best out of them as a human resource, then we need to engage with them genuinely as people. A good example of this is the work of Buber (1958) who distinguished between I–Thou and I–it relationships. The former refers to interactions between people that are based on respect and which are affirming and enriching. I–it relationships, by contrast, lack respect and are purely instrumental. Importantly, Buber argued that, in engaging in I–it relationships, we not only dehumanize the person we are treating in this way, but also dehumanize ourselves. Authenticity, then, is a key aspect of a genuinely human approach to the people dimension of working life. Authenticity helps to achieve win-win outcomes, so everyone benefits.
- *Leadership*. We have seen a significant shift in recent decades away from the traditional idea of management command and control towards the idea of leadership, where managers and human resource professionals are called upon to pull people in an appropriate, empowering direction by motivating them, rather than to push them in a manipulative way into doing what is required of them. Leadership, then, is an important part of the genuinely human approach I am advocating in this manual. There is a chapter specifically about leadership, but it will also be a theme that relates to many of the individual chapters.
- *Meaning*. People do not come to work simply to earn a living. Work is an important part of people's lives and often of their identity. In this sense, it can be seen as a spiritual (but not necessarily religious) matter, in the sense that it is a question of meaning. Our work can help us make sense of our lives, our sense of who we are as people, and how we fit into the wider world (Moss and Thompson, 2020). The basic principle here is that, if work is not meaningful to the people who are being asked to carry it out, then it is highly unlikely that they will fulfil their potential and achieve optimal results.

As we go through the various chapters, then, it will be important to bear in mind these four key elements of the Staying CALM approach.

Figure 0.1   Staying CALM

Is this a theoretical manual?

The short answer to this is yes and no. It is not a theoretical manual in the sense of containing a great deal of explicit theoretical exposition or analysis, but it is a theoretical manual in the sense that what is contained within it is based on a wide range of theoretical ideas that I have come across in my 40+ years in the people professions. A hallmark of my work is a blending of theory and practice based on the view that theory without practice is of little value, and practice without theory is a dangerous undertaking, as it involves relying on limited understanding.

This manual is therefore theoretical in the sense that the ideas contained within it are not just so-called 'commonsense' ideas but are rooted in a variety of theoretical insights drawn from various disciplines and from a significant body of research. I do not discuss the research here, as that would distract from the main focus of the manual, which is attempting to optimize people management. However, there are various textbooks that can offer a background in the theoretical aspects. One I particularly value is Linstead, Fulop and Lilley (2009), but that is one that focuses specifically on management and organization. The approach I have adopted here is to draw on a much wider range of theory (psychology, sociology, organizational theory, social theory, philosophy, social work and social policy), but my aim here is not to provide an exposition of what that theory base is or where it has come from. Butt (2004) is very helpful in relation to the people focus of this manual.

Will this manual tell me all I need to know?
The short answer to this is: no, it will not. There are lots of things that are missed out here which are widely available elsewhere. Given the tendency mentioned above for the literature to dehumanize people and to present them in a very technical way, much of the existing literature is, in my view, of limited value, but that is for you to judge for yourself (for a critique of much management theory, see Stewart, 2009). What I want to promote here is a basis of critically reflective practice. What I mean by this is an approach that values theory and research but does not put them on a pedestal and fail to adopt a critical approach to them. Critically reflective practice emphasizes that people management (and professional practice more broadly) is not simply a matter of 'painting by numbers' (that is, unthinkingly following procedures) to get the 'right' answers. It is more a case of wrestling intelligently and sensitively with the complexities involved to develop a well-informed, carefully thought-out approach to the challenges involved. For a fuller explanation of critically reflective practice, see Thompson and Thompson (2018).

As Armstrong (2020) reminds us, drawing on the work of Lawler (2003), what managers have to do is 'treat people right'. This involves: (i) recognizing them as individuals with their own specific needs and wants; (ii) rewarding their achievements; (iii) helping them to develop; and (iv) treating them with consideration as human beings, particularly in terms of helping them to feel, valued, supported and safe.

This recognition is at the heart of high-quality people management.

PART I: THE FUNDAMENTALS OF PEOPLE MANAGEMENT

Introduction

In this first of three parts the focus is on what I see as some of the key elements of good practice in managing people. Significantly, the first chapter is on equality, diversity and inclusion, as I want to make a clear, strong statement right from the beginning that high-quality people management has no place for discrimination, whether against individuals or groups or categories of people. We will certainly not get the best out of people if we allow unfairness and disadvantage to be features of our working environments. People are far more likely to flourish and deliver of their best if they know that they are working with people managers who are genuinely committed to promoting equality and valuing diversity. This initial emphasis sets the scene for the whole manual, so the contents of the subsequent 29 chapters should be understood as being based on a foundation of fairness and dignity. To disregard or play down the significance of equality and diversity would run counter to the people-focused approach the manual seeks to promote.

It is sadly the case that many organizations regard equality issues as an 'add on', something they will give attention to if they have to, but their main focus is on minimal compliance. In my view, this is a very misguided and counterproductive approach. If we want to get the best out of people, then it is important that we make sure that we take seriously the values of dignity and respect, which of course means that we must work towards developing workplaces that promote equality and value diversity.

The second chapter addresses another crucial aspect of good practice, namely communication. If, as people managers, we are not able to communicate effectively, then we are highly likely to struggle with the other duties that befall us. The lessons to be learned in this chapter are therefore very important ones indeed.

My overall aim in this first part of the manual is to provide an introduction to such key specific aspects of people management as induction, supervision and handling grievance and disciplinary proceedings and a basis for further learning about them and related matters.

CHAPTER 1: EQUALITY, DIVERSITY AND INCLUSION

In this chapter you will learn about the central role of equality, diversity and inclusion not only as morally important, but also significant in terms of getting the best out of people.

Introduction

Of course, it has to be recognized that we will not be able to get the best out of people if we treat them unfairly or allow others to do so. We therefore have to have a strong focus on fairness. This is usually encapsulated under the heading of 'equality and diversity'. Historically, organizations have placed emphasis on equal opportunities, but more recently we have moved away from this to talk about equality and its companion term, diversity. What these approaches have in common is a recognition that discrimination can be a significant problem in the workplace and is therefore something that needs to be given careful attention.

As an example of this, Brewis and Linstead (2009) highlight the significance of gender:

> Gender is a powerful principle in the organization of our lives. An individual's identity as either male or female, possessing masculine or feminine qualities, makes a difference to the way in which he or she experiences his or her social world. It is therefore significant to consider the influence of gender when examining what managers do and how they do it.
>
> (p. 90)

In this chapter I will give an overview of the move from equal opportunities to equality, diversity and inclusion and emphasize why these are crucial issues for people management professionals. In doing this I am laying the foundations for the remaining chapters, in so far as getting it right in relation to equality and diversity is an important precondition for achieving success in so many other areas of people management practice.

Equal opportunities

'Equal opportunities' was the traditional term used for many years. It is still used from time to time today, but it has largely been superseded by notions of equality and diversity. It was based on the idea that, if people could be given a fair starting point (in the sense of not being disadvantaged in terms of what opportunities were available to them), then this would be sufficient to ensure fairness. However, over the years that approach has been criticized for being too naïve and too individualistic, for not taking account of wider factors that stand in the way of fairness. To give somebody equal opportunity alongside somebody who has a much stronger starting point (in terms of social privileges, for example) is hardly fair (Barry, 2005). For example, a woman applying for a management post in a male-dominated organization with a strong 'macho' culture and an all-male senior management team technically has the same opportunity to get the job as a man does. The reality, of course is very different, which is why dissatisfaction grew with this approach and new ways of understanding fairness at work started to emerge.

What also contributed to the decline of interest in equal opportunities was the recognition that it had become a very defensive endeavour, in so far as a very strong tendency had developed to concentrate primarily, if not exclusively, on ensuring compliance with anti-discrimination legislation, to be concerned with the letter of the law, rather than its spirit (and the value of a commitment to fairness on which it was based). It is for this reason that I use the term, 'defensive', as the major concern had become one of 'not getting into trouble' – that is, avoiding litigation, employment tribunals, grievances and so on.

We have therefore seen a movement away from the idea of equal opportunities to an emphasis on equality, which is a similar concept but a more sophisticated one. Linked to this has been a growing emphasis on diversity, which involves the importance of recognizing difference as an asset, a positive aspect of organizational life. Notions of equality and diversity have not replaced a commitment to equality of opportunity, but rather extended it to show that there is much more to promoting fairness than giving people an equal starting point in terms of their opportunities.

Equality
Unfortunately, this important term has been misinterpreted by many people to mean 'sameness'. While this is understandable, in so far as in its literal sense, equality can be seen to mean sameness, in its moral or legal or political senses, this is very much an oversimplification, and potentially a very dangerous and counterproductive one. Equality (or 'equity') is best understood as a matter of treating people with equal fairness (Thompson, 2018b) and can be encapsulated in the idea of 'fairness for all'. It is about ensuring that people have equal rights and are not treated as 'lesser than' other people without good reason. In a sense, equality can be understood to mean an absence of unfair discrimination. Promoting equality and tackling discrimination are two sides of the same coin.

What is also unfortunate is that progress towards equality has been hampered by not only the defensiveness described above, but also the common tendency to see equality issues as something separate from mainstream organizational life. This is perhaps because discrimination hinges on relations of dominance (it is generally the more powerful, dominant majority groups that have the capacity to discriminate and the less powerful, subordinate minority groups who are more likely to be on the receiving end of such discrimination). This can lead to considerable complacency around discrimination, as members of dominant groups may have little understanding of how significant such matters are for minority groups who are discriminated against (for example, non-disabled people may have little understanding of how often disabled people encounter discrimination and how much harm it can do – Barnes and Mercer, 2010).

Referring to the work of Kandola and Fullerton (1998), Marchington and Wilkinson (2008) make the important point that: 'It is only when "women's, disabled or black issues" are recast as "people's issues" that any real moves towards equality can take place' (p. 25). This is a key consideration, as we are unlikely to make any substantial progress towards 'fairness for all' if such concerns are seen as minority issues and therefore of limited interest to people who are in the majority. If men see gender equality as a matter for women; if white people see racial equality as a black people's concern; if non-disabled people see disability equality as an issue limited to disabled people, then fairness for all will remain a minority pursuit, with limited impact. However, if we can make a commitment to equality a concern for everybody, then we have a very different picture emerging. This is part of the challenge for people management, and so I shall return to this point below.

Discrimination
Literally, to discriminate means to identify a difference. However, in its legal, moral or political sense, to discriminate refers to discriminating *against* an individual or group of people. That is, it involves not only identifying a difference, but also treating unfairly the people identified as different in some way. The technical term for this is a 'detriment' – people suffer a detriment or disadvantage if they are discriminated against. However, a detriment can be relatively minor, a slight inconvenience or disadvantage. It is for this reason that, in discussing discrimination, people often talk in terms of oppression – recognizing that discriminating against people can produce very serious negative outcomes; discrimination, as a source of oppression, can ruin people's lives (Thompson, 2018b).

> *Practice focus 1.1*
> Margaret had been aware of discrimination and knew that it meant that people on the receiving end of such unfair behaviour or attitudes could be disadvantaged by it. However, she had not realized just how much harm discrimination could do until she got to know her new colleague, Lakshmi, and found out about the

circumstances behind why she and her family had moved to the area. Where they had lived previously they had been subjected to a racially motivated hate campaign, with a group of young white men taking every opportunity to make family members' lives a misery, including throwing a brick through their kitchen window. The family had been very badly affected by this onslaught but had originally decided to stay put and weather the storm in the hope that, after a while, it would all subside, the perpetrators would get bored and would go off to do something else for their kicks. However, they changed their plan and moved out of the area altogether when their 14-year-old son Anvik made a very serious suicide attempt because he felt he could no longer take the strain that this hate campaign was placing on him and the rest of the family. Margaret was moved to tears when she heard of this and started to realize that the problems associated with discrimination were much more serious in their consequences than she had recognized.

An important point to note is that, while Practice focus 1.1 gives an example of a very serious situation involving deliberate, intentional discrimination, this is not the only type of discrimination. It can be intentional or unintentional, and the reality of the situation is that most discrimination is in fact unintentional. For every example of deliberate, fully intentional discrimination, there will be many more where the discriminatory outcomes produced were not intended (for example, when people make assumptions that disabled people are incapable). It is based on inaccurate or distorted assumptions that people make or the way systems work in such a way as to exclude certain people or to assign them a lower status or reduced set of rights compared with others. It is therefore a significant mistake to assume that, if we are not deliberately discriminating against people, then discrimination is not an issue that we need to consider.

KEY POINT

An important concept here is the idea of institutional discrimination. This refers to forms of discrimination that are in some way built into the way organizational or wider social systems work or the way people operate on the basis of established habits and cultures. They have become 'institutionalized' as patterns of thought and behaviour, established as the unquestioned, taken-for-granted norm (hence the term, *institutional* discrimination). It is important that people managers, whether senior managers, line managers or HR professionals are aware of the significance of this and do not fall into the trap of assuming that an absence of intentional discrimination is therefore an absence of discrimination *per se*.

The existence and prevalence of institutional discrimination mean that discrimination is far more common than people generally realize. Because of this it is very easy for us to fail to notice discrimination when it occurs. For example, we can become so used to people being treated in discriminatory ways that it often does not register with us as discrimination. A significant illustration of this would be the use of language that excludes women ('chairman', 'manpower', 'manning the phones'). Even though this tendency for some forms of language use to paint a picture that reinforces the notion that 'it is a man's world' has been strongly criticised for decades (Cameron, 1998), it is still commonly used today. For example, in a book strongly committed to promoting racial equality, Parekh (2006) consistently uses terminology that excludes women – for example: 'Liberalism is a substantive doctrine advocating a specific view of man [*sic*]' (p. 14). What can then also happen is that people who try to raise awareness of discrimination can come to be seen as people who are 'rocking the boat', rather than people who are genuinely trying to promote fairness for all.

Diversity
Literally, diversity means variety, and the reason this term has become so prominent in recent years is that it has come to be recognized that it is important to value diversity, in the sense that we need to be aware that differences are an asset to an organization. To have everybody the same would be problematic for any organization. The variety of experiences and outlooks that people bring to the enterprise is something we should appreciate and recognize as an important basis of organizational effectiveness. The opposite of this is known as 'cloning'. This refers to the tendency of some organizations to want to recruit people of the same ilk and to encourage people to think alike. Of course, it does not take much logic to work out that this is a dangerous strategy and leaves organizations vulnerable, because they are not well equipped to deal with the complexities of the external environment if there is such a narrowness of thought and approach. Diversity is therefore an asset, something to be valued and even celebrated. Consequently, a good people manager is somebody who recognizes the significance of this and promotes the valuing of diversity in various ways. Perhaps the most important way is encouraging everyone to see diversity as a benefit and to help them move away from potentially discriminatory assumptions about different groups of people (based on stereotypes, for example).

It is important to note that diversity and difference are complex notions and we have to guard against adopting oversimplified approaches to the subject (or 'reductionism' to use the technical term). Unfortunately, the tendency to look for simple answers was a feature of the equal opportunities approach that some people have carried forward into contemporary thinking about equality and diversity (see Thompson, 2019a, for a discussion of this danger and how to avoid it).

Miller and Katz (2002) are critical of such simplistic approaches which they describe as 'diversity in a box':

> Unfortunately, most organizations end up with a *diversity in a box* strategy. They see diversity as getting in the way of success by forcing the organization to do something it doesn't want to do. Or they see it is an issue to be managed, shaping it and getting it to "fit" in the existing structure of the organization. Still other organizations see diversity as a value and end in itself, unrelated to the mission, vision and purpose of the organization. The result: either a singular focus on representation and awareness or ignoring the issue altogether.
>
> (p. 5)

In the early days of the valuing diversity approach many people used the term 'managing diversity'. However, this terminology is now being used less and less, partly because it implies that diversity is a problem to be managed or 'smoothed out', rather than an asset to be valued, and partly because it is being recognized that diversity is not something that can or should be managed – it is something to be capitalized upon, rather than managed.

In terms of valuing diversity, it is also important to note that, like the equal opportunities and equality approaches before it, it is prone to oversimplification. Diversity is a complex aspect of social life and we do no one any favours by adopting a simplistic understanding of it or approach to it. There is now a significant literature base that warns against adopting an oversimplified diversity approach (Malik, 2008; Michaels, 2016). In particular, we need to be wary of approaches to diversity that 'sanitize' discrimination and fail to capture any real sense of its significance (as I have argued previously, we need to understand *adversity* as well as *diversity* – Thompson, 2021a).

Equality, diversity and inclusion
For some people, there is a contradiction between equality and diversity. This is because they interpret the terms too literally to mean sameness and difference respectively. In reality the two are entirely compatible. This is because the philosophy behind equality, diversity and inclusion is based on the idea that, through having differences amongst people, we have great strengths but we also, because of those differences, have the potential for discrimination. Promoting equality and valuing diversity is therefore a matter of recognizing that we can achieve 'unity in diversity' (Kallen, 2004); that we can have different people who can work effectively and supportively together and that there is no need for people to be treated unfairly or excluded simply because they are different in one or more ways from the majority. Valuing diversity is therefore not simply a matter

of avoiding discrimination, but actually going so far as to recognize the benefits of having different perspectives, different strengths and different ways of looking at situations.

> *Practice focus 1.2*
> Paul worked in a closely knit team for almost three years. It felt very comfortable to work there, as the six members had a lot in common and were very similar in their approach to the work. However, when he started his new job he was surprised to find how different the set up was. He knew he was going to be working in a bigger team, but he had not realized that there would be so much variety across the team. He felt quite unsettled at first, as this was very different from what he was used to. However, over time he started to realise that there were distinct advantages in having so many different people, with so many different approaches. He felt very comfortable in his previous team – perhaps too comfortable, he was now starting to realize – but the team could hardly have been called dynamic or productive; they just got themselves through the day as best they could. Paul could see that his new team might be prone to more conflict from time to time because of the differences across individuals, but he felt that would be worth it because of the buzz in his new team that he had never encountered before. Work in his new team seemed much less of a chore.

There are various reasons why it is important to promote equality and value diversity, not least the following:

1. *The ethical or humanitarian case.* This is based on the idea that we need to be fair to people, that it is unethical to discriminate against people. This, of course, in itself is a powerful argument in favour of equality and diversity: a basic commitment to fairness as a part of our value base. A key part of this argument is the idea, to paraphrase Edmund Burke, that all that is necessary for the evil of discrimination to flourish is for good people to do nothing. As Miller and Katz (2002) express it:

> To support oppression and discrimination, all a person or group, or institution need do is take no action. To keep the isms alive and powerful – to keep the dominance of the one-up group alive, to convince some that the one-down group deserves its plight, to keep "us" feeling threatened by "them" – all that is needed is a comment here and an inaction there, ...
>
> (p. 99)

2. *The legal argument.* There are various laws which require organizations to refrain from discriminating against people on various grounds. There is therefore a legal compliance argument for equality and diversity, although from my own point of view, I

would argue that it is dangerous to rely too heavily on this argument, as it is possible for individuals, or even whole organizations, to get round the law in various ways. Also, it fails to engage with the positives of equality and diversity and presents such matters narrowly as a challenge of legal compliance, rather than a much broader question of making the most of the human resources within the organization. So, while this is an important argument, it is not enough on its own.

3. *The business case.* This is a question of arguing that the benefits of diversity are good for business (meaning organizational effectiveness – it does not just apply to private sector organizations). If an organization values diversity, there will be fewer problems related to discrimination, conflict and tension and related matters. There will also be the benefits that accrue from having a diverse workforce where people are valued for what they bring, for their contribution to the breadth of vision, knowledge and skill that effective organizations need.

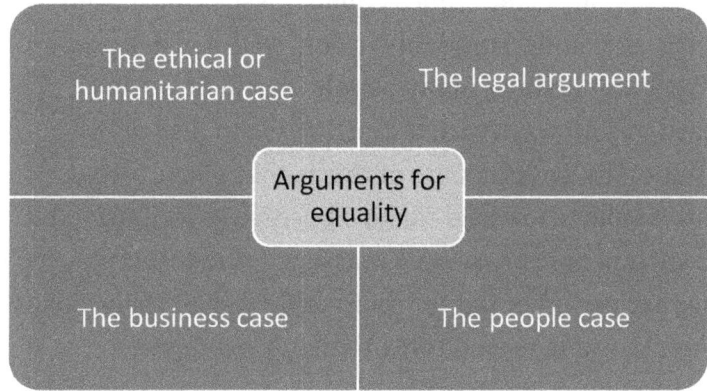

Figure 1.1 Arguments for equality

4. *The people case.* For me, this is the most important argument. It is based on the fact that people management is about getting the *best* out of people, not the *most* (as discussed in the Introduction). That is, it is not simply a matter of manipulating people into doing as much work as possible, but, rather, creating the right environment where people will want to achieve their best, where they will want the enterprise – whatever it might be in that particular organization – to succeed. This will not occur if there is discrimination taking place and people therefore resent being treated unfavourably. So, if we want to have high morale and therefore high motivation and the effectiveness that these can contribute to, then we have to ensure that we have a workplace free of discrimination.

Conclusion

It is no coincidence that this topic forms the basis of Chapter 1. I deliberately chose this to emphasize that everything that follows rests on our commitment to equality and diversity. So many of the good practices I will be talking about in the chapters that follow will be seriously undermined if they are not underpinned by a strong foundation of equality and diversity. Discrimination undermines morale, fuels tensions and conflicts, exacerbates stress, blocks learning, stymies communication and generally acts as a brake on organizational progress. People managers therefore need to take the challenges of equality and diversity very seriously and move away from the common problems associated with addressing such issues. There are three of these problems that are worth commenting on:

1. *Dismissing or trivializing them.* Unfortunately, there are some people managers who do not appreciate the significance of equality and diversity and are therefore likely to dismiss such concerns as 'political correctness' and not give them the attention they deserve. These are likely to be people who have either not had direct experiences of how harmful discrimination can be or they have not learned from those experiences.

2. *Fearing them.* In certain places and at certain times equality issues have been dealt with in confrontational ways that have understandably produced defensive and fearful responses. This then has the result of making many people fearful of getting involved, and they therefore work hard to find ways of avoiding having to deal with discrimination issues or related matters. The sad outcome of this is that equality and diversity issues become sidelined and people who could make a positive contribution to 'fairness for all' do not do so. Where such people are people managers, the result is particularly problematic, as it means that the potential for them to do well at their jobs is severely diminished and others in their workplace who rely on them for support, guidance and leadership are likely to lose out unnecessarily.

3. *Oversimplifying them.* A common example of this is the tendency to assume that equality means sameness, that the way forward is simply to treat everybody the same. The flaw with this logic is that it does not recognize the fact that treating everybody the same reinforces existing inequalities in many situations (Thompson, 2018b). Another example would be the grossly oversimplified approach to the relationship between language and discrimination. While some forms of language can indeed be highly discriminatory, the assumption that all that is needed is to pressurise people into using certain words instead of certain others (without any real understanding of how language can reinforce discrimination) is dangerously naïve (Thompson, 2018a). One unfortunate result of this is that it reinforces problem 1. (in so far as it gives unconvinced individuals the excuse to dismiss equality issues as 'political correctness gone mad') and problem 2. (by adding to the confusion and uncertainty that reinforce fear).

A key feature underpinning all this is trust. As we noted earlier, if we are to have a genuinely human and humane workplace where people are valued rather than exploited, then there has to be a strong element of trust. As Kouzes and Posner (2017) argue. At the heart of collaboration is trust. It as the central issue in human relationships within and outside organizations, they contend. They go on to state that, without trust, you cannot lead or get extraordinary things done. People who cannot trust others fail to become leaders because they cannot bring themselves to be dependent on others. They can end up doing all the work themselves or supervise work so closely that they become overcontrolling (which can be seen as a form of bullying). Their lack of trust in others can work two ways, in the sense that it can result in others not trusting them.

There can be little or no trust where there is discrimination. Our commitment to promoting equality and valuing diversity therefore has to be rock solid as a foundation for effective people management. We are not expected to be experts, nor are we expected to get it right every time, but there certainly is a strong expectation that we do our best to make a reality of equality as a basis of fairness for all and diversity as a platform for allowing people to fulfil their potential rather than be discriminated against because they are 'different'.

Points to ponder
1. What is meant by diversity?
2. Why is diversity important in terms of human resources management?
3. Why is it important not to see equality as 'sameness'?

Exercise 1
What examples of actual or potential discrimination can you identify in your workplace (or where you are studying)? How might such discrimination prevent people from achieving their best?

CHAPTER 2: COMMUNICATION

In this chapter you will learn how to make sure your communication is as effective as possible.

Introduction

At the end of Chapter 1, I made the point that so much of what we are trying to achieve in people management will collapse if not built on the foundation of a commitment to equality and diversity. Much the same can be said about the topic of this chapter. Without skilful and effective communication, organizations will struggle to achieve their aims. In fact, there cannot be any real organization without communication. To bring people together with common goals which is, after all, what organizations are all about, cannot happen unless there are patterns of communication that connect people to one another and to the information they need to share.

Similarly, we could say that managing is itself a form of communication. If we are not communicating, then we are not managing. Indeed, the importance of communication cannot be overemphasized: 'Effective communication is key to managing change, resolving conflict, tackling absence, dealing with disciplinary and grievance issues, promoting equality – it is the backbone running through everything you do' (ACAS, 2015).

This chapter has therefore been written to give you an overview of what the key issues are in relation to communication as a foundation for effective people management. It covers a number of key points that should be sufficient to give you a platform of understanding on which to build over time.

We begin by looking at the unavoidability of communication and its implications.

We cannot not communicate

This is a central point about communication in general, but has a particular resonance for people management. As human beings we are constantly giving off signals, and that in effect is the primary basis of communication: transmitting signals or messages to other people and receiving messages from them. While much of our communication will be deliberate and intentional, we also have to recognize that we are likely to be giving off signals without realizing that we are doing so. For example, not turning up for a particular meeting to which we have been invited will communicate a certain message (perhaps about our lack of interest in that topic), whether or not we intended to give that message. What this means is that communication is not one hundred per cent within our control, and so it is important that we do what we reasonably can to control what messages we are giving people.

A key part of this is what is known as a 'meta-message'. 'Meta' is the Greek word for above or beyond, and so a meta-message is what is communicated above or beyond what we intend to communicate. For example, if someone says to a colleague: 'When can I expect that report from you?', then this is superficially a simple request for information. But, if it is said in a harsh tone and accompanied by body language that conveys dissatisfaction, then the message is likely to be received as not simply a request for information, but a strong expression of disapproval, accompanied by a degree of criticism that the report has not yet been completed. We therefore have to be very clear about what messages we are giving people, as we may be undermining what we are trying to do if our messages are mixed or convey a meaning that we did not wish to convey.

> *Practice focus 2.1*
> Ken was a deputy team manager who was confident that he would get the team manager vacancy after Jackie left, as he felt he had been doing a very good job and had had no complaints. In particular, he was proud of how hard he had been working over the past two years in his current post. However, he was very disappointed when he was told that he had not even been shortlisted for the post – he regarded that as quite a kick in the teeth. He therefore asked to have some feedback about his application so that he could get some idea about why he was not felt suitable for the job. After making a formal request through the Human Resources Department, he was offered a meeting with Marlene, the section head. Marlene clearly felt uncomfortable in the meeting and that made Ken feel even more uncomfortable, leading to a very tense atmosphere. Despite this, Marlene managed to explain to Ken that the problem was that she had sought feedback from the team about what they wanted from their new team manager, and this feedback was not in Ken's favour. Concerns had been expressed that Ken always seemed to be very busy and was giving off signals that he was too busy to listen or give anyone any support. Ken protested that this was unfair, as he was always willing to listen and the fact that he came across as so busy was because he was such a hard worker. Marlene tried to get across the point to him that a key part of his job was to support staff and that, if he seemed to be communicating to them that other aspects of his job were more important, they would understandably interpret that as not having time for them. Ken was grateful to Marlene that she had been so honest with him, even though she was clearly uncomfortable in saying what she had to say, but he was disappointed that what he saw as a strong point (his industriousness) had been seen as a weak point (being too busy to

listen). There was a painful message in this for Ken that he had to be much more careful about what message he was giving people to make sure that he was not giving them the wrong message.

This is just one example of a misleading meta-message. Other examples are not too difficult to find. Consider the following not uncommon scenarios:

- Steve is very keen to help, but he is very tired. He does not realize that he is coming across as tired, and that this is undermining the message of support he is trying to convey.
- Carla likes to look her best, and so she always dresses smartly and wears make up. Some people at the tenants' meeting she attends interpret this as her feeling superior and being condescending towards them.
- Lora wants to encourage more team participation, and so she develops a rota for individual team members to take it in turns to chair team meeting. However, she does not explain the reasoning to the team, and so it comes across to them as an abdication of duty, that she is getting them to do her job for her.
- Dennis finds Lisa very attractive, but he is happily married and respects Lisa as a colleague, so he has no intention of doing anything about the attraction he feels. However, he does not realize that his feelings towards Lisa are very apparent in his interactions with her, which leaves her feeling very uncomfortable and ill at ease.
- When Fiona is busy, she has a tendency to speak very fast. At such times she is not unduly anxious and is coping well with the situation, but the rate at which she speaks gives the impression that she is anxious and struggling to cope.

When we also add into the mix the positive side of meta-messages (that is, when we use them appropriately to reinforce an important message we are trying to put across), we start to recognize how complex such matters are and therefore how well informed we need to be about them. For example, as people managers, we will often need to give a message of authority to win the respect we need to get their job done. This can be an important part of establishing our credibility as leaders. However, we should not confuse authority (the legitimate use of power) with authoritarianism (throwing our weight about and losing respect and credibility in the process). We therefore have to make sure that the message we are conveying is one of authority and not authoritarianism.

KEY POINT

We need a degree of self-awareness if we are going to be effective communicators as part of being effective people managers (see Chapter 1 of People Skills – Thompson, 2021b). If we are not tuned in to how our communications are shaping the circumstances we are in, we will miss out on significant opportunities to influence the situation in a positive direction and may actually make it worse.

Getting our message across

Communication is all about conveying and receiving messages, sending out – and receiving – the signals that enable us to form relationships, to work together and to keep one another informed. It can be divided into a number of subsections, depending on what medium of communication we are using (speech or writing, for example). Consider the following elements:

What we say

When we talk to people, the words that we use can, of course, be very significant indeed. We should therefore choose our words carefully. For example, using jargon terms that other people may not understand is likely to alienate them and give them the impression that we are not making any genuine commitment to communicating with them. It can give the impression that the interaction has to be on *our* terms when it comes to the language that *we* feel comfortable with, and not necessarily what *they* feel comfortable with (this is, of course, another example of a meta-message).

This does not mean that we should risk getting tongue tied by having to weigh up every single word we use, but there is a need for a certain awareness of the forms of language we are using and whether or not they are appropriate in those circumstances. The technical term for this is 'register'. We choose the appropriate register. For example, we would probably not use informal slang terms in a job interview, and nor would we, in all likelihood, use highly technical terms in talking to a four-year-old child. This ability to switch the style of language we use to suit the circumstances is what the idea of register is all about. We therefore need to make sure that we are choosing the appropriate register, matching our style of language to the circumstances. You can probably remember occurrences where people have got this wrong, thereby creating embarrassing situations where the language used did not suit the circumstances. For example, someone using informal language in a situation that calls for formality can come across as overfamiliar, while someone who uses formal language when it is not called for can come across as though they do not fit in, as though they do not understand the context they are operating in.

How we say it

This is what is referred to as 'paralanguage'. It relates to the factors that accompany the language we use when speaking. It includes the pace at which we speak, the pitch or tone that we use, how loudly we speak, and so on. All of these factors can give different meanings. For example, speaking quickly can show enthusiasm or anxiety, while speaking slowly may indicate that someone is uninterested or possibly even slightly depressed. These are important aspects of communication, and a skilled people manager will be able to use these to good effect, not only in the way he or she speaks, but also in picking up clues from how other people speak to him or her and the way they use paralanguage. This is an important part of emotional intelligence (Howe, 2008), the ability to tune in to people's emotions by picking up on the signals they give off, and paralanguage, in turn, is a key part of that. It can be a very useful and insightful exercise to listen to two or more people talking (whether in real life, on television or in cinema) and focus carefully on how they are using paralanguage. This can be a difficult thing to do at first, as we are so used to reacting to paralanguage without realizing that we are doing it that we may struggle to pick out what exactly it is people are doing to convey particular meanings through tone, pitch, pace, loudness and so on.

What our body says
Alongside the actual language we use and the paralanguage that accompanies it comes body language. A key point to recognize here is that body language is more powerful than other forms of language. For example, if we say that we are happy, but our body language suggests that we are not, then the message people will take on board is that we are not happy, despite what we have actually said. We therefore have to make sure that our body language is congruent with our language – that is, that it does not contradict what we are trying to say. A heightened awareness of body language can be a very useful tool for people managers, and time and effort spent developing a more advanced level of ability in this area are well spent.

This is a point worth emphasizing, as often what makes the difference between a good people manager and an excellent one is the latter's ability to use nonverbal communication at a more advanced level – to put people at their ease; to win trust and respect; to convey concern and empathy; to get our message across clearly and accurately; to create a sense of security and thereby boost confidence; to create clarity about where we are going and how we are going to get there; and to establish a strong rapport. These are, of course, all important parts of leadership in particular and people management in general. There is therefore much to be gained by developing a more advanced level of nonverbal communication in whatever ways we reasonably can.

If we consider, for a moment, the A of *Staying CALM*, we may recall that this refers to authenticity. Being able to use body language effectively and to pick up on the signals from other people's body language is an important part of this authenticity. If we are saying one thing and our body is communicating something else, we will not come across as genuinely interested in supporting staff. It will come across that we are being dishonest or disingenuous, neither of which is a firm basis for effective people management.

What we write

It is not only the oral use of language that counts, there is also the way we use written language to communicate. A good example of the importance of this is email. In these days of intense email use, it is not uncommon for problems to arise because somebody dashed off an email too quickly without checking it and without thinking about how it might be read by the person on the receiving end. But that is just one example of how we need to be careful in terms of what we write, especially as the written word may be available for people to consult years or even decades later. Written communication has a certain in-built formality because of its longevity. Even if we write in an informal style there is still a certain formal status that is attributed to written communications.

> *Practice focus 2.2*
>
> Martin was a very committed manager, but he often found it difficult to get his message across. This was largely because he was seen as a mild-mannered, rather than assertive, person. However, one day he attended a training course on communication skills and he took the opportunity to talk to the trainer during the coffee break in order to get her advice on how he might be more successful in getting his team members to take more notice of him. Her advice proved to be very significant, as she suggested that he should commit very important matters to writing and make it clear that he was doing so because of the importance of what he was trying to get across. This proved to be a very worthwhile move on his part, as the extra weight of written communication gave his team a very clear message that he 'meant business'. (source: Thompson, 2018a)

How we write it

This can be understood in two senses. The first sense is the style of writing that we adopt, how effective we are in getting our message across clearly, accurately and without creating confusion or any basis for misunderstanding. But this can also be seen to refer to the written medium we use. Letters are being used far less these days due to the development of email, but, at times, a letter is what is called for. For example, in issuing an apology for a mistake made or an inconvenience caused, a letter is likely to have far more impact than an email. In becoming the best communicators that we are capable of being, we therefore need to take account of not only what we write, but also how we write it and the medium in which we write it.

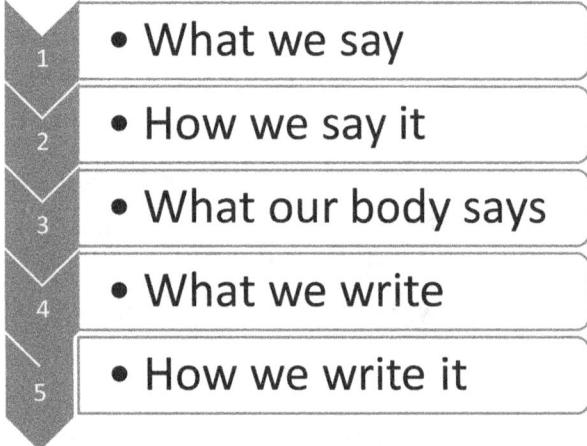

Figure 2.1 Getting our message across

The importance of listening

If we want staff to feel valued rather than exploited, appreciated rather than manipulated, valued rather than taken for granted, then we have to be able to listen. In particular, we have to be able to undertake what is known as 'active listening'. This takes us back to the question of body language. For example, if we are genuinely listening, but our body language is giving off signals that contradict that (for example, if we are concentrating on what we are hearing and, in concentrating, we are perhaps looking down and not making eye contact, then we may be contradicting the message we are trying to give that we are indeed listening). Active listening is therefore a matter of showing that we are listening – for example, through appropriate eye contact, occasional nodding of the head and also perhaps at times feeding back what has been said to us to check out that we have properly understood.

In terms of effective listening there is an interesting concept that derives from Australian Aboriginal thinking known as *dadirri* listening. This refers to the idea of not just paying attention to somebody, but fully listening, listening with our heart and soul, really connecting with that person. As Tehan (2007) puts it:

> The art of patient, contemplative listening has been in existence for many thousands of years ... Ungenmerr-Bauman describes dadirri listening as: 'a special quality, a unique gift of the Aboriginal people, is inner deep listening and quiet still awareness'. (p. 215)

You may have already come across people in your life who are good at this (even though they may have never come across the concept itself), those who are able to give a sense of real warmth and human connection in the way they listen to people. The closer we can get to that ideal the better.

Dealing with 'noise'

Noise can be a barrier to communication in a literal sense (for example, when trying to have a conversation in a noisy pub). However, the term 'noise' is also used metaphorically to refer to anything that can stand in the way of effective communication, any barrier between the message we are trying to express and its being received by the appropriate person(s). This can include, but is not limited to:

- *Tension* Where there is a degree of tension in a situation the result will often be that people get distracted and lose sight of what is being said. Tension can also distort communication in so far as a tense person may filter out aspects of what they are hearing by focusing on some aspects at the expense of others (for example, listening out for potentially threatening aspects of a situation).
- *Conflict* Conflict can lead to raised tensions which may then distort communication as described above. However, there can also be conflict at the heart of the communication, in the sense that the participants may have conflicting agendas or differing expectations about what the basis of the interaction is.
- *Confusion* There are various ways in which confusion can stand in the way of effective communication (including tension and conflict), mainly because a lack of clarity can act as a fog blocking the transmission of information.
- *Haste* Sometimes busy people can communicate too hastily and therefore not do a very good job of putting their message across. Equally, people who are in a rush may also do a poor job of listening and taking in the information being given to them. Where both parties to a communication are in a hurry, the quality of the communication can be very poor indeed.
- *Cultural differences* The ways in which cross-cultural communications can go awry are well documented (see, for example, Jandt, 2015). Cultures are full of taken-for-granted assumptions and unwritten rules. Where we are interacting with someone whose assumptions and unwritten rules are different from our own there can be considerable scope for miscommunication.
- *Gender differences* Research has shown that there are significant gender differences in communication styles (Tannen, 2001), and so this too can be a source of 'noise', in the sense that men and women can get in each other's way in trying to communicate.
- *The setting* The environment in which communication takes place can be a key factor in determining whether or not messages get through. There can be various distractions that can get in the way, but the setting itself can provide a meta-message. For example, trying to carry out formal business in an informal setting can be difficult because the informal setting can in itself contradict any formal messages that we are trying to convey.

 Dealing with noise is important for anyone who needs to communicate effectively. However, for people managers it is particularly significant, as we are required not only to communicate effectively as far as possible in our own right, but also to promote effective communication wherever and however we reasonably can (see the discussion of managing communication in Thompson, 2018a). It can therefore be helpful to have this wider understanding of communication and appreciate how it can be blocked by various forms of 'noise'. This will then make us much better equipped to remove or avoid such obstacles or at least keep their impact to a minimum.

Conclusion

It should be clear from the discussions in this chapter that communication is a central feature of effective people management. If we are to succeed in our endeavours to be good at our job, then we need to make efforts to maximize our communicative abilities. What can sometimes hold people back is that they will have learned, of course, the basics of communication from their upbringing. It is therefore very easy to be complacent and to assume that we are already good communicators and not put any effort into becoming the best communicators that we can be. The difference between ordinary, everyday communicative skills and the most advanced level possible is huge. We therefore need to take seriously the challenge of building on our existing communication skills and trying to get as close to the ideal as we possibly can.

Points to ponder

1. Why is it essential to make sure that our body language is appropriate?
2. What are the likely consequences of failing to listen properly?
3. What is 'noise' and why do we need to be aware of it?

Exercise 2

What do you see as your strong points in terms of communication? How you can you improve them even further? What do you see as your not so strong points? How can you develop your skills in these areas?

CHAPTER 3: SUPERVISION

In this chapter you will learn how to supervise staff in ways that help them achieve their potential.

Introduction

Supervision can be understood as a form of leadership carried out on a one-to-one basis. Leadership is in part about getting the best out of people, and this can be done collectively through the leadership of a team, division, or whole organization at a macro level or individually through supervision at a micro level. It is a process of offering guidance and support to enable employees to produce the best quality of work that they are capable of and to learn from the process, so that their personal and professional development are adequately catered for. Supervision involves establishing a healthy balance between the destructive extremes of, on the one hand, intrusive micro management (where the manager gives far too detailed a set of instructions on how the work should be carried out, leaving little or no room for autonomy and a sense of pride in one's work) and, on the other hand, where there is laxity about supporting people to achieve their best (where they are, in effect, simply left to get on with it, without adequate management support).

Hawkins (2008) highlights the importance of supervision: 'Supervision used to be centred on those who were still in training. Now it is much more recognized that supervision is for life not just for trainees. In the "people professions", when you stop learning, you stop being effective' (p. 11). This chapter looks at a range of key factors relating to supervision to provide a foundation for further development of the knowledge and skills that are important underpinnings of effective people management.

Supervision sessions

Supervisors (that is, managers in a supervisory role) have two main sets of responsibilities in terms of supervision. One is an overall oversight of the staff members' work (super vision literally means over sight), but there is also the responsibility for individual supervision sessions (sometimes also referred to as supervision meetings or simply one-to-ones).

Such supervision sessions are a key part of making sure that supervision is a helpful process. To make the best of them, it is important that there is clarity about the following issues:

- *Frequency.* Different organizations have different expectations in terms of frequency of supervision, but a very common pattern is for supervision to be weekly during the person's induction period, changing to monthly thereafter, but this is certainly not set in stone. It is therefore important for you to be familiar with the supervision policy of the organization concerned and ensure that you are at least fulfilling the minimum requirements in terms of frequency.

- *Length and timing.* This again varies considerably from organization to organization, and there is no hard and fast rule about what is an appropriate length of time. A basic guideline is that it should be sufficient for its purpose. In some settings and for some posts, that may be relatively brief; in others, much lengthier sessions may be needed. It may also be the case that the length of session varies depending on the current circumstances relating to that particular employee or the team as a whole. In terms of timing, I have found it useful to look for the best times of day for supervision sessions in terms of the supervisee's preference. For example, some people are morning people and are at their most productive and thoughtful in the early parts of the day and may fade out in late afternoon. For such people, a late afternoon supervision session may be far from ideal. Similarly, somebody who is not a morning person and takes a while to get going and then fulfils their potential in terms of work capacity later in the day, an early morning supervision session may not be helpful. There are also our own preferences to take into account, in so far as we need to be at our best as well where possible. So, there is no simple or ideal answer to the question of when supervision sessions should take place, but it is important to give some thought to this, rather than just sprinkle them randomly throughout our diary and potentially be suffering the consequences of doing that.

- *Shared agenda.* In our efforts to move away from a command and control mentality in the workplace to one that is based on leadership, it is important that it is not simply the supervisor who sets the agenda, but also invites the supervisee to contribute to the agenda-setting process. This makes sure that they have a voice and that their issues and concerns are receiving attention. Supervision should be seen as something that we do *with* supervisees, not *to* them.

- *Venue.* This can be very significant. I have come across people who have made the mistake of trying to hold supervision sessions in open spaces, with other people sitting around (I once had the misfortune of hearing a supervision session taking place at the table next to me in a Little Chef diner!). There needs to be a venue that will not allow interruptions to take place and will allow confidential material to be discussed without fear of being overheard. Where possible, it should not be in the manager's office (but I recognize that it may have to be in many work settings). If it is in the manager's office, then efforts should be made to arrange appropriate seating; the manager behind his or her desk clearly presents an obstacle and, going back to the discussion in Chapter 2 of body language and nonverbal communication, clearly gives the wrong message in terms of trying to work in partnership, trying to achieve that connection, as in the C of *Staying CALM*.

These are not the only factors to be taken into consideration, but they are certainly important ones that we should make sure we do not neglect.

> *Practice focus 3.1*
> Steph had worked in the same team for just over a year when the manager left and was replaced by Reena. Steph's supervision sessions had often been cancelled in the past and, when they did take place, they were generally little more than a chat about how things were going with her workload. Reena's approach to supervision, though, was very different. She made strenuous efforts to make sure that nothing got in the way of a scheduled session and, while they were taking place, she was very focused and made full use of the time to help Steph develop her practice. Steph felt a little uncomfortable at first, but soon settled into what she recognized to be a much more helpful and productive use of supervision sessions. She started to realize how wasteful of time her previous sessions had been, as they had not made any positive contribution to developing her practice.

The four elements of supervision

Based on the work of Morrison (2006) we can identify four key elements or aspects of supervision and it is worth exploring each of these in turn.

1. *Standard setting*

This relates to the responsibility of the supervisor to ensure that supervisees are producing work of an acceptable quality that is in line with policy, legal and ethical expectations. This aspect of supervision is therefore concerned with accountability. While the employee concerned is responsible for his or her own work, the line manager or supervisor has a degree of accountability, in the sense that they can be 'called to account' in respect of the supervisee's work. It is therefore important that the supervisor is aware of the work that is being undertaken and is satisfied that it is of an acceptable standard.

A key aspect of this is the ability to give sensitive, constructive feedback so that staff know where they stand – they know what their strengths are, so that they can build on them and what their not so strong points are, so that they can build them up (this idea of 'building on and building up' is one to which we will return later). This takes us back to the subject matter of Chapter 2, communication, as the skills needed for giving effective feedback involve being able to communicate at a high level of capability. If, by contrast, supervisors do not succeed in giving constructive feedback, then staff will have little by way of a benchmark from which to judge how their practice can improve. It is important to note that, as no one is perfect, every supervisee (and every supervisor, for that matter) will have scope for improvement.

A key aspect of giving feedback is the role it can play in making sure that staff know what is expected of them. Unclear expectations can be a source of stress, and we can hardly expect employees to achieve their best if they are not entirely clear what it is that they need to do to succeed. As Hyter and Turnock (2005) point out: 'Many, if not most employees ... do not know what it really takes to succeed in a particular company, and their managers don't know how to guide them' (p. 138). A skilled supervisor can therefore be of immense benefit in helping to establish precisely what is expected of each supervisee so that they get the benefits of that clarity.

In giving feedback the key term is 'transparency'. Staff will benefit from having clear and helpful feedback about their performance, whereas a lack of such transparency can lead to confusion, ill feeling and low morale. These are important considerations in relation to appraisal and performance management, and so we will return to this topic in Chapter 7.

2.   *Staff development*

This aspect of supervision is concerned with maximizing learning, helping supervisees to draw out the learning from their work. It is not simply a matter of arranging for them to attend appropriate training courses. It is, as we shall see in Chapter 19, also about helping to prepare them for such training and to draw out the lessons thereafter. However, there is also an important supervisory role in terms of drawing out the learning from everyday practice and not just from training workshops. This is an example of critically reflective practice, encouraging supervisees to think about what they are doing, to plan accordingly and to have a reflective or mindful approach to their work (Thompson and Thompson, 2023). As Carroll *et al.* (2005) comment: 'Learning-in-action, the cyclical interplay of thinking and doing is increasingly important for organizations as environments and required capabilities become more complex and interdependent' (p. 575).

Staff development can be understood as a process of building on and building up. This refers to building *on* existing strengths, so that good points can get even better, and building *up*, which involves identifying the not-so-strong points and strengthening them where possible through the development of appropriate knowledge, skills and values.

This can be quite a skilful job, as it involves being able to help staff review their performance and identify their learning needs, something that many staff struggle to do and which many others are reluctant to open up to discussion (perhaps for fear of being criticized). Some participants on supervision courses I have run have expressed concern that they do not have the appropriate skills for promoting learning because they have no background in a training and development role. Each time this has happened I have responded by saying that such a background is not needed. It is a matter of using our analytical skills to identify (in partnership with each supervisee):

- What aspects of their practice are strong and what needs to happen so that they can get even stronger;
- What aspects of their practice are not very strong and what needs to happen to strengthen them;
- What lessons can be learned from their practice (whether strong or not) so that they are learning from experience over time (rather than just having the experience and not getting any learning benefit from it);
- In preparation for attending a training course: what do they hope to get out of it? What can they do (preparatory reading, for example, or talking to a more experienced colleague who is well versed in the subject matter of the course)?
- After a training course: what will be done differently now? What ideas or tools from the course will be used in practice? How?

KEY POINT

If this sort of work is not undertaken, then significant opportunities for learning will be missed and staff will not be able to achieve their best. There is, of course, a time commitment involved in this, but we should see this as an investment rather than a cost, as we should see a significant return on the time and effort invested in learning and development.

If there is an effective appraisal system in place (see Chapter 7), then the groundwork for much of this will have been laid through that process. Ideally, appraisal and supervision should support one another over time.

An example of how supervision can usefully promote learning is the way in which a skilful supervisor can help the supervisee identify when their thinking is being distorted by fear or anxiety. As Argyris (1999) explains:

> Defensive reasoning encourages individuals to keep private, the premises, inferences, and conclusions that shape their behaviour and to avoid testing them in a truly independent, objective fashion.
> Because the attributions that go into defensive reasoning are never really tested, it is a closed loop, remarkably impervious to conflicting points of view. The

inevitable response to the observation that somebody is reasoning defensively is yet more defensive reasoning.

(p. 131)

If sensitively handled, such reasoning can be gently and constructively challenged in supervision, enabling the supervisee to develop their understanding and thus take their practice to a higher level.

3. *Staff support*

This is about promoting workplace well-being (to be discussed in more detail in Part III) in which staff feel that they are being adequately supported and valued for their contribution. A key part of this is listening and being prepared to address any obstacles that may be getting in the way of the supervisee achieving their best. This is not a matter of counselling employees, as that is something that is best left to specialists, but there is a strong element of forming a supportive rapport that will act as an important foundation for effective people management.

Support can take many forms, chiefly the following:

- *Appreciation.* Simply saying 'thank you' or 'well done' can make a very positive impact, while the absence of these touches of appreciation can leave people feeling undervalued, taken for granted and thus exploited. It saddens me that I have met many managers over the years who do not understand this simple but crucial aspect of people management and who either see no value in showing appreciation or they have never given the matter a moment's thought and are unaware of what a negative impact their lack of appreciation is likely to be having. Of course, the appreciation has to be genuine (reflecting the A, for Authenticity, of *Staying CALM*) rather than something that is done mechanistically without any real commitment to staff support.
- *Listening.* This reflects the C, for Connection, of *CALM*. If staff feel they are not being listened to, then they are once again likely to feel undervalued, taken for granted and exploited – the exact opposite of what staff support is intended to achieve. Listening does not mean having to agree or doing everything a staff member wants you to do, but it does mean showing that person respect by taking their concerns seriously. It should be clear by now, even at this relatively early stage of the manual, that listening is a key component of effective people management. Not listening means not connecting, and that means our trust, respect and credibility as leaders are on the line.
- *Guidance* Wherever the setting and the nature of the work allow, and in a spirit of promoting empowerment and boosting confidence, we should issue direct instructions only where we need to (Huq, 2016). However, even the most confident, empowered, self-directed staff can benefit from guidance from time to time. Such guidance can include

suggestions for how a particular task or piece of work can best be addressed. Providing helpful guidance can be experienced by staff as very supportive. It can help them feel more secure in rising to the challenges of their job.

- *Signposting* This refers to situations where we may not be able to help directly, but we can point the staff member of concerned in the direction of a person, service or organization that may well be of assistance. This can be particularly helpful when someone is distressed or anxious as there may be sources of help that they are aware of but do not think about because of their anxiety or distress.
- *Putting things in perspective* A good supervisor will have an overview of the supervisee's workload and the challenges involved, but will also have a certain amount of distance. This distance can be very helpful when it comes to keeping things in perspective. This is because staff can sometimes get so enmeshed in a situation that they get too close to it and lose that sense of perspective. The slightly removed view of the supervisor can therefore be very helpful and supportive.
- *Transparency* The importance of letting people know where they stand was mentioned above. If they are clear about what their strengths and areas for development are, they can feel reasonably secure about delivering to an acceptable level of performance. By contrast, if people do not know where they stand, they can become unnecessarily anxious on the one hand or complacent on the other.
- *Leadership* We will explore this topic in more detail in Chapter 11 where we focus on this L of *CALM*, but for now it is important to emphasize that staff tend to find being supervised by someone with clear leadership skills a source of security and thus support. By the same token, supportive supervision can help to establish a leader's credibility and thus a baseline of trust and respect, essential foundations of effective leadership.

One of the benefits of the staff support element of supervision is that it can help with the standard setting aspect. For example, if staff feel well supported, morale is likely to be higher. If morale is higher, error rates are likely to be lower, and standards of work will generally be higher, thereby presenting fewer problems of accountability.
A further benefit is that it can also support the staff development aspect, in so far as well-supported staff are more likely to be open to learning (and, conversely, staff who are learning and developing are likely to find this supportive, a boost to their confidence and overall morale).

4. *Mediation*
This refers to the process of identifying, and attempting to resolve, any conflicts or tensions that may be preventing the supervisee from achieving optimal levels of work. As we shall see in Chapter 25, conflict is an inevitable feature of the workplace. Very often, conflicts can be quite destructive and can prevent people from doing their work to an optimal standard and may, at times, even prevent them from achieving an acceptable

standard. The ability to identify such issues and be suitably supportive in addressing them is therefore an important part of our repertoire.

Practice focus 3.2

Jan was a manager in a voluntary organization with responsibility for over 30 staff. Sometimes staff would fall out with one another and create a very tense atmosphere that could be very problematic for everybody. At first Jan just crossed her fingers and hoped that not too much harm would be done while she waited for things to die down. However, over time she realized that this was not the most helpful way of dealing with conflict situations, as she was aware of how much tension and ill feeling could be generated. In her early days in her post she did not have the confidence to deal with conflict issues, but she now felt that she needed to adopt a different approach and try to tackle conflict situations directly rather than adopt an ostrich approach to them. While her first efforts to address conflict situations in supervision were a bit nerve wracking for her, she soon came to the conclusion that this was a much wiser and much more effective tactic and she regretted that she had waited so long before summoning up the courage to tackle conflict as and when required.

As Practice focus 3.2 illustrates, it can be a little anxiety provoking to tackle conflict to begin with, but I would argue that it is important to get past this, partly because leaving conflicts unresolved means that we are not succeeding in getting the best out of people, and partly because not having the courage to address conflict will give staff the strong and understandable impression that we lack credibility as leaders and are not to be trusted.

We will return to the subject of leadership in Chapter 11 and to the subject of conflict in Chapter 25.

Figure 3.1 The four elements of supervision

Effective supervision

To be an effective supervisor we need to make sure that we are covering all four elements of supervision as discussed above. It can be highly problematic if we simply stick to our favourite aspects and do not look at the situation holistically. This is not simply a matter of, for example, dividing an hour-long supervision session into fifteen minutes for each of the four sections. A skilled and experienced supervisor will be able to weave together the different elements. For example, asking the question: 'How are you getting on with X?' can provide opportunities to discuss standard setting (Is the work being carried out within appropriate parameters?); staff development (Are opportunities for learning from this being drawn out?); staff support (advice, guidance, encouragement and reassurance can be given alongside thanks and appreciation for the work done); and mediation (identifying any conflicts or tensions in this situation and seeking to address them). Of course, this will not work in all situations, but it is a good example of how we need to seek to blend the elements, rather than to see them as separate issues.

What we also need to do to be effective supervisors is to make sure that supervision sessions are not simply a tedious process of working our way systematically through the supervisee's workload. This is something that I like to refer to as 'painting the Forth Bridge', which involves going through a supervisee's workload from start to finish, either in one session or across a series of sessions, only to begin the process again when it is completed, and thereby largely neglecting other elements of the supervision relationship. What is far more appropriate and helpful is a reflective, analytical approach where, instead of routinely going through the whole workload, there is a focus on the most important aspects, so that, in effect, what is happening is that the supervisor and supervisee are prioritising together what are the key issues that supervision needs to address under one or more of the four headings described here.

An effective supervisor also has to be committed to equality and diversity (to ensure that a culture of fairness and openness exists as a foundation for staff achieving their best) and has to be a good communicator to ensure that supervisory interactions are positive and helpful. Supervision can therefore be seen as something that builds on the insights we have covered in the first two chapters (and lays the foundations for many of the chapters that follow).

Conclusion

My experience has taught me that supervision can make all the difference between bad practice and good practice on the one hand, and between good practice and excellent practice on the other. A skilled and confident supervisor can help to bring out the best in a supervisee, help them to fulfil their potential in terms of achieving optimal standards of work, while also taking opportunities for maximizing learning and developing in the process. Supervision is therefore a vitally important process in terms of people management and well worth the investment of time and effort to build up the knowledge, skills and confidence we need to be the most effective supervisors we are capable of being.

Perlmutter *et al.* (2001) describe what is needed for effective supervision:

> First, it is essential to create an *organizational culture* that both unites diverse professionals and supports and recognizes their unique expertise. Second, managerial supervisors must develop (1) an in-depth awareness of their own *professional identity* and a recognition of what other professionals bring to the organization, (2) an up-to-date knowledge base about multiple professional requirements and standards, and (3) the leadership ability to mobilize this awareness and knowledge into action.
>
> (p. 14)

This highlights the demanding nature of supervision. This may seem daunting to new supervisors, but it is important to recognize that the knowledge, skills, values and confidence needed for high-quality supervision can be developed over time – there is no need to have it all in place on day one.

To work out whether or not supervision is working, the litmus test is to see whether supervisees look forward to supervision or not. Because it is intended to be a helpful, constructive process that helps them to achieve their best, then it should be something that they appreciate and therefore look forward to. If, on the other hand, it is the case that they are dreading supervision, or least not looking forward to it at all, then that is giving a very strong message that supervision is not fulfilling its potential. Commonly, people complain that supervision is a tedious process of checking up (what is sometimes referred to as 'snoopervision'). Clearly this indicates that supervision is not working. What needs to happen is for a skilled supervisor to be able to use the time together to discuss key issues that will enable the supervisee to become the most effective, most confident and most skilful practitioner they can be.

KEY POINT

Everyone benefits from good supervision. The employee is helped to achieve their potential. The team therefore benefits from the improved contribution from that particular member, as does the organization and all its stakeholders. But, of course, managers also benefit in the sense that an employee who is finding supervision helpful will present fewer problems and will make the manager's job easier and more successful. And, of course, HR professionals benefit, in the sense that, if supervision is working well, then they will be faced with fewer problems to address in the wider scheme of things.

Points to ponder
1. Why is giving effective feedback important?
2. What is meant by building on and building up?
3. What are the likely consequences of staff feeling unsupported?

Exercise 3
From your own experiences of having been supervised or of wishing for better supervision, what lessons can you learn about what is helpful and what is unhelpful in the context of offering supervision?

CHAPTER 4: RECRUITMENT, SELECTION AND WORKFORCE PLANNING

In this chapter you will learn about important issues to bear in mind when recruiting and selecting staff and in overall workforce planning.

Introduction

Without people there can be no people management, without staff there can be no employing organization, and so the question of recruiting and selecting appropriate employees and undertaking workforce planning is an important part of our endeavour. Getting the right people can be crucial; getting the wrong ones can be disastrous, potentially creating problems for years to come. This therefore raises two important questions. First: how do we attract and select the best people? and second: how do we plan for what our staffing needs will be? These are the two main topics to be covered in this chapter.

Attracting the right staff

There are various ways in which people can be encouraged to become employees of your organization. The following are the main ones:

- *Advertising vacancies in the right places (including online).* This refers to making sure that the place we advertise is consistent with the type of people we require. For example, if we advertise in the Times, then we should not be surprised if Times readers apply for the post, but if the people we are seeking to appoint are not likely to read the Times (reception staff, for example), then clearly that was not a wise use of our advertising budget. Increasingly now we are seeing online recruitment opportunities, but the same argument can apply (see the end of the chapter for information about this). Different people will use different online resources to seek employment, and so it is important that we are mindful of which online resource(s) is likely to be our best bet. The question of choosing 'the right places' to advertise also needs to take account of equality and diversity issues. For example, if an organization's workforce is not representative of the local community in terms of ethnic make up, then there could well be a good case for advertising in specialist media that are more likely to be seen by potential applicants from minority ethnic groups.
- *Other recruitment methods.* There are also other approaches to consider. For example, there are what are sometimes called milk rounds, which is where one or more companies attend a university or college to present the opportunities that exist for graduates in that organization. This type of event can also happen at conferences and exhibitions in some cases. In addition, there are now employment agencies that can

provide staff on a part-time, full-time, temporary or permanent basis. Again, it is important to be clear about how best to use the budget available for recruiting staff. It is also important to be clear about the equality and diversity implications. It is essential that we make sure that the recruitment method(s) we choose do not have in-built biases that will significantly reduce the involvement of underrepresented groups.

- *Reward packages*. This is not just simply a matter of salary. Prospective applicants will want to know what else is on offer that is likely to attract them to the job. This will vary from organization to organization and job to job, but there are likely to be quite a range of different opportunities for employees to gain rewards from the post (for example, is there a relocation allowance for people who would need to move house to take up the offer of a post? Are there crèche facilities?). It is important that reward packages are described in ways that will attract potential applicants, but which are also fair and accurate and not at all misleading. We should also bear in mind that rewards are not simply financial or finance related. Other important attractions that could potentially be mentioned would be: a full, thorough induction programme (see Chapter 5); regular supervision (Chapter 3); training and development opportunities (Chapter 19) and so on.

- *Clear expectations*. We will need to develop, at the very least, a role or job profile which specifies what is involved in the post, and this will need to be accompanied by a person specification which spells out in some precise detail what it is we are looking for in the likely successful candidate. If we do not provide this clarity of expectation through such documents (and through, for example, advertisements), then we risk wasting our own organization's time and the time of people who apply who soon recognize that it was a mistake to do so (when they realize that the job is not what they thought it was, or the person specification you were looking for is not what they thought it was). It can also be helpful to provide background information about the organization in order to give potential applicants a good picture of what they can expect.

- *Choosing the right criteria*. If we advertise that we need people with certain qualifications, skills or experiences and these are not strictly necessary for the job, then we may well be excluding good candidates who could have achieved a high level in that post. We could also potentially be guilty of discrimination if we are unfairly excluding people who could have been effective employees. It is therefore important that considerable thought is given to the role or job profile and person specification to make sure that they do not contain any unnecessary or inappropriate criteria. A common and helpful step is to distinguish between *essential* and *desirable* criteria – that is, being clear about which criteria will rule out certain applicants if they are not met (that is, the *essential* ones) and which will not rule anyone out if not met, but which will be an advantage if they are (the *desirable* ones).

Clearly, then, a lot of thought and effort needs to go into the process of attracting the right staff. Thinking of placing an advert without going through the processes that are needed to clarify how we will get the best person is not a wise way of tackling these issues. In particular, it is very easy for ill-thought-through approaches to introduce discriminatory elements – reflecting the point made in Chapter 1 that most discrimination is unintentional.

Practice focus 4.1
Chris was surprised to find that there had been only two applicants for the vacancy in his team and that there was now going to be a very inconvenient delay while the post was re-advertised. Previous vacancies had attracted quite a few applicants so he wondered what had gone wrong this time. When he made enquiries about this, he was very disappointed to learn that, due to budget cutbacks, the post had not been advertised in the appropriate professional press as before, and the only notice relating to the post had been placed in the local newspaper, which was much cheaper. Chris was annoyed by this, particularly as the need to re-advertise meant that the recruitment process would now end up costing more than would have been the case originally.

Selecting the right staff
Once we have succeeded in attracting appropriate applicants, we then have the important task of selecting the best person for the job. The most common way of selecting people is through inviting application forms to be completed and then shortlisting on the basis of those. However, some organizations prefer to invite applicants to submit a curriculum vitae (CV) with an accompanying letter of application, so one thing we will need to do is to check what the policy of the organization is, and, if it allows for a CV and letter of application to be submitted, rather than the traditional application form, we will then need to consider which is going to be more helpful to us in making the decision.

One factor that we would need to take into consideration in making such a decision is: how helpful is the application form? Over the years I have seen a wide range of application forms and they have varied in their fitness for purpose. Some have been of excellent standard and appropriately focused to supply the necessary information to make decisions about shortlisting, while others I have seen have been far from adequate in doing that. We will therefore need to make our own judgement about whether the application form is sufficient or whether we would get a better basis of information for making our decision from a CV and letter of application.

Once we have the application forms (or CV and letter of application) in, we will need to begin a process of shortlisting. For this we will need to ask at least two questions. First of all, we will need to ask:

- *Who needs to be involved?* For example, is it sufficient for one person to be the interviewer or is a panel required? If a panel, who are the best people to be on it? Single-person interviews are the most cost effective, but they also bring the potential for claims of discrimination (for example, a woman employee complaining that a male interviewer did not appreciate her perspective as a woman), and so panel interviews tend to be favoured more these days in many organizations. But it is important to make sure that the panel is no larger than it needs to be, partly for economic reasons in terms of the time costs involved, and partly to make it fair on applicants that they do not feel that they are being interviewed by too large a group of people (the bigger the panel, the more nervous people tend to get – including members of the panel themselves in many cases). Of course, the bigger the panel, also the greater is the risk of disagreement and difficulty in making a satisfactory decision. If the panel is too large we are, in effect, adding a further, unnecessary criterion, in so far as the question of how well candidates come across will, in part, be dependent on how well they are able to respond to large panels – something that will be irrelevant to most jobs.
- *What are the criteria?* Whether a single-person interview or a panel interview, this is an important question, as there has to be clarity about the basis on which the decision is being made. Without that clarity, we are quite rightly open to criticisms of discrimination, as there could be considerable inconsistency in terms of how people's applications and presentation at interview are being perceived.

In order to have a successful interview, or set of interviews, we need to make sure that the practical arrangements are in place – for example, a suitable venue, notifications to the appropriate people (candidates and panel members), the availability of refreshments and waiting facilities. We will also need to make sure that timings are appropriate. For example, if we allow too short a time for each interview, we will quickly get behind schedule and inconvenience everyone involved. We therefore have to be realistic in terms of allocating an appropriate time slot for each interview, allowing some time for discussion and reflection on the part of the panel before beginning the next interview. It will also be necessary, of course, to timetable short breaks. It is not wise to expect panel members to be able to concentrate fully in a series of interviews without appropriate comfort breaks.

KEY POINT

It is good practice to have a criteria grid available for interviewers – that is, a chart that lists the relevant criteria and has space for making notes, so that, when the discussion takes place after the interview, everyone is singing from the same hymn sheet in terms of what they are focusing on. Similarly, if it is to be a panel interview, we will want to consider having a standard set of questions and whether or not supplementary questions are permissible. The need for this is based on attempts to be fair and not allow discrimination to creep into the process.

Some organizations like to ask candidates to make presentations. This raises a number of issues. First of all, if we are going to do this, we will need to make sure that the appropriate facilities are available. For example, it can be unfair if chaotic circumstances knock candidates off their track, and it also puts the organization in a bad light. For example, I have been both an interviewer and an interviewee in circumstances where the facilities were not working properly and caused chaos. But a more fundamental issue to address is: what is the purpose of asking people to make presentations? If the job involves giving presentations, then it makes sense to test people out in doing this, but if making presentations is not part of the job, then asking candidates to make their presentation as part of the selection process can be misleading, as we may get, for example, a mediocre candidate overall who has exceptionally good presentation skills, being preferred over an excellent candidate overall who is not particularly effective at making presentations.

Some organizations use assessment centres, which is a term that refers to a set of observed work-related activities and tests that can take place over one or two days. This is a very expensive approach in terms of time, money and the use of facilities, and is not necessarily more effective than the traditional use of a structured interview. However, this is not to rule it out altogether; it remains an option, but should only be used where there are compelling reasons to prefer this to more conventional means.

Some organizations also rely on psychometric tests – for example, tests of personality and/or intelligence. These do have certain limitations (see, for example, Newell and Shackleton, 2017), but can be useful if used as part of an overall package of measures. However, they should not be used on their own, as they will not give a full picture of the candidate and their circumstances.

Regardless of the method used, it is likely that references will be required too. It is important to make sure that these are from relevant people and that they are up to date. There may be little value in a reference from, for example, a former employer in relation to a job which is very different from the job in which the candidate was previously employed. The reference will not be completely without value, in so far as it can offer comments on the employee's reliability and so on, but it will not give us a sufficient picture in terms of how suited they are to the current job. Similarly, if a reference is several years old, we have to question how valuable that is, because so much could have changed during that time.

Different methods have different levels of validity – see, for example, Armstrong (2020). But, what is important is that we select methods that we feel are going to be suited to the particular circumstances that apply in relation to this specific post. There is no 'right answer' when it comes to staff selection methods, but there is much we can learn by weighing up the alternatives and considering them carefully.

Whatever methods are chosen, the question of appropriate checks will also need to be addressed. Depending on the circumstances, this could involve the following:

- *Criminal record checks.* These are necessary for some posts, especially those that involve working with children or vulnerable adults (that is, adults with physical or learning disabilities; older people; people with mental health problems). It will be important to check the policy and related procedures of the organization concerned in order to be clear about in what circumstances such checks are to be used and what precise steps need to be taken to comply with the appropriate requirements.
- *Qualification checks.* It is general good practice to ask for evidence of qualifications claimed, but this is essential in situations where a particular qualification is a *requirement* for the post. It is not unheard of for people to claim that they have qualifications that they do not in fact possess, and so it is vital that appropriate documentary evidence is seen. Where the qualification was gained abroad, then enquiries may need to be made to the appropriate authorities to ensure that the qualification is actually equivalent to what is required – for example, a diploma from one country may not be equivalent to a diploma in another country.
- *Professional registration check* If the post requires the successful candidate to be registered with their appropriate professional body, then it is essential that confirmatory evidence of that registration is obtained.

Failing to make the necessary checks can result in major difficulties if, at a later date, it is discovered that someone who was appointed should not have been. This is not only embarrassing for the organization in general and the individuals involved in the appointment in particular, but also a considerable inconvenience (and expense) in terms of having to go through the process of having to dismiss the person concerned and appoint someone else in their place. However, potentially of much more importance, there may be things that employee has done that are no longer valid. For example, there may be worrying circumstances in which someone claimed to be duly qualified to make particular professional or clinical decisions who was not actually authorized to do so, thereby potentially rendering the whole process invalid (perhaps a health and safety inspector who has passed certain equipment as safe without the necessary knowledge, qualifications or accreditation to do so).

One final point in terms of selecting the right staff is that I believe it is important to have some degree of sensitivity in notifying unsuccessful candidates. I have come across many instances of poor practice where, for example, candidates have been told they will be informed within, say, forty-eight hours, and have not received any communication during that time, and may not receive any communication at all. They are just left to assume that they were unsuccessful. I have also come across examples of very poorly written standard letters that have been quite problematic in terms of the message they convey, which then cast the organization in a very poor light. Some cynics may argue that this does not matter, as these are the unsuccessful candidates we are talking about, and it is the successful candidate(s) who is important. However, what we have to remember is that unsuccessful candidates on this occasion may be potential applicants for future vacancies, and we may lose potentially excellent candidates if they are declined insensitively on this occasion. There is also the broader issue of a genuinely people-focused approach to people management. How can we square treating unsuccessful applicants so shabbily with a genuine commitment to valuing people and the contribution they make?

> *Practice focus 4.2*
> Jean was a human resources officer in a large organization. She had never been involved in appointing staff before until a reorganization of duties meant that she now had responsibility for making the appropriate arrangements. At first, she was quite anxious about the situation, as it was a lot to take in. What motivated her to get it right was that she had had previous bad experiences of applying for posts and encountering all sorts of problems – chaos, confusion, apparent unfairness, unreasonable delay and so on. Also, when she talked to her family and friends about her new duties she was told many stories of bad experiences people had had at the hands of organizations that had not got their act together when it came to appointing staff. Jean was therefore determined to make use of her organizing skills to make sure that any appointments she was involved in would not leave people feeling disgruntled by poor organization.

Workforce planning

So far, we have looked at the situation of recruitment and selection at a micro level in terms of dealing with individual vacancies as and when they arise, but we also have to consider the bigger picture, the macro level, of workforce planning. This involves having a wider strategic focus and not just looking at individual posts. It is a matter of developing an overall picture of what human resources are likely to be needed, with what knowledge, skills and values. For example, there is little sense in a restaurant having enough chefs and kitchen staff if they do not have enough serving staff to wait on the tables – or vice versa.

Simply dealing with vacancies on an *ad hoc* basis may leave us in a difficult position if, for example, there is a change in the external environment that we could have anticipated which now leaves us with inappropriate staffing levels or with people who do not have the appropriate skills, qualifications or accreditation. Some degree of planning is therefore a wise option to ensure that the right people are in the right place at the right time.

 There is much to be gained from thinking strategically about the bigger picture of workforce planning by not allowing yourself to get bogged down in the details of filling a particular post or posts.

The sort of questions that workforce planning needs to address are:

- *Do we have the right balance or skills mix?* For example, there is no point in having highly paid professional staff wasting time doing their own filing and photocopying because of a shortage of clerical or administrative staff. That is, of course, a poor use of organizational resources.
- *Are there succession plans in place, especially for key people?* For example, if there is somebody who has been around for a long time and has a lot of knowledge about the organization, but is now approaching retirement, what plans are there in place to ensure that all that knowledge is not lost when he or she leaves the organization? This is important not only for the organization (and the employees who will benefit from having that knowledge available), but also for the retiring employee who is likely to feel valued and validated if his or her knowledge is seen as worthy of holding onto within the organization.
- *Are we planning appropriately for changes ahead?* This can refer to changes within the organization. Can we anticipate anything that is likely to happen (a reorganization, for example) that may have implications for staffing levels or the type of people and skills that will be needed? We also need to anticipate changes in the external environment. For example, where we know of coming changes in the law or likely changes in the market as a result of new technology, then it would be foolish not to plan for what implications that they have for our workforce needs.

Workforce planning is not an exact science but, by the same token, there are considerable costs involved in not taking seriously the challenge of trying to anticipate what the organization's needs will be in terms of its most important resource, its people. Of course, there will be a number of unforeseen (and sometimes unforeseeable) factors that may crop up and spoil our plans, leaving us having to adapt to new circumstances as effectively as possible. However, this is a situation that is far preferable to having no plans and leaving the fulfilling of staffing needs to chance.

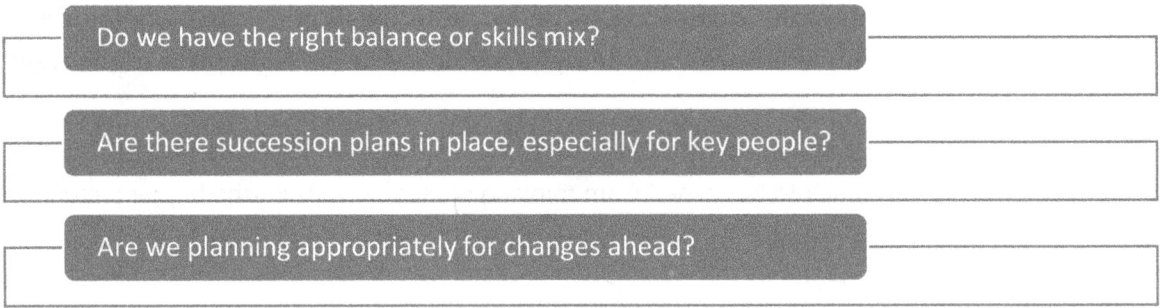

Figure 4.1 Workforce planning

Conclusion

This chapter has shown that it is very important to have the right people in the right place at the right time. It is extremely important to get this right as far as we can, in so far as the price of getting it wrong can be very high indeed. Employing people who are not suitable for the job brings with it a whole array of potential problems, some of them very serious indeed. If we skimp on this aspect of people management, then we take a very serious risk. It is therefore vitally important that we are well informed about the issues involved, and it is to be hoped that this chapter has provided a good basis for continuing to develop that knowledge and understanding.

Points to ponder
1. Why is it essential to establish clear expectations?
2. What do you see as the pros and cons of using psychometric tests?
3. In terms of workforce planning, in what ways is the skills mix important?

Exercise 4

What experiences have you had of applying for jobs? What lessons might you be able to learn about good practice in this area of people management form your own experiences (or those of friends or colleagues)?

CHAPTER 5: INDUCTION

In this chapter you will learn about how to make new staff feel welcome so that they get off to a good start and are well prepared for their role and duties.

Introduction

We are all generally aware of the importance of first impressions, and this is a particularly important consideration when new members of staff join an organization. It is therefore important that the induction process is taken seriously and given the attention it deserves. New employees who are largely left to fend for themselves are likely to have a poor impression of the organization and get a very clear message that it is not a supportive people-focused organization. It can take a long time to eradicate such a negative perception, and for some people in some circumstances, it may never be removed.

Induction – or 'onboarding', as it is often known – is very important in terms of laying a foundation for motivation and commitment. Someone who has an unhelpful induction period may find it difficult to identify with the organization and its goals, to feel part of the enterprise and committed to it. They are likely to feel that they have not been accepted fully as part of that organization and are therefore likely to be less engaged and motivated than might otherwise have been the case. They are therefore highly unlikely to achieve their best.

Armstrong (2020) highlights the importance of induction by emphasizing that it reduces the cost and inconvenience of early leavers. Due to the importance of first impressions and the impact of the first four weeks of employment, staff are far more likely to resign during the initial months. Such early resignations are disruptive and costly – for example, in terms of the costs of obtaining replacements, induction, training, lower productivity from new starters, and gaps between one person leaving and another one arriving. It should be clear, then, that the tendency I have sadly seen many, many times in my career for induction to be skimped on is a very dangerous and costly error to make.

There are also implications in terms of retention (as we shall discuss in Chapter 16). It is unfortunately the case that, in some organizations, a significant proportion of newly appointed staff will leave within a matter of months, some within weeks or even days. So, if we are to make sure that the efforts that went into recruiting and selecting the best staff are not wasted, we have to follow up our efforts with a proper induction programme.

If we do not, then the price we could pay for that is not only potentially that particular member of staff being disaffected or even leaving, but also low morale across the team, work group or even whole organization. This is as a result of the understandable perception that an organization that does not bother to welcome its staff properly and prepare them for their duties is an uncaring organization and one that is not to be trusted. We therefore have to ask ourselves how we can make induction as effective and fruitful as possible. This chapter should therefore go some way towards setting you on the right track for making induction a positive and empowering aspect of people management that sets new recruits on a positive pathway.

The chapter is divided into four main parts. The first one tries to establish a common baseline of understanding by asking the key question: what is induction? The second and third cover issues relating to induction before arrival and on arrival respectively, while the fourth introduces a helpful framework for making a success of induction, the A to E of induction.

What is induction?

Induction is the 'joining' process whereby a new recruit is welcomed into the organization and helped to settle in. It involves clarifying what each party can expect of one another with a view to laying the foundations for an effective partnership whereby the organization will get the best out of their new employee and they, in turn, will achieve their best and get the full benefits of being a valued employee.

Armstrong (2020) outlines the following four aims of induction:

1. Smooth the preliminary stages when everything is likely to be strange and unfamiliar to the starter.
2. Establish quickly a favourable attitude to the organization in the mind of new employees so that they are more likely to stay.
3. Obtain effective output from the new employee in the shortest possible time.
4. Reduce the likelihood of the employee leaving quickly.

To this I would want to add:

5. Establish a foundation of trust and respect as a basis for good working relationships.
6. Introduce the new recruit to the culture of the organization, so that they can be aware of its positive and negative points.

7. Begin a process of learning that will be sustained and developed by other organizational processes: supervision, training and development and possibly coaching and/or mentoring.
8. Begin to integrate the new person into their team or working group so that they can both benefit from, and contribute to, effective teamwork (see Chapter 14).
9. Introduce the new recruit to key people as part of a process of establishing positive working relationships.
10. Begin the process of identifying any potential difficulties the new staff member may encounter and consider ways of addressing or avoiding them.

KEY POINT

What makes induction particularly important is that it reflects in microcosm the basis of people management. It is (or at least should be) the starting point of the mutually beneficial partnership that effective people management is intended to achieve (and on which it relies for its potency). It paves the way for so many other important components of successful organizational life. It is for this reason that we need to make sure that we do not see induction as simply a straightforward administrative process. It is a crucial foundation for helping organizations and the people within them to fulfil their potential.

Before arrival

The induction process does not begin on day one. Before the new recruit arrives there are things that need to be done in preparation, in an effort to ensure that all goes as well as possible. For example, it can be very helpful to notify key people of the new person's planned arrival (for example, reception staff), so that they are aware of when he or she will be arriving. In this way, it can be arranged that they can be the first to provide a welcoming smile and positive greeting right from the start. I cannot emphasize enough how important this can be. The difference in impact on a new member of staff between a workplace that offers a warm welcome and one that does not is immense. It reflects the C, for Connection, of *Staying CALM* – it is about making important human connections right from the start.

There may also be considerable value in the new recruit having informal contact with the team that he or she is going to be part of if time for this can be found. It can be quite daunting for somebody to go into a new job on day one not knowing anything about the people they are going to be working alongside. Some sort of informal get-together can therefore be very helpful, if it is practicable at the time.

There is also the question of the provision of relevant information to be addressed. Some of this information can be provided in advance, although it is not fair to expect somebody who is not yet on the payroll to read reams and reams of information. Some of this information can be provided on day one, and can therefore be part of the first day induction (looking at relevant information as part of forming a better picture of the job and the setting is an important part of induction). It is particularly important to provide concrete information for new recruits, rather than take the lazy way out of simply referring them to the organization's website.

It is also important to arrange practicalities in advance – the provision of resources and facilities, for example. Imagine the emotional impact of these not being in place when someone arrives. Imagine the strong message of not being welcome, of being unimportant (see Practice Focus 5.1). The damage that this can bring about can be quite significant and may prove to be irreparable in many cases. Even something as simple to avoid as this can create an initial negative impression that can last for a very long time, a small but possibly quite significant obstacle to the staff member concerned fulfilling their potential.

Some organizations have a 'buddy' system which means that each new member of staff is assigned a mentor from the team. This mentor will be the key person in making the induction a successful and positive experience. Where such a system is used it is important that: (i) the appointed buddy is made fully aware of the importance of induction and the dangers of skimping on it; and (ii) is given adequate time to prepare for their role (that is, they are not told about it the day before the new colleague arrives!)

There is clearly much that can be done, then, to pave the way for making the new recruit's entry into the organization a very positive and indeed potentially excellent start, while neglecting these issues can mean that potential goes unfulfilled, trust and positive working relationships are not fully established, and success becomes much harder to achieve for both employee and employer.

On arrival: the first day
It is essential that this first day is handled sensitively. For example, it is important to communicate a clear time of arrival and one that will dovetail with your availability (or the availability of the appropriate person who will be getting the induction process going). It is a poor start, for example, to have someone arrive at 9 a.m. only to be sitting waiting while the person who is taking responsibility for greeting them is making telephone calls or working their way through their email before getting into the main business of the day. It would be much better to invite that new person to start day one at, say, 10 am after the key person with person with responsibility for welcoming them and settling them in has had the opportunity to clear the decks, as it were.

It is also important to make sure that there is an appropriate balance of work on day one – not too much, not too little. Overloading somebody on their first day will give a very negative impression and could get things off to a very bad start. Similarly, having a new team member sitting about twiddling their thumbs is not an auspicious start to a new post. It is therefore important to think about what they will be asked to do on that first day, to make sure that the balance is right.

It is also very wise to make sure that practical information is provided early on that day – for example, where the toilets are, what the arrangements are for tea and coffee and so on. In addition, if the person concerned is going to be working as part of a team, ideally a seating plan of the team should be provided, so that they are quickly able to work out the names of the people they will be working with. Even a simple practical measure like this can be a very positive step in making someone feel welcome and therefore valued. By contrast, if no effort is made to make settling in easier for the new staff member, then a very negative impression can be created.

Practice focus 5.1
Roy was delighted to be offered the job as it was a significant promotion for him, even though it meant that he would have a long commute. He had equipment he needed to bring with him and he also needed to have internet access to continue with the project it had been agreed he would bring with him to his new post. His office was on the second floor and so it was agreed that a porter would be available on his arrival on his first day to help him take his equipment to his office. It was also agreed that there would be a brand new computer on his desk, linked to the internet. When he turned up at the agreed time on his first day in his new post there was no sign of a porter being available to help him take his equipment up to his office. He walked over to the porter's desk in the next building but was told that no arrangements had been made and there was no one available to assist. Roy was disappointed by this very poor start, but fortunately one of his new colleagues arrived and was able to help him get the equipment up the stairs. However, the next thing that disappointed him was that the brand new computer linked to the internet he had been promised was nowhere to be seen. Instead, he had an antique machine on his desk with no internet connection. It turned out that this extremely poor induction process was not atypical of the organization's approach to staff, and, within a matter of months, Roy had tendered his resignation and was in the process of developing a freelance career for himself.

It can be helpful for the new appointee to meet some key people on the first day, but if that is going to happen, make sure such meetings are relatively short, as there is a limit to how much information somebody can take in on a first day. It should not be underestimated how much of a challenge it can be to try and absorb so much information in a context that is largely new to the person concerned. Even for people who already have a good feel for the organization and a lot of knowledge about it would struggle to take in a lot of information from a series of meetings with key people. So, for somebody who is still finding their way around the building and trying to remember the names of their colleagues, the information provided in meetings may be more or less completely wasted, in so far as much of it will not be retained. The key, then, is to keep such meetings short and for them to be followed up with fuller meetings in the not-too-distant future.

With these thoughts in mind, it is also worth arranging for the first day to be a short day rather than see out the whole day and to go well beyond our capacity for information retention. It can be kinder, more fruitful and give a positive message to the new employee to allow them to finish earlier than would normally be the case. This is not only wise in terms of information overload dangers, but also gives a positive message that you are concerned about their well-being and are not going to overload them.

> *Practice focus 5.2*
> Lynn regularly supervised students on placement from the local university. She had been doing this for years and had it down to a fine art. She had worked out a structured induction programme that worked a treat after it had been modified a number of times since she first developed it. It covered all the practicalities; enabled the new student to meet some key people but without being overwhelmed; provided a nice balance of information – not too much, not too little; and generally did an excellent job of making the student feel welcome and valued. This also worked well for the team, as everyone knew where they stood and what was happening. The students really appreciated the time and effort that had gone into getting them off to such a good start. It gave them a really good launch pad for their learning and development throughout the period of the work placement. Lynn had put so much effort into making induction work well as she had had some very negative and demoralizing experiences as a student herself and as an employee. She wanted to make sure that the students she was responsible for did not have the same bad experiences that she had had in her day.

The A to E of induction

Having clarified what we mean by induction and considered what needs to happen before the new colleague's arrival and on their first day, we now turn our attention to a wider picture of induction. We are going to explore these under the heading of the A to E of induction, a framework I have developed to cast light on some of the important issues involved.

This framework is based on the fact that we can identify five key areas of induction that conveniently spell out A to E. This goes beyond the first day and accounts for a full induction programme which can be anything from a week to months (depending on the organization, the post, the person and the circumstances). This will depend in large part on the amount of learning that needs to be done by the new recruit. It may be worthwhile to check the policy of the organization concerned to get a clear picture of what constitutes an appropriate period of induction (if such a policy exists – not all organizations have one).

A refers to *Adapting existing knowledge and skills*. No one will be starting a new job with a completely blank slate, as it were, and so a key task of the induction process is to give the new recruit the opportunity to see how their existing knowledge and skills can be brought to bear in the new work setting. This will be a useful baseline for later supervision and appraisal and will also enable the new colleague to consolidate existing knowledge and skills by developing an understanding of how they can be used in a new context. Adapting in this way is something that many people find quite straightforward and will therefore require relatively little support in this regard. Others, by contrast, may struggle to see the connections between what they have learned to date and the new setting and could therefore need quite a lot of support and guidance, to begin with at least.

B refers to *Briefing*. This means being provided with the information needed to make sense of the confusing new circumstances that they now find themselves in. If appropriate information is not provided through such briefing, then they may form a false view of the situation through a lack of information, or they may be given unhelpful information – through gossip and rumour, for example. I have already emphasized the importance of not overloading new colleagues, especially on the first day, but we also need to make sure that we do not provide them with too little information. What is particularly important is that the induction period teaches them not only the basic knowledge they need, but also – just as importantly – how to find out more as and when they need it.

C refers to *Cultural transmission*. Induction is a process by which a new recruit learns about the culture they will be working in. Cultures have both positive and negative aspects, and it can be important for people managers to emphasize the positives and encourage the new member to engage with these positive aspects while trying to keep the negative aspects at bay, so that they are not unduly influenced by any problematic aspects of existing cultural assumptions, habits or values. That way, the introduction of a new recruit can be not only a matter of him or her learning about the culture, but also the new member of that culture being in a position to influence it in a positive direction. In Chapter 11 on leadership, I explain that it is not only managers that can be leaders (that is, people who influence the culture in a positive direction). Indeed, part of a leader's role is to help others become leaders. This is also an important consideration in relation to teamwork (see Chapter 14).

D refers to *Developing new skills and knowledge*. There will be knowledge and skills that are specific to that particular setting which may well build on existing knowledge and skills but will be important issues in their own right. The induction process should enable us, together with the new recruit, to begin the process of identifying what those are and make a start on developing them. Being in a new post will provide lots of learning opportunities for the new staff member, even if they have occupied a similar role in one or more previous posts. It is understandable that someone in a new environment will feel a little insecure and will want to stick to their existing strong points in terms of capabilities. However, there is much to be gained by gently encouraging new recruits to look positively at what new learning challenges the new post offers – and to see this as an opportunity for growth and development, rather than as something to be concerned about.

E refers to *Expectations*. These need to be both clear and realistic. Induction should give a crystal clear picture of what is expected of the new recruit. This is important for reasons of morale, in the sense that a person who is not clear about what is expected of them can be quite prone to stress and a sense of insecurity, whereas clear expectations can be a source of great help (see the discussion of giving feedback as part of supervision in Chapter 3). Similarly, expectations have to be realistic. If people are asked to do the impossible, then they may well choose to look for another job sooner rather than later. It is therefore very important that the induction process is successful in establishing both clear and realistic expectations for the new team member. It should also help the new colleague by making it clear to them what they can expect from their manager, the team and the organization more broadly.

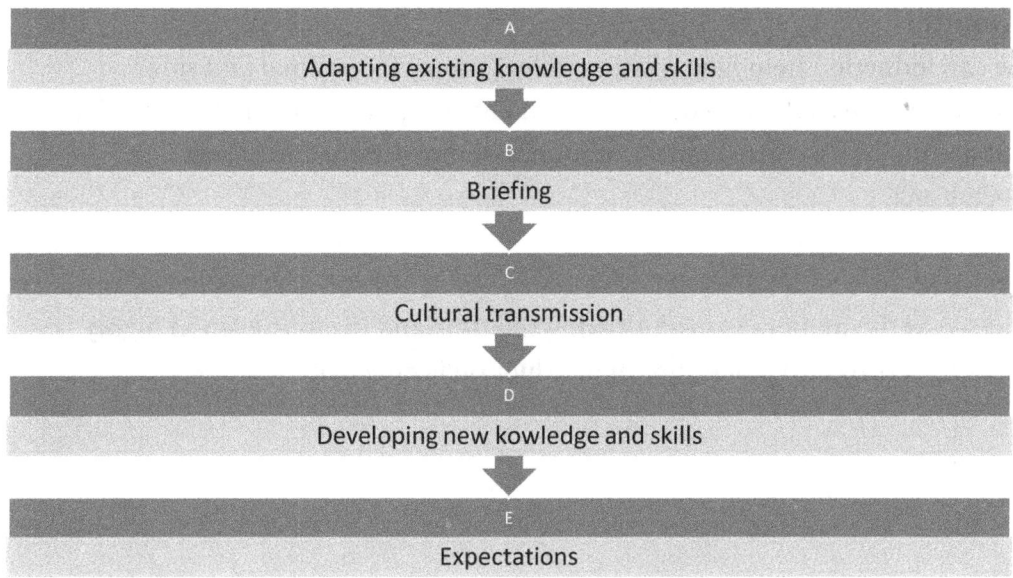

Figure 5.1 The A to E of induction

Thinking of induction in terms of this A to E framework does not offer magic answers, of course, but it can be a useful mnemonic to help to make sure that we are taking induction seriously and investing in it the time, effort, energy and thought it deserves.

Conclusion

In Chapter 4 we noted the importance of getting the right people in the right place and at the right time. We can now see that it is also crucial to start them off on the right track. If we are tempted skimp on this, we can undo all the good work we have done in making sure we appointed the best person for the job. Some people unfortunately see induction as a very straightforward matter and largely provide very little by way of support and structure to such a process. They simply leave the new recruit to get on with it, perhaps basing their thinking on the dubious idea that throwing people in at the deep end teaches them how to swim. Some of those who are thrown in the deep end in this way may well learn to swim, but they are likely to learn how to swim badly – just enough strokes to prevent drowning – and may therefore be less than well equipped to carry out their duties.

While it would be unwise to go to the opposite extreme and micro manage an induction process (and thereby give people the disempowering message that they cannot be trusted), there are significant dangers in not taking seriously the need to make sure that induction is as effective as possible. It is to be hoped that this chapter has given a clear picture that induction deserves much more time and effort than many organizations generally give it.

Points to ponder
1. How can induction help new recruits to feel supported, valued and safe?
2. What do you see as the role of the team in ensuring that induction is effective?
3. What are the likely consequences of induction not establishing clear expectations?

Exercise 5
What do you see as the main reasons for taking the time and trouble, even in highly pressurized work settings, to make sure that induction is effective?

CHAPTER 6: WORKLOAD MANAGEMENT

In this chapter you will learn about the importance of making sure that workloads are kept within safe and manageable limits.

Introduction

Maximizing productivity can be seen to be an important part of a manager's role – in effect, a key element of the rationale for human resources management. The challenge of making sure that people have appropriate workloads (so that they are able to produce optimal results in terms of quantity and quality of work) is something we therefore need to take seriously. In this chapter we will be looking at some of the key issues that we need to be aware of if we are to try and make sure that we are successful in this task of maximizing productivity.

Getting the balance right

It is vitally important that, when it comes to workload, we are able to get the balance right in terms of what we expect from people. Giving people too little work means we are not maximizing productivity and, ironically, this can prove stressful for workers. This is because, as we will note in Chapter 21, one of the potential sources of stress is not only too *much* pressure, but also too *little* pressure, as a result of which we can feel understimulated. Too little work can also lead to what is known as 'atrophy' – that is, a situation in which people lose their momentum and their sharpness, and the quality and quantity of their work go down. They become less effective employees overall if they are not adequately stretched, but, equally, giving people too much work can lead to stress and possible sickness absence, and that, in itself, can potentially lead to litigation. There is clearly, therefore, a lot to be lost by overstretching people by giving them more work than they can reasonably cope with.

An important concept here is that of 'creative tension'. If what we are asking people to do is slightly beyond what they are currently doing, then the tension between the current situation and the desired situation is small enough to be positive and motivating. However, if the gap between current levels of work and expected levels of work is too great, then there is no creative tension. The gap is perceived as unrealistic, and it is likely that this will demotivate people. What that can then do is to create a situation where people feel they are being set up to fail, which is then likely to result in a decrease in the quality of work and an increase in the error rate, both of which can lead to other problems (an increase in the level of complaints, for example). We therefore have to be clear that asking people to do more than is realistically possible is likely to decrease work output. It can also lead to low morale, low concentration, tiredness, sickness absence, conflicts and tensions, dangerous cutting of corners – and even departures when staff leave because they perceive that they are being overloaded and therefore feel that they are being manipulated and exploited, rather than valued and supported.

This is not to say that staff should not have a high workload, but there is a world of difference between a high and manageable workload on the one hand and one that is too high on the other. What we need to do, first of all, is ensure that people have a suitable workload and then seek to maximize productivity from that. One way of doing this is by encouraging *smart* working – that is, to support people in being creative and using their intelligence in how they go about their work (a key element of critically reflective practice, as discussed in the Introduction).

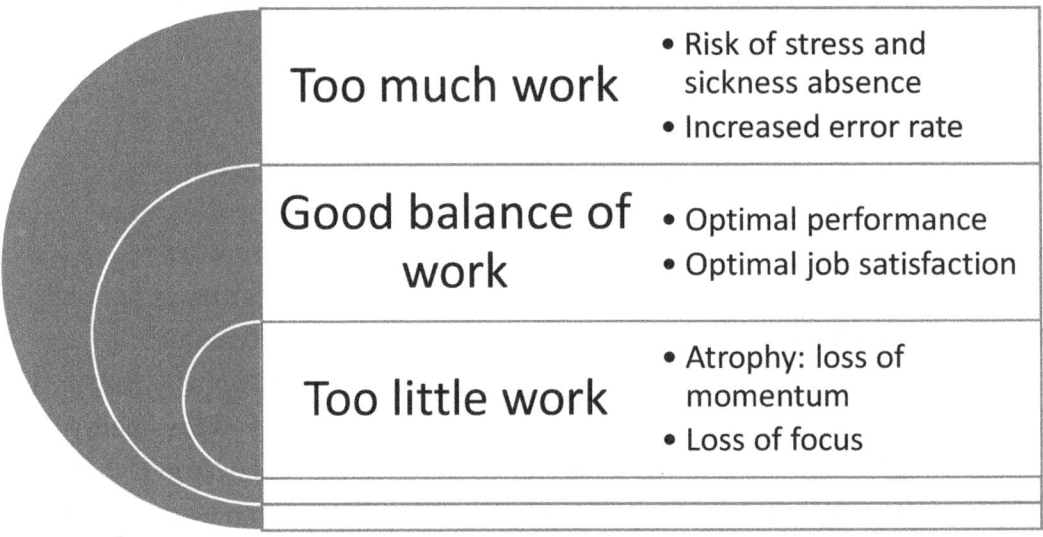

Figure 5.2 The importance of workload balance.

Managing motivation

There are also issues of motivation to consider, in the sense that a motivated worker is likely to be able to achieve far more than somebody who is demotivated. Chapter 15 explores issues of motivation and morale in more detail, but for now we should note that managing our workload is not simply a matter of managing time; it also involves being able to manage our motivation. So, from a people management point of view, we need to take account of motivation issues at an individual employee level and morale at a team or organizational level. In this regard, Adams's (2007) comments are of interest:

> In a recent literature review of the effects of disease prevention and health promotion on workplace productivity, Riedel *et al.* (2001) reported that the most important moderator of job performance was morale. Morale, according to these

authors, can be increased substantially when companies invest in the well-being of their employees, such as including employee health priorities in business objectives and linking employee satisfaction and performance to financial indicators. In fact, Riedel and his colleagues reported that in the Fortune magazine's top 100 companies to work for, all of which were rated highly on employee morale and performance, particular attention has been paid to the recognition of employee well-being. Nevertheless, according to Riedel *et al.*, these companies represent a minority; most companies ignore issues of employee morale, or fail in their attempts to enhance performance and morale because they are addressed inadequately.

(p. 124)

My own experience reinforces the significance of morale, as my consultancy work has involved me in a wide range of situations where low morale has proven to be very destructive – poisonous even. I will return to this point in Chapter 15.

Motivation is a key factor in relation to workload management in the following ways:

- *It aids concentration.* A low level of motivation is likely to prove to be a distraction and can therefore lead to confusion and a lack of clarity. High motivation, by contrast, is likely to lead to clearer thinking and therefore a higher level of concentration and better focus. This, in turn, is an important basis for reflective practice. However, it is important not to allow a high level of motivation to lead to an overzealous approach, as going overboard in this way can lead to *reduced* concentration and thus less focus.
- *It energizes people.* People who are motivated are likely to work faster and more effectively and therefore to be far more productive. This can produce a virtuous circle – that is, the more productive we are, the more job satisfaction we are likely to get, and the more job satisfaction we get, the more motivated we are likely to be, and so on. This can also apply in terms of the effect on other people, in the sense that, if some people are motivated, it can rub off on their colleagues by creating a more positive atmosphere. A more positive atmosphere can then feed motivation.
- *It promotes teamwork.* Following on from the point above, we can see that high motivation can form the basis of a supportive team atmosphere. Team members are far less likely to support one another if they are dissatisfied, disaffected and demoralized. As we shall see in Chapter 14, effective teamwork can make a huge difference to how team members experience their time at work. Anything that supports effective teamwork can therefore be seen to be of value.

- *It reduces mistakes.* Of course, no workplace is going to be completely error free, but working environments characterized by low levels of motivation and thus low morale can have significantly increased error rates due to poor concentration, possible feelings of resentment and the possible tensions and conflicts that often accompany them. Unlike the virtuous circle mentioned above, low motivation can create a vicious circle in which a tense atmosphere creates more tensions, more dissatisfaction and more ill feeling, which, in turn produce low morale.

Practice focus 6.1
When Siân took over as team manager she was concerned that most members of the team really seemed to be struggling to cope with their workload. People were creaking under the weight of pressure. She was therefore not surprised to note that levels of motivation seemed to be quite low. She was an experienced enough manager to know that there would be no simple or magic answers, but she was also sure that there must be ways of improving the situation. The first thing she did was to put the matter on the team meeting agenda, as she worked on the basis that the first step to solving any problem is to acknowledge that the problem exists in the first place. This proved to be a very positive move, as the team really appreciated her honest approach and her willingness to tackle problems head on. That in itself was an excellent start, as the fact that the team now perceived her as a good leader served in its own right to increase motivation.

KEY POINT

It should be clear, then, that people managers, including HR professionals, would do well to take seriously the demands of promoting morale on a collective basis to supplement efforts to promote individual motivation. Much of this involves getting things right, as far as possible, in terms of our other people management duties.

Each of the following will be important as a potential contribution to high morale:

- *Supervision.* Part of the supervisor's role is to show appreciation and to value staff. That, plus the positive impact of helpful guidance and help with learning, can be very beneficial in terms of generating positive feelings and thus motivation. By contrast, poor or non-existent supervision can be a source of resentment and therefor an obstacle to motivation.
- *Appraisal and performance management.* Having clarity about our strong points and our areas for development can be very motivating, as can being helped to establish clear goals and develop a plan of action for achieving them. When

carried out skilfully and constructively, appraisal and performance management can be very beneficial (see Chapter 7).
- *Learning and development.* Learning in itself is often a source of motivation, but being helped to learn can also boost motivation, as it amounts to a message that we are valued and that our development is important. By contrast, working environments where people just 'get on with the job' with little or no learning taking place are generally not characterized by high levels of motivation.
- *Leadership.* We return once again to the L of *Staying CALM*. As Practice focus 6.1 illustrates, leadership can be a major source of motivation. It can create a sense of safety and security rooted in trust and respect for the leader. Indeed, leadership can make all the difference when it comes to levels of motivation.
- *Teamwork.* Good leadership should also lead to good teamwork. I will be arguing in Chapter 15 that motivation is generally seen in individual terms, whereas in reality much motivation comes from how we relate to the people around us and the context in which we are working. Teamwork is clearly a key part of this.
- *Problem solving.* Several of the chapters in this manual, especially in Part III, revolve around the theme of problem solving. This is based on the idea that, in order to get the best out of people, we need to (i) be aware of any problems (drug and alcohol misuse and/or mental health difficulties, for example) that can stand in the way of optimal levels of work and optimal results; and (ii) be reasonably well equipped (in terms of knowledge, understanding and confidence) to tackle those problems constructively.

Given the importance of workload management, the challenge of developing high levels of motivation where possible is clearly a very important one.

What is an appropriate workload?
Workload management is an important topic, and so this is a key question. How do we know what constitutes 'appropriate' in terms of someone's workload? The first thing to note is that there is no definitive, scientific way of knowing. Some organizations rely on what I would regard as a (pseudo-)mathematical workload weighting system, but this can be very misleading. It is important to note that different people have different workload capabilities, depending on a number of factors, and so allocating scores to particular tasks can be largely meaningless. The factors to take into consideration include:

- *Experience.* This is not simply a matter of the *quantity* of experience, but also the *quality*, in the sense of how much the person concerned has learned from their experience. Somebody with ten years' experience who has learned little or nothing from it will be nowhere near as well equipped as somebody with less than half that amount of experience, but who has drawn out of it every last bit of learning possible.

- *Knowledge and skills.* Different employees will have different levels of knowledge and skills, and so we should not expect everyone to be able to produce the same quality and quantity of work. That is simply not realistic.
- *Motivation.* Some people may well be in a job that is ideally suited to them and they may feel that they are being well supported and fully appreciated. Their motivation may therefore be at an optimal level. By contrast, other workers may be in what is basically the wrong job for them and/or in a setting where their manager does more harm than good in terms of being supportive, and so their motivation is at an all-time low, perhaps verging on burnout or actually within the realms of burnout. So, as we have already noted, different levels of motivation will produce different levels of output.
- *Confidence.* Of course, there is also going to be a variation in the levels of confidence across employees. A confident employee will be far more capable of achieving higher standards of work than somebody who lacks a degree of confidence. There is therefore an important role here for people managers to focus on boosting confidence wherever possible, as that will also boost morale and thereby boost productivity.
- *Intelligence.* There will be differences in terms of intelligence – for example, in terms of the pace at which people think. Some people are very deep thinkers and are very effective at coming up with important ideas, but may take a long time to do so. Other people may be not so capable of thinking so deeply, but they think very quickly, and that has advantages and disadvantages too, so these are factors that we need to take into consideration.
- *Training and qualifications.* Some people can be excellent at their job without having a formal qualification, but it has to be recognized that having studied for a qualification generally gives people an advantage in terms of how effective and productive they are likely to be. In-service training occupies a similar role, in so far as it can play an important part in developing a worker's capabilities (and, as indicated above, their confidence).
- *Personal circumstances.* People do not live or work in a social vacuum. There will be things going on in their lives, either within the workplace or outside it, that can have either a positive or a negative effect on their appetite for work and their abilities to get it done. Of course, we are not expected to be able to resolve any difficulties our staff encounter, but we should, at the very least, be aware of them and take them into consideration.

- *Health and fitness.* It is unquestionable that health can be an important variable when it comes to productivity. Somebody who is struggling with health problems may be seriously disadvantaged in terms of how much work they can get done or what quality of work they can achieve. However, we should also not forget fitness. Somebody who lacks physical fitness, who is, for example, overweight, and has a sedentary lifestyle, may lack the energy that somebody who is physically fit and exercises regularly is able to devote to the job. These factors can then interrelate with other important issues, such as levels of motivation and confidence.

It is therefore clear that there are a number of variables that we need to include in our deliberations in terms of working out what is likely to be an appropriate workload. One of the implications of this is that it is important for us to know our staff as far as reasonably possible. This is likely to involve monitoring their work to a certain extent and maintaining an ongoing assessment of how each employee is responding to their pressures. The work of Arroba and James (1992) on stress is helpful in this regard. They define stress as your response to an inappropriate level of pressure). We should also be aware that pressure relates to both *amount* and *level* of work. It is not simply a matter of quantity, but also how difficult the tasks are that people are being asked to do. (We shall return to the important topic of stress – and the significance of how it is defined – in Chapter 21).

One other helpful aspect of determining what constitutes an appropriate workload is to encourage honest feedback. We need to make sure that the people we are allocating work to are aware of (i) the importance of getting the balance right; and (ii) the fact that it is unfair on their colleagues for them to do too little and dangerous for them to try to do too much. An interesting concept here is that of 'Goldilocks' tasks (Pink, 2018). This means making sure that we are allocating the right tasks to the right people (and also giving people an appropriate level of variety and range of learning opportunities in the process).

Practice focus 6.2
Siân was pleased that raising the issue of workload management had produced an early positive response. However, she realized she would have to do more than just talk about the problem if she was going to make a positive difference. She remembered form her training the importance of 'job design' – that is, making sure that there was a good match between the person (and their knowledge, skills, experience and level of confidence) and the specifics of the job. She therefore decided that her efforts to tackle the workload problem would include

working with each staff member in supervision to establish the best fit possible between what they brought to the team and what the team needed from them.

Managing our own workload

While there are clearly important factors to take into consideration in terms of allocating work to others, we also have to make sure that we are managing our own workload effectively. If we allow ourselves to become overloaded, then we are going to be ill equipped to support the people who are relying on us. It is therefore crucial that we do not allow our work pressures to get the better of us and thereby risk letting those people down.

In terms of the lessons we can learn about managing our workload, the chapter in my *People Skills book* (Thompson, 2021b) is a good starting point for initial guidance, but you are encouraged to do further reading – and undertake training where available – to increase your effectiveness in managing a heavy workload. It is also important to get support from your own line manager, as often a supervisor's slightly more removed view of a situation can help us to gain an overview and get a clearer picture of what we need to do to manage efficiently and effectively.

However, one particular concept that should prove helpful in this regard is what I like to refer to as the five Ds of task management. This is a useful framework for categorizing the tasks we face, so that we can have a clearer picture of how best to respond to them:

- *Do it.* This involves getting the task out of the way and giving ourselves more space in our diary and – just as importantly – more thinking space in our head. We are also likely to get a sense of satisfaction from completing a task, and this can spur us on, an important factor in terms of morale and motivation. If, on the other hand, we do not 'clear the decks' of tasks, they can add up and weigh us down, undermining our sense of control (which, as we shall see in Chapter 21, can be a major source of stress).
- *Delegate it.* This is not simply a matter of dumping tasks on others (a common misinterpretation of what the term 'delegation' means). If done skilfully, delegation can be beneficial for everyone, and a good learning experience for the people we delegate tasks to.
- *Delay it.* We can give ourselves some space by delaying or deferring low priority tasks if we need to, but *only* if we need to. It is important not to get into the habit of procrastination and thereby putting off things that are more wisely done sooner rather than later (see *Do it* above).

- *Dump it.* Are we sure it needs doing at all? Sometimes we can get so busy that we become unfocused and may end up taking on tasks that are best left to others or do not need doing at all. Also, at times of high pressure, it can be safer to abandon some low-priority tasks, rather than risk high-priority tasks not getting done.
- *Decline it.* If we take on too many tasks, we do ourselves no favours, and we could end up letting down our superiors and the people we are meant to be supporting. The lesson of 'not biting off more than we can chew' applies to ourselves as well as to the staff we supervise. Sometimes people make the mistake of thinking that they will be looked down upon or considered uncommitted if they do not say yes to everything they are asked to do. However, in reality, someone who takes on more tasks than they can reasonably complete to a satisfactory level and within an appropriate timescale is likely to come across as unreliable and a poor task manager – and that will do far more damage to our reputation than declining certain tasks.

This framework is not guaranteed to solve all your task management problems, but it can one the less be a useful starting point for establishing that important degree of control that we need to be able to manage our workload effectively. It is, of course, also a useful tool that you can introduce your staff to, so that they too are better equipped to deal with the challenges of workload management.

Conclusion

Workload management is possibly one of the most important issues in contemporary workplaces. This is because levels of pressure have increased significantly across the private, public and voluntary sectors for various reasons. The net result is that there is considerable vulnerability to stress and taking on a workload that is greater than we can reasonably deal with is a dangerous move. It is therefore vitally important that people managers – both line managers and HR professionals – are aware of the significance of keeping workloads within manageable limits. It is a false economy to give people more work than they can cope with, as the net result will be a higher error rate, lower levels of morale and motivation and thus, poorer results than would have been the case if they had been given a reasonable, if high, workload. If the overall work that needs to be done is greater than the combined capacity of the team, then this is an issue that needs to be dealt with strategically *as a team*, rather than having managers and possibly HR professionals simply encouraging individuals and teams to try to do the impossible.

Points to ponder
1. Why is it important to achieve a balanced workload?
2. What part does motivation play in terms of workload management?
3. What factors will shape what constitutes a reasonable workload?

Exercise 6
What steps can take to ensure that you do not get overloaded with work? How can you also make sure that the staff you are responsible for do not become overloaded?

CHAPTER 7: APPRAISAL AND PERFORMANCE MANAGEMENT

In this chapter you will learn about what is involved in effective appraisal and performance management.

Introduction

Appraisal is intended to be a constructive organizational process that can have positive outcomes all round. By reviewing work performance and learning, employing organizations are able to work towards getting the maximum return on their investment in terms of human resources, in so far as the process is designed to help employees achieve their best. By the same token, employees can be helped to maximize their potential, to achieve optimal job satisfaction and to identify opportunities for continuous learning and development. In this way, the process can be a good basis for career planning (see Chapter 17). Other stakeholders of the organization (customers, clients, patients, for example) can also therefore benefit from what the process has to offer.

Appraisal is therefore an important part of people management and can be linked to the broader concept of 'performance management'. This relates to the responsibility of people managers to ensure that employees are maximizing both their quality and quantity of work, and, where necessary, to help them achieve at least minimal standards. This latter aspect applies to situations where, for whatever reason – or combination of reasons – an employee's standard of work is falling below an acceptable standard in terms of legal, policy or ethical requirements.

This chapter therefore reviews the important role of appraisal and performance management in ensuring that optimal outcomes are achieved for the benefit of all concerned. It also includes a discussion of how performance management can go wrong, as the process can also be quite destructive if it goes awry or if it is poorly managed or executed.

What is appraisal?

Appraisal, also known as performance review, is a process of evaluating the past year and planning for the year ahead. It normally takes the form of an annual meeting (or six-monthly or even quarterly in some organizations) in which what has happened in the past year is explored with a view to highlighting the strengths and weaknesses of performance and the lessons that can be learned from what has happened during the year. In this way, it fits well with supervision, as discussed in Chapter 4, in the sense that it allows a process of building *on* (the strong points) and building *up* (any areas for development).

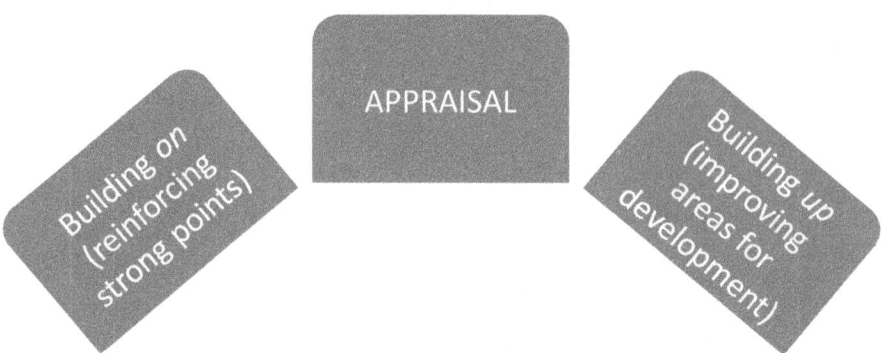

Figure 7.1 Appraisal: building *on* and building *up*

It can involve simply the employee and his or her line manager (what is known as the 'parent model') or the employee, line manager and the line manager's line manager (the 'grandparent model'). This latter model gives a further degree of objectivity (but, of course, complete objectivity is not possible in such matters).

There can also be 360° appraisal which involves seeking feedback, as the name implies, all round – from not only superiors, but also colleagues, anyone who is supervised by the person being appraised (the 'appraisee') and sometimes by clients, customers or

KEY POINT

Ideally, appraisal should interrelate with supervision, in the sense that what is discussed in appraisal should set the learning agenda for the coming twelve months. Supervision should then dovetail with what has been discussed (in terms of trying to ensure that the learning outlined is actually achieved), and the performance management issues identified are appropriately addressed.

The overall purpose of appraisal can be broken down into the following components:

- to review performance since the last appraisal meeting and identify ways of improving it (building *on* and building *up* again); this should apply to all employees and not simply any whose performance is causing concern – it is important that appraisal is not seen as something shameful and to be avoided, as such stigma can prevent the benefits of appraisal from being realized.
- to identify (and consolidate) learning gained and identify opportunities for future learning; this can be an important way of validating the employee's contribution

and giving due emphasis to the lessons that can be learned from the past year's experience.
- to identify obstacles to performance improvement and learning, and develop strategies for removing or sidestepping these obstacles, or at least minimizing their impact; this is a way of optimizing learning. As we will note in Chapter 19, learning can happen spontaneously, but it can also be reinforced in various ways – including appraisal.
- to boost morale and confidence by congratulating employees on their achievements and offering support in addressing any problems that may be getting in the way of optimal outcomes; this is an important dimension of appraisal, but can at times be absent, making the process appear to be simply a bureaucratic means of checking up on staff. This can lead to resentment and defensiveness – see the discussion below of how performance management can go wrong.
- to set goals for the coming year, ensuring that such goals are realistic and therefore a source of motivation, rather than unrealistic and a source of demotivation; it is important that this aspect is taken seriously and not just dealt with mechanistically. Reflecting the M, for meaning, of *Staying CALM*, it is essential that the goals are meaningful.

In some organizations, appraisal is also the basis for determining bonuses and/or levels of pay (performance-related pay, or 'PRP'). This can be problematic, in so far as it can encourage employees to hide any learning needs or aspects of their work they are struggling with and hype up the positives of what they have achieved, with a view to gaining a higher bonus or pay rise.

> *Practice focus 7.1*
> Clive was very anxious in the days leading up to his appraisal meeting. He was worried that his boss would be very critical of him in front of the divisional manager. On the morning of the meeting he felt very tired and lacklustre, as he had hardly slept the night before due to his nervousness. However, he soon perked up once he realized that the meeting was not as he had expected it to be. The main emphasis was on how well he had done, and how he had managed to maintain high standards of work in difficult circumstances (including severe staff shortages for part of the year). There was also discussion of aspects of his work that could be improved, but these issues were tackled sensitively and constructively. What Clive found particularly helpful was that they were able to identify concrete, manageable steps that he could take to improve his practice. He still felt a little uncomfortable about being the centre of attention and having his

practice open to scrutiny, but he realized that all his earlier anxiety had not been necessary. It had given him and his line manager plenty to discuss in forthcoming supervision sessions, and he looked forward to building up his strengths and building on the not-so-strong aspects of his work.

Making appraisal work

In order to get the best out of appraisal and ensure that it is as effective as possible, it is important to address a number of issues. The first of these is preparation. Both the appraiser and the appraisee have to have some clear ideas about what the focus of the appraisal will be. This usually involves a report being prepared for the meeting. This can sometimes involve self-assessment, in which case the appraisee plays a part in writing the report but, very often, it is a case of the appraiser writing a report in such a way as to encompass the perspective of the appraise as far as possible. There is no hard and fast rule about how to achieve this, but, either way, it is helpful to have a report prepared well in advance, so that there is a clear set of issues to be discussed. The absence of a clear agenda can add to the anxieties illustrated in Practice focus 7.1.

It is also important that there is clarity and a degree of transparency throughout the process. This is a matter of open communication of course, which, as we noted in Chapter 2, is a vital part of effective people management. Any appraisal process that is seen as underhanded or less than a hundred per cent honest is doomed to failure, as it will create mistrust and will discourage appraisees from being open about identifying areas for development (reflecting the A, for authenticity, of the *Staying CALM* approach to people management). Therefore, instead of it being a constructive process of mutually beneficial growth and development, it can become a defensive process of trying to push positives to the fore and keeping less positive aspects of performance well hidden. People managers involved in appraisal processes therefore have to be very skilful in putting people at their ease and creating a positive and trusting working relationship (reflecting the C, for connection, of *Staying CALM*).

In addition, it is important that appraisal is successful in establishing clear goals. This applies in two senses. There have to be goals *for* the appraisal – that is, people need to be clear about what it is all about and what they need to get out of the time and effort that go into it. But, goals also need to be what comes *from* the appraisal, in the sense that the outcome should be a set of clear goals.

It is also important to emphasize that those goals should be phrased in terms of outcomes, rather than activities (this is a common mistake where people identify activities such as 'to focus more closely on communication in writing', which is not an outcome in itself, but, rather, a process geared towards meeting an as yet unidentified outcome. There needs to be clarity and precision about what exactly is to be achieved, what the desired outcome should be (for example, to avoid complaints from clients about unclear or misleading letters).

The goals should therefore be measurable in terms of whether or not the outcome has been achieved. This will then be an important factor to feed into the next appraisal and supervision sessions that take place in the meantime. This notion of clarity about outcomes links well with the idea of systematic practice discussed in Part III of *People Skills*, where it is emphasized that it is important to have clarity about (i) what we are trying to achieve (our goals, objectives or desired outcomes); (ii) how we are going to achieve it (our plan or strategy); and (iii) how we will know when we have achieved it (What will success look like? How will we know when we have finished?).

Managing poor performance
This is another aspect of performance management that merits our attention. It is not just a matter of having a constructive process of appraisal whereby the appraisee is helped to fulfil their potential. There also needs to be provision for those circumstances where a member of staff's work falls below an acceptable standard and some form of remedial action is required. A clear danger in such situations is for the people managers concerned to 'turn a blind eye' to this and pretend that it is not happening. This ostrich approach is a very dangerous and unwise strategy. It can lead to a wide range of problems, not least that of the people manager concerned losing any credibility as a people manager, because they are – understandably – seen as weak and unwilling to tackle difficult issues. What can also happen is that the situation can get worse and become much more difficult to deal with at that point.

It is also important not to go to the other extreme and to overreact and be heavy-handed about matters of poor performance. We have to get the balance right in terms of how we handle such challenges and this is important because if we get this right, then everyone benefits.

The organization as a whole and its stakeholders benefit from not having to suffer the problems associated with poor performance (for example, poor customer service). The team will benefit from matters being appropriately dealt with because poor performance not being tackled can lead to considerable resentment and ill-feeling and, again, the reputation of the line manager/HR professional suffering significantly in terms of credibility and respect.

However, the employee concerned will also benefit from having poor performance dealt with constructively. This will prevent them from entering into a vicious circle in which their poor performance leads to lower confidence and poor morale, and therefore potentially even worse performance. It also prevents conflict between this person and the wider team or organization. In addition, it prevents the possible need for later disciplinary or capability procedures, and also enables the member of staff to be clear about what is expected of them and gain the satisfaction of being able to achieve that with the appropriate support.

If we are to avoid the minefield of difficulties associated with this aspect of people management, there are some important guidelines that we need to follow in terms of managing poor performance:

- *Do not wait for appraisal.* Raise in supervision, or even before that, any matters of performance falling below an adequate level. If it is serious enough, it may need to be dealt with more or less on the spot, but if that is the case, make sure that you do so in private. Public criticism can be deemed a form of bullying. There is an important balance to be struck here, in so far as we need to be able to react promptly where required, but without acting precipitately when it would be wiser to choose our moment more carefully.
- *Give balanced feedback.* Even if an employee is falling below an acceptable level in some respects, it is highly unlikely that they are falling below an acceptable in all respects. That is, while they may be doing some things wrong, they are bound to be doing lots of things right as well, so it is important that we are not purely critical of their performance, that we give them balanced feedback. This will involve congratulating them and praising them in terms of the positives, but also making it clear that there are aspects of their performance that need to change in order to reach an acceptable level. It can be difficult at times to get the balance right. If we give too much weight to the negatives, the overall effect can be quite counterproductive, losing any sense of balanced feedback. But, if we give too much weight to the positives, we may give the impression that we lack courage in addressing those aspects of working practices that are unacceptable.
- *Give constructive feedback.* Telling somebody off or simply pointing out that their standard of work is not good enough is not only unhelpful, it may also actually prove very detrimental all round (for example, by creating tensions and resentment, and even possibly sabotage or reprisals). What is much more effective is to give *constructive* feedback. That is, if somebody is going wrong in some way, we should not simply point out the fact that they are 'going wrong', but actually help to make it clear what they need to do to get things right and, where necessary, help them to do so (see below). It is, of course, unfair to do otherwise.

- *Give specific feedback.* It helps if the feedback can be behaviour focused, rather than more general or possibly vaguer than that. For example, saying to people that their performance is unsatisfactory without specifying precisely in what way it is unsatisfactory is not likely to be perceived as a helpful point to make. However, if we are specific in terms of saying exactly what needs to change to make the performance acceptable, then that is much fairer on the individual and gives them a much higher chance of being able to make the changes necessary. Being specific in this way helps to ensure that the employee concerned understands why change needs to happen and what exactly the changes need to be. In this way, they are more likely to be committed to bringing about such positive changes and get the benefit of doing so.
- *Support the employee in making the necessary changes.* It is not simply a matter of letting them get on with it. There may be reasons why they have struggled to meet the required standards and may therefore need further support in being able to reach the level that is required of them.

Giving effective feedback is quite a skilful undertaking, and so it is essential that we build up our skills over time. Relying on our everyday skills will mean that basic competence is likely to be the most we can hope for, while making the effort to develop our skills (through reflective practice, reading, attending training courses and so on) can help to take us to a more advanced and thus more effective level.

> *Practice focus 7.2*
> Clive's manager, Jean, had found it difficult to give feedback to staff in supervision or appraisal meetings. She had felt very self-conscious and unsure of what she should say. However, when she attended a two-day course on supervision skills, one of the emphases of the training was on giving feedback. She learned a great deal from this which, in turn, encouraged her to read up on the subject. The net result was that she became much more confident and skilful in giving feedback. This started a virtuous circle, in so far as she was able to see the positive results of her enhanced capacity for giving constructive feedback in the responses of her supervisees, and that then further boosted her confidence. So, when she started the appraisal meeting with Clive and she could see that he was very anxious, she recognized that this would be a good opportunity to put her skills into practice. The result was a positive outcome for all concerned. Her own manager, who was present at Clive's appraisal meeting, made a mental note to congratulate Jean on her feedback skills when it came time for her appraisal.

Many organizations now have what are called capability procedures. They are parallel with disciplinary procedures but instead of focusing on behaviour that is unacceptable in terms of moral or legal aspects of the situation, the focus here is on unacceptable performance – that is, performance that falls below an acceptable standard. It is therefore important to check whether the organization concerned has capability procedures and, if so, what your duties are in terms of these procedures. In organizations that do not have capability procedures, then it is likely that such matters will be dealt with as a subdivision of the disciplinary procedures. If this is the case, then again you will need to be familiar with the appropriate policies and procedures in connection with this. To stumble on, dealing with such matters on an ad hoc basis, without being aware of what policy framework you are expected to work within, is a potential recipe for disaster – and, once again, will not do your credibility any good.

Problems with performance management

As we have seen, appraisal in particular and performance management in general have the potential to make an extremely positive contribution to organizational effectiveness overall and to individual staff members achieving their best. However, there are various ways in which the processes involved can go wrong and, in the worst cases, do a great deal of harm. It is therefore important to consider some of the common ways in which problems with performance management can emerge, and that is precisely what we are going to do now, by focusing on three key pitfalls to avoid. These are by no means the only ones, but they are certainly important ones.

Whitewashing

This is a term used to refer to the tendency shown by some people managers to gloss over key issues and try to 'sanitize' the process. This can happen in supervision and can then be carried over into appraisal and the wider relationship with staff. It involves being very vague and not really getting to grips with the issues that should be the focal point of the process. This can have its roots in a misguided view that it is safer to gloss over such matters than actually address them. Where this happens, the whole ethos of performance management can be undermined, and it can be viewed cynically by staff who see no value in what will come across to them as playing a game.

A punitive approach

This can be a form of bullying (see Chapter 24). It involves giving undue emphasis to the negatives associated with someone's performance, taking the opportunity to 'give them a hard time'. This abuse of power can do a great deal of harm for the individual concerned and can also undermine the value of performance management overall if what is happening (or has happened) becomes known to other staff members. This punitive approach can be the result of a lack of skill and sensitivity on the part of the people manager concerned (especially if this approach is applied to staff in general). Alternatively, it can arise on a more individualized basis where, for example, there have been circumstances that have led to a poor relationship (perhaps rooted in a particular conflict). Either way, the results can be very detrimental all round.

Process re-engineering and managerialism
Management fads have created major difficulties for people managers over the years (Stewart, 2010). The private sector has been beset for quite some time by the fad of process re-engineering which had its heyday in the 1990s (Micklethwait and Wooldridge, 1997). This approach led to large-scale 'downsizing' (often euphemistically referred to as 'rightsizing'), with large numbers of people losing their livelihoods. This in turn led to the remaining staff often having unrealistically high workloads to contend with. In such situations performance management can become a process of pressurizing staff into trying to reach unrealistic targets – a case of unscrupulously trying to get the *most* out of staff (regardless of the consequences for the staff concerned), rather than ethically trying to get the *best* out of them (and trying to create win-win situations).

The public sector has been beset by managerialism (Clarke *et al.*, 2000), an approach to public service that involves a strong emphasis on performance indicators and targets that has had the effect of demoralizing a high proportion of the workforce (Thompson, 2016) due to (i) the targets often being unrealistic; and (ii) the way in which the targets have often distorted what public service is all about (for example, counting the number of times a phone is allowed to ring before it is answered, rather than the quality of human interaction and service offered once it is answered).

What we can learn from these lessons is that goals or targets need to be both realistic and meaningful (consistent with the organization's purpose and strategy). If they are not, then not only can the value of performance management be lost, but also the process can become oppressive and counterproductive.

Conclusion
As we have noted, some people find it very difficult to give feedback to employees about their performance – whether that is positive or negative feedback – but it is important that we are able to do so systematically, consistently and constructively. Without such feedback, employees will not know where they stand. They will not know whether they are doing well (or how well they are doing) and will therefore not get job satisfaction from knowing that they are doing a good job and, equally, if they are not doing so well, they will not have the support of constructive feedback and concerted efforts to create a better working situation for them and for everyone else.

It is therefore important that people managers are well aware of what appraisal and performance management entail, why they are important and why it is dangerous to neglect them or to undertake them without a proper understanding and a good platform of knowledge on which to base future skill development.

Points to ponder
1. What do you see as the advantages and disadvantages of 360 degree appraisal?
2. What are the likely consequences if poor performance issues are ot addressed?
3. What is meant by 'whitewashing' and why is it to be avoided?

Exercise 7
In what ways might performance management and appraisal be badly handled? What could you do to prevent these problems from arising?

CHAPTER 8: STAFF DEPARTURES

In this chapter you will learn about good practice in handling situations where staff leave.

Introduction
One aspect of people management that receives relatively little attention in the literature or in training programmes is the question of staff departing – that is, leaving the employment of the organization concerned. Despite this gap, it is a very important subject, as the way an organization treats people who are leaving says a great deal about that organization and to what extent they are people focused. How the departure of a member of staff is handled also gives a strong message to remaining staff and to other organizational stakeholders about how seriously it takes the idea that an organization's most important resource is its human resource. Sending out a very negative message can do a lot of harm to that organization (for example, in terms of how partner organizations perceive it in terms of trustworthiness and reliability or how attractive the organization might appear to potential applicants for jobs.

Furnham and Taylor (2004) make the important point that: 'Companies ... have a hard time distinguishing between the cost of paying people and the value of investing in them. (Thomas Stewart, US Journalist, US Capital)' (p. 67). And, of course, it is not just companies that this applies to, but any employing organization. Staff – the human resource – represent a significant investment, and so it would be very unwise not to learn the lessons from the departure of a staff member. If people are indeed to be treated as a valuable resource and not just as replaceable cogs, then the tendency to neglect the issues that arise when someone leaves can be seen as an unhelpful one.

This chapter therefore addresses the question of what we need to be aware of to manage staff departures as effectively as we reasonably can. We should not allow the fact that these issues are often given very little attention to distract us from realizing how significant they are and how important it is for us to know what we are doing in handling such situations. We begin by asking the key question: why do people leave? That leads on to a discussion of the implications of staff leaving and, finally, of how not to handle staff departures – that is, of the pitfalls to avoid.

Why do people leave?
There is, of course, a variety of reasons why people will choose to move on. Some of these are connected with the organization itself in terms of how it treats its staff (see Chapter 16 on the subject of staff retention). Some reasons will be connected with the career

plans of the individuals concerned – for example, a promotion or a sideways move to broaden their experience (perhaps in preparation for a promotion at a future date). Other reasons will have to do with personal circumstances. It may be, for example, that someone's partner has obtained a better job in another area, and so the family are moving to that area. There are various ways in which a person can leave the organization. The main ones are the following, and it is worth exploring each of these to consider their implications:

- *Retirement.* An important question to ask ourselves here is whether the organization concerned has some sort of 'preparation for retirement' scheme. Many organizations now do have such a scheme which is intended to prepare retirees for their future circumstances. This can be a helpful, humane undertaking, but can also help the organization to ensure that the person leaves on good terms and is therefore more likely to be willing to co-operate with passing on important knowledge and information to other staff and to work to their full capacity until they depart. This helps to avoid the phenomenon of being 'retired in post'. This lighthearted term is none the less a serious problem at times. It refers to situations in which, for a period before someone retires, their commitment to the job is minimal, with possible detrimental effects for many people (not least for team colleagues who may have to pick up the pieces as a result of the lack of commitment). It is, of course, also important that retirement should be well handled in order to show appreciation to the person retiring for their contribution over the years. It would be a tragedy for someone who had provided good service over a number of years to leave on a negative note because their departure had not been well handled.
- *Moving sideways within the same organization.* This can also arise for a variety of reasons, but the most common is to get a broader range of experience. However, we have to be aware that this is not the only possible reason. We should not assume that there is nothing else at play here. For example, the fact that somebody is taking a sideways move from our team or section may be highlighting that there could be particular problems in our section. This could be as a result of conflicts or tensions, or even a means of escaping bullying. It may also be that they have 'grown out of' their job, in so far as they are now so experienced that they no longer find it challenging or stimulating. If that is the case, then it is providing valuable information for us about who we might want to avoid that in future by helping even very experienced staff to find opportunities for challenge and learning. Of course, we should also not go to the opposite extreme and assume that there are sinister reasons for every departure – we need to keep an open mind and weigh up each situation carefully.

- *Moving sideways to a different organization.* This could once again very well be because of the desire to get a broader experience, and getting this in a different organization will mean that there are extra dimensions to the breadth of experience on offer. This is because there will be not only a different setting, but also a different organization altogether, with, in all likelihood, a different culture, and so there is much to be learned in those circumstances. But again, it is important to establish whether or not the person is leaving because of dissatisfaction with aspects of their current role or setting that we could perhaps have addressed if we had known about them sooner.
- *Promotion.* This can be an important development for the member of staff concerned, and is perhaps a sign of success, in so far as it tends to suggest that they have been succeeding in their present post. There are important lessons to be learned from this in terms of looking at what it is that we have done as people managers that has helped this person to gain promotion. In particular, we could usefully look at what has been done that has helped them to develop, so that we are more aware of how to do more of the same (or do even better) for other employees who may need that help.

Practice focus 8.1
Gyatri was studying part-time for a Master's degree in human resources, as part of which she was undertaking a research project. Her focus was on promotion and how well equipped people felt for their new role. She therefore interviewed six people across her organization to try to find out how their previous job had prepared them for their new role. Interestingly the sample she had chosen (at random) was split down the middle. Three of the interviewees felt they had had good support and had been helped to learn and develop, which had stood them in good stead for their new, more demanding role. However, the other three felt that they had been promoted as a result of their own efforts, with little or no support from their employers – in fact, one commented that she had managed to get promoted *despite* the way her manager in particular and her organization in general had treated her. Gyatri was saddened to hear this, but it taught her that the way people are supported (or not) varies considerably, not only from organization to organization, but also within the same organization.

- *New career direction.* Sometimes people leave not only their job, but their particular vocation or profession. This may be because they have had a longing to do something different and have only now got the courage, confidence or opportunity to do so. But again, it may be telling us that there is something about their current work that was problematic.

- *Downsizing.* This is a euphemism for staff being laid off or made redundant. An important issue to recognize here is what is known as survivor's guilt. This is a concept that is quite significant in explaining the reaction of people who are not made redundant or laid off. They can feel somehow guilty that they were spared from the axe, as it were. This is a form of grief where people are trying to adapt to the loss of one or more valued colleagues. It can be quite and profound in its impact, just like any other form of grief. We have to be very careful not to underestimate its significance, as not recognizing grief can make it harder for the grieving person(s) to deal with it (see the discussion of 'disenfranchised grief' in Chapter 27). Of course, there will also be significant grief issues for the person(s) leaving, as they will have put in a considerable emotional investment to something that they are now losing.
- *Dismissal.* When a disciplinary matter gets to a sufficient level of seriousness to warrant dismissal, it strongly suggests that there have been problems of some kind leading up to this. It may well be that these are matters entirely beyond the control of people managers, but it may also be the case that there are again important lessons that can be learned here. Also, it is important to recognize that, while confidentiality is an important consideration, if someone is dismissed, it will be necessary for remaining staff to have at least some understanding of the circumstances, so that they do not harbour any feelings that a colleague has been unjustly or harshly treated (or fear that they will be harshly treated). There is also the danger that people will take sides (those who feel it was right that the person concerned was dismissed and those who do not), and so it is important that, as people managers, we feel able to handle such situations calmly and sensitively.
- *Death.* While many people are reluctant to discuss issues relating to death, dismissing them as a morbid preoccupation, we do, of course, have to be realistic and accept that death affects everybody. The workplace is no exception to this. The challenges involved in this are discussed in more detail in Chapter 27, but for now it is important to note that there are significant risks associated with disregarding the significance of death (and other sources of grief) in the workplace (Thompson, 2009).

The implications of people leaving

It should be clear from my comments already that there are potentially quite a number of lessons that can be learned from why people are departing, but there are other considerations we need to be aware of as well. For example, we need to begin the process of preparing for a replacement, if there is indeed to be a replacement for the person who has departed (that is, the post has not been deleted for some reason). The sooner we begin this process, the shorter will be the period of additional pressure on the remaining staff members between the departure of the outgoing member of staff and the arrival of the new member of the team.

Similarly, there may need to be arrangements for interim cover to be put in place. It is often the case that teams or groups of staff have to simply get by without the absent member of staff until a new person arrives, but sometimes the nature of the work is such that it can be dangerous for certain tasks not to be done, and so some form of interim cover has to be arranged – the deployment of agency staff, for example.

Figure 8.1 Main reasons for departure

 What can be particularly helpful when staff leave is to hold an exit interview. Some organizations do this informally, and so the final supervision session becomes a means of reviewing the overall situation and seeing what lessons can be learned and what insights gained by getting feedback from the departing employee.

Many organizations now have a formal policy for exit interviews. Such interviews will often be undertaken by HR staff or by a manager who is not the departing member of staff's immediate line manager (to offer the opportunity to speak freely about the line management relationship, as it is likely that this will have been an important part of the staff member's experience, and may even be part of the reason why they are leaving). An exit interview should be carried out not as an interrogation in a spirit of defensiveness, but, rather, as a genuine means of identifying what can be learned – for the benefit of other staff – including the new person who will ultimately fill the vacancy now created – and the organization as a whole. Furnham and Taylor (2004) offer helpful comment when they argue that:

> An exit policy based on the principles of dignity, fairness, transparency, caring and respect for the law and organizational rules will contribute significantly to

the loyalty and commitment of existing staff and reduce the potential damage of those who have left. (p. 20)

This is an important consideration. It would be naïve to think that much of what is discussed in an exit interview will not be fed back to the staff who are remaining. So, if the exit interview is badly handled, it is not only the departing member of staff who gets a raw deal. The impact on morale for those who remain could be very significant.

> *Practice focus 8.2*
> Carole had worked for the same organization for over twenty years. There had been ups as well as downs during that time, but what had spoiled things for her was that, in her last year in post, there had been a major reorganization that had been poorly handled in some ways. As a result of this, morale had been quite low, and Carole's line manager seemed to have been overwhelmed by this as he had become quite negative and was often quite dismissive towards Carole and other colleagues. When Carole was invited to an exit interview with someone from the human resources department she was at first reluctant to attend, as she did not want to be untruthful, but nor did she want to depart on a negative note. However, she did decide to go in the end, and she was glad that she did. The member of the HR staff who conducted the interview very skilfully put her at her ease and helped her to understand that the focus of the interview would be what the organization could learn from her experience over the years. Carole therefore spoke openly about the negativity associated with her last year and how disappointed she had been that good leadership seemed to be lacking, but she was able to balance this out by talking about many of the good things she had enjoyed over the twenty years as a whole.

There is also the humanitarian issue of supporting the departing employee. Even if they are departing in not entirely favourable circumstances, we still have a duty of care to employees, and there is still much to be gained by treating people *as people*. Of course, in focusing on people who are leaving, we should not lose sight of the remaining staff and their support needs. This is not just in terms of issues relating to cover for the absent colleague, but also to address any issues that may have arisen for the staff. Much of this will depend on the reasons for the departure, but we have to recognize that this can be a sensitive and important matter for remaining staff group, and it would be very unwise of us – and potentially dangerous – to fail to take notice of that fact.

One significant implication for the remaining staff group when someone leaves is the effect that this can have on the team dynamics. We will discuss team development in more detail in Chapter 14, but for now we should note that the departure of one or more staff can sometime have a significant impact on team dynamics. For example, if the person who has left had a calming effect on people, then his or her absence may change the emotional climate within the staff group. Similarly, if someone who was good at getting colleagues to stop and think is no longer in the team, there may be less of a focus on reflective practice. And, when the new member fills the vacancy created by the earlier departure of the team member, the dynamic can shift again depending on what contribution the new person makes.

In terms of the arrival of a new person, we also need to consider induction – that is, in the majority of cases, when one person leaves, the scene is set for a new person arriving (see Chapter 5). This can be a good opportunity for bringing people together by making induction a team process – it can help the team handle the departure together (see the discussion below of rituals of transition).

In a similar vein, as the saying goes 'when one door closes another one opens'. Staff departing can therefore create openings for remaining colleagues – new opportunities arise. For example, if the person who has left was a member of a particular committee, then this now creates an opportunity for someone else to be involved and therefore to broaden their horizons. If we are not alert to such possibilities, then valuable opportunities for learning and development can be missed.

Importantly, there is also the question of how we manage change and the grieving that so often accompanies it. This will be an important consideration in Chapter 27 where the point is made that grief arises as a response to any significant loss and not just to a bereavement.

How not to manage departures
A recurring theme of this manual is that people need to be understood (and treated) *as people* – we are not just cogs that can be slotted into a system and replaced by other cogs as and when required. An approach to workplace issues that presents people as cogs is likely to be a dangerous and problematic one, as it not only oversimplifies some very complex issues, but also risks alienating staff. Dean and Liff (2010) make the important point that: *'labour is human* and therefore incapable of being purely a commodity' (p. 423).

However, Bolton and Houlihan (2007) are aware of the tendency to treat people purely as a resource and gloss over the all-important *human* element of the term, 'human resources'. They argue that: 'whilst the 'soft' rhetoric of people as an organisation's greatest asset is universally maintained, here too ... observation of practice indicates that 'people' figure largely as part of a balance sheet equation' (p. 1).

KEY POINT

Treating people, even people who are leaving, as just a resource is not a good way to handle staff departures. We need to apply the learning about people management in general to the specific task of working with employees who are leaving.

We need to make sure we do not do any of the following:

1. Allow people to leave without any formal recognition of their contribution. This recognition can take various forms, depending on the circumstances, but for someone to leave without this recognition can create considerable ill feeling – especially if staff who are remaining are aware of this omission.
2. Behave insensitively towards departing staff – for example, by implying that their contribution will not be missed: 'Perhaps when we get our new team member we will be able to reduce the time it takes to process orders'.
3. Make obvious any changes to office layout, procedures and so on before the person has left.
4. Underestimate the change to team dynamics or the sense of loss or relief that others might feel.

Conclusion

Even in times of great stability there will be some degree of staff turnover, and so we have to recognize that staff departures are a fact of life. In some settings they are very common indeed. For example, in some organizations, there will be a high turnover of staff for a variety of reasons (see Chapter 16 on staff retention).

The question of staff leaving therefore presents a number of challenges for us, but it also presents a number of opportunities for learning and development. It is to be hoped that the brief introduction provided by this chapter will enable you to move in the right direction in terms of being equipped to rise to those challenges and to draw out the lessons to be learned.

Much of the success (or otherwise) with which we handle staff departures will depend on how effective we are in recognizing, and responding to, the human dimension of significant change. In this respect, staff departures can be seen as a form of litmus test in judging how people focused an organization is. Those which are not at all people oriented can encounter significant difficulties in relation to staff departures, while those that take seriously challenge of developing a genuine people focus can learn a great deal from such changes and earn the respect of key people in the process.

Points to ponder
1. What should an exit interview achieve?
2. What impact is a person's departure likely to have on remaining staff and how would this need to be handled?
3. Why should you not underestimate the impact on team dynamics of a person leaving?

Exercise 8
How would you want to be treated if you were leaving your job? What does this teach us about how best to manage staff departures?

CHAPTER 9: DISCIPLINARY MATTERS

In this chapter you will learn how to manage disciplinary matters sensitively and effectively.

Introduction

This is the first of two chapters relating to what many organizations refer to as 'Fairness at Work' policies. What the two chapters have in common is a sense of dissatisfaction, the dissatisfaction that characterizes many workplace situations. This first chapter is a discussion of disciplinary matters and therefore reflects dissatisfaction on the part of the organization towards one or more of its employees, while the next chapter addresses grievance procedures, which reflect dissatisfaction on the part of an employee towards the organization or some aspect of how they have been treated by it.

This chapter provides an overview of why disciplinary matters are an important part of people management and explains why we need to take them seriously. The whole topic of disciplinary matters can be an anxiety-provoking one for many people, which means that there is a danger that it will be avoided wherever possible. This, as we shall see, is not a wise approach to such matters. It would, of course, be much wiser to develop a fuller understanding of what is involved and therefore feel better informed and more confident in dealing with disciplinary matters as and when they arise.

What constitutes a disciplinary matter?

Traditionally, disciplinary matters were deemed to be either an unacceptable level of *performance* or an unacceptable level of *behaviour*, but now, as discussed in Chapter 7, many organizations have 'capability procedures' which address unacceptable levels of performance. What I am therefore going to focus on in this chapter is how organizations can respond to what is seen as an unacceptable level of behaviour – that is, where the member of staff concerned acts in such a way as to cross a line in terms of what is considered acceptable (in relation to the law, policy, ethics and so on). Capability matters relate to situations in which an employee appears to be *unable* to perform to an unacceptable standard, while disciplinary matters relate to situations in which an employee is *unwilling* to adhere to particular requirements or is negligent in doing so. Capability procedures are geared towards helping struggling employees to reach an acceptable level of work (in terms of quality, quantity or both), while disciplinary procedures are geared towards reducing or eliminating unacceptable behaviours.

Of course, different people may have different ideas about what constitutes unacceptable behaviour, but, in general terms, unacceptable behaviour is defined as anything that is likely to be detrimental to the organization or its stakeholders or to fellow employees. This can cover a wide range of actions that, in some way, contravene the written or unwritten rules of acceptable workplace behaviour.

It can be divided into misconduct and gross misconduct. Which category it falls into will depend on the seriousness of the behaviour concerned. For example, swearing at a colleague may be deemed to be misconduct, whereas the more serious matter of physically assaulting a colleague is likely to be deemed gross misconduct. However, inevitably, there will be differences of opinion in some cases as to which is the appropriate category.

Another important factor to take into consideration is that of persistence. That is, even minor misconduct can become a serious matter if it becomes persistent – for example, problems around punctuality. Somebody who is late once or twice may not be presenting a problem to the organization, but where levels of punctuality are such that it has become a persistent problem, then it is necessary for the organization to do something about that.

There are various ways in which unacceptable behaviour can arise, not least the following:

- *Breaching organizational policies*. This can happen through omission (not doing something that needed to be done) or commission (doing something that should not have been done). An example of omission could be where someone is required to fulfil a particular procedure (completing a health and safety risk assessment, for example), while an example of an act of commission could be a member of staff doing something that is expressly forbidden in policy (such as utilizing the organization's equipment for personal use).
- *Acting unethically or unprofessionally*. This may be defined by reference to an internal code of conduct or to an external source, such as the requirements of professional registration for those people who need to be registered with a professional body. In the former case, the matter can be dealt with internally within the organization, but in the latter case it may be necessary to report the breach to the professional body concerned. Examples of such behaviour would include deception, racial discrimination or having a romantic or sexual relationship with a client.
- *Breaking the law*. Of course, organizations cannot condone or tolerate instances of illegal behaviour and have to take appropriate action. Whether or not the organization needs to dismiss the member of staff will depend on the seriousness

of the offence, the circumstances surrounding it and the post occupied by the person concerned. For example, it would be necessary in most situations to dismiss someone who works with vulnerable people if their offence included an element of violence or deception.

- *Acting against the interests of the organization.* This can take various forms; sometimes quite open and at other times more subtle, but what this amounts to is doing something which is in some way likely to harm the organization. This could include passing on confidential or commercially sensitive information, undermining the reputation of the organization or anything else that could be seen as detrimental to the employing organization – whether through deliberate sabotage or through negligence.

If you are faced with situations that may fall into any of the above categories, it is important that you seek advice and discuss this matter with a senior colleague and/or HR adviser. This is because you may well be dealing with a very serious problem that could have significant consequences. Also, as I mentioned above, dealing with disciplinary matters can be quite anxiety provoking, and so it can be helpful to have support in responding to the challenges involved. It is less daunting in dealing with such matters to be working with a more experienced colleague.

Practice focus 9.1
Roger was aware of tensions in the team, but he had not felt comfortable in dealing with them, so he had simply hoped they would sort themselves out. However, as time went on, he felt more and more uneasy until he reached the point where he knew he had to do something about it. However, before he could take any action, he was approached by three members of the team who asked to have a confidential discussion with him. From this discussion he learned that one of the long-standing members of the team had been stealing stock. This had become apparent to colleagues a few months ago, and this had split the team into two factions: those who felt that he was doing no real harm, as the company could easily afford the losses and those who felt that stealing was wrong, whatever the circumstances, and therefore felt very uncomfortable knowing that their colleague was, in effect, pilfering. Roger was not a very experienced manager, and so he felt quite threatened by this situation and was not sure what to do. He raised the issue with his line manager and, as a result of this, a three-way meeting was held, involving Roger, his manager and an HR adviser. Roger found this meeting very helpful and was reassured that he was not alone in dealing with a very difficult situation.

Disciplinary procedures

First of all, we need to make sure that we are familiar with the policy and procedures of the organization concerned, as these can vary considerably from one organisation to another. However, despite the variations, there are commonly four main stages to a disciplinary process:

1. *Informal discussion.* This is where it has become apparent that there is unacceptable behaviour taking place or some form of misconduct has taken place and steps are being taken to resolve the difficulties before they reach a more serious level. This can take the form of a verbal warning where it is made clear to the individual concerned that whatever has happened must not happen again. This can also be a useful point for engaging in problem solving. Depending on the circumstances, it can be helpful to see whether the unacceptable behaviour is linked to one or more problems. It may well be the case that, by addressing the problem(s), the unacceptable behaviour can be stemmed. For example, if someone is behaving rudely or aggressively towards a colleague, this could be as a result of an underlying conflict. Taking steps to resolve the conflict could be enough to prevent any further rudeness or aggression.
2. *Formal written warning.* This happens where either an informal warning has been ignored or the matter is serious enough to warrant an immediate formal written warning. This can be a significant blemish on an employee's personnel record, and so we should not take this step lightly. However, we also need to make sure that we do not fail to issue such warnings where they are necessary. A clear and balanced view of the situation is called for.
3. *Second (and final) written warning.* This is, in effect, a situation where the organization is saying: we have already warned you in writing once about this, but you have not complied with our requirements. We are now giving you a second warning and this will be a final warning, in the sense that, if the matter arises again, the next step is likely to be dismissal. Clearly this is also a very serious step, but if we do not take it when it is necessary, we can pay a high price.
4. *Dismissal.* This can happen as a result of moving through the three stages highlighted above or it can amount to instant dismissal. This refers to incidents where the behaviour is serious enough to justify on the spot dismissal (or at least dismissal after the organization has had the opportunity to investigate the matter and establish the facts). This would include such serious matters as theft and/or violence.

Again, it is important to emphasize that you will need to be familiar with your particular organization's policies and procedures as what is described here is very common but not universal. It is therefore very wise to be clear about the specifics that affect your particular workplace.

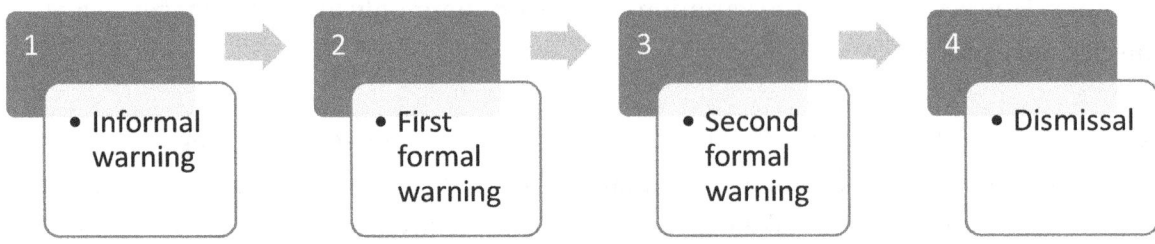

Figure 9.1 Common disciplinary stages

Making the process work
The UK Arbitration, Conciliation and Advisory Service have produced guidelines on disciplinary (and grievance) procedures (ACAS, 2015). These offer useful guidance on good practice in this area and make an important contribution to casting light on helpful steps to take. The following pointers are based in part on this guidance.

Establish the facts
As in all aspects of people management, disciplinary matters need to be carried out with complete fairness. It is therefore essential to establish the facts of the situation as soon as reasonably possible. This is so that we are not acting on the basis of false assumptions or misleading understandings, and thereby being unfair.

We have to be clear that an investigation to establish the facts is not the same as a criminal investigation, just as a disciplinary hearing is not the same as a trial. However, there is a degree of overlap, in so far as, in both cases, there is a need to ensure that there is a clear and accurate understanding of the circumstances in question.

In some cases, it may be sufficient to talk directly to the employee concerned, but in other cases, there may need to be a formal investigation to gather the relevant information. This could involve one or more meetings, depending on the complexity of the matter at hand. However, meetings to establish the facts of the situation should not be confused with formal hearings which have a different standing and a different purpose (see below).

If the facts that emerge from an investigation suggest that it is not appropriate for the person concerned to continue at work pending a formal disciplinary hearing, it may be necessary to suspend him or her. This can be a formal suspension where the seriousness of the circumstances dictates this, or, depending on the specific policy of the organization concerned, an informal suspension – what is often referred to as 'garden leave'. Once again, such matters need to be carefully thought through, and with appropriate consultation and support.

Communicate

Situations involving disciplinary matters can become quite fraught, and so it is important to keep the channels of communication open, partly to prevent misunderstandings adding unnecessary complications and partly to make sure that we have a clear and accurate understanding of the situation we are dealing with, so that we are better equipped to manage it effectively.

This communication needs to include the following elements as appropriate:

- Informal discussion to prevent problems developing, as mentioned above.
- Informing the person concerned that there are concerns about one or more aspects of their behaviour. The timing of this will depend on the circumstances (for example, if the alleged misconduct is bullying, it may be necessary to take prior steps to safeguard the person(s) at potential risk of a backlash), but should take place as soon as reasonably possible. This is because undue delay can create bad feeling and further unnecessary complications.
- Notifying the person concerned that there is a case to answer. Where the gathering of information has enabled a decision to be made that there is s disciplinary case to answer, then the member of staff to whom this refers needs to be notified in writing of this. There may be specific guidelines about this in the policy of the organization concerned, and so it will be important to check these before proceeding. The ACAS code of conduct advises that:

    > This notification should contain enough information about the alleged misconduct or poor performance and its possible consequences to enable the employee to prepare to answer the case at a disciplinary meeting.
    > (ACAS, 2015)

- If meetings are required (whether an investigatory meeting to gather facts and develop an understanding of the situation or a decision-making meeting – often referred to as a 'hearing'), then communication at them needs to be open and transparent. This is important for three reasons: (i) to facilitate effective practice in taking the procedures forward; (ii) in the interests of fairness; and (iii) to prevent providing grounds for an appeal (see below).

- We also need to get the practicalities right in terms of letting appropriate people know the time, date and venue for relevant meetings – important details that can sometimes be overlooked in fraught circumstances. We also need to make sure that the employee has been informed that they may bring someone suitable with them to the meeting (unless the specific procedures of the organization do not allow this – for example, in fact-finding meetings).

These examples of key aspects of communication should be sufficient to establish just how important it is that we give the communication aspects of disciplinary matters our full attention. And, as I have already noted, disciplinary matters can be anxiety provoking, and anxiety can distort or even halt communication altogether.

Coming to a conclusion
It is in nobody's interest for disciplinary proceedings to take any longer than is necessary. However, it is also important to make sure that we do not act hastily. What can help us to get the balance right is clarity about the process we are going through, from establishing the facts through to making a decision about how to bring the matter to a conclusion. It is therefore essential that a clear, fully supported decision is made and the situation is not allowed to drift on or fizzle out. This decision-making process can lead to the following possible outcomes:

- *No further action*. In effect, the case is dismissed. This could be because of a lack of evidence; the original complainant withdraws their complaint; new evidence come s to light that changes how the situation is perceived; or any other reason that makes taking any further action inappropriate.
- *Formal or informal warnings* As discussed above, organizations generally have a system of warnings and these can often prove to be sufficient to put an end to the inappropriate behaviour or prevent a repeat of the misconduct.
- *Sanctions* The possible sanctions will vary from setting to setting, but will include loss of certain privileges and/or demotion.
- *Dismissal* If the offending behaviour is serious enough, the result can be the termination of the staff member's employment.

Pitfalls to avoid
In order to make sure that we get it right when dealing with such potentially complex and sensitive matters as disciplinary proceedings, there are some important issues that we need to be aware of, some pitfalls that we need to avoid if we are to be successful in dealing with these important matters. The following are some of the main ones that we

would do well to keep in mind, so that we can try to ensure that we do not fall foul of them.

The ostrich approach
Perhaps most importantly of all, we need to recognize that adopting an ostrich approach is dangerous. That is, if we try to pretend that unacceptable behaviour is not taking place and/or fail to take ownership of the situation, then we are taking a number of significant risks:

- For one thing, we are failing to nip problems in the bud, and we are therefore risking that they will escalate and become much more serious further down the line. Clearly, this is not a sensible course of action, as we are missing important opportunities to prevent later difficulties.
- We are also risking a certain degree of resentment or ill-feeling in the team or staff group if they are aware that unacceptable behaviour is or has been taking place and they either know or suspect that you are aware of it but are doing nothing about it. It should not be underestimated just how much bad feeling such a set of circumstances can generate.
- Once again, this is likely to have an adverse effect on our reputation, thereby destroying trust and credibility, putting us in a much weaker position in terms of people management. For example, in terms of the L, for leadership, of *Staying CALM*, we will note in Chapter 11 that effective leadership hinges on being able to win the trust and respect of staff if we are to have any credibility and influence as leader. If we do not grasp the nettle when it comes to disciplinary matters, we are likely to come across as weak and ineffectual leaders who cannot be trusted.
- Also, what can easily happen is, if we do not address a disciplinary matter in the somewhat naïve hope that it will simply go away, then we risk being in a very embarrassing situation later. Consider, for example, if it later becomes known that there was unacceptable behaviour that we were aware of, but we did nothing about it. We may then find ourselves in a position where we are facing disciplinary proceedings in our own right for not having carried out our duties to an acceptable level.

Being overzealous
At the other extreme, being overzealous can be dangerous too. This may happen because we are perhaps fuelled by taking personally the behaviour concerned – for example, if the disciplinary matter relates to one or more incidences of insubordination that have been disrespectful or even humiliating towards us. We have to be very careful that we are balanced in how we tackle such issues and, if there is a matter of personal affront

involved, then it is wise to seek support from our own line manager to make sure that we do not let our own personal feelings get in the way of doing our job properly, thereby leaving us open to significant criticism at a later date. Also, if we approach disciplinary matters with what comes across as more gusto than the situation calls for, we may unsettle staff who may come to see us as 'authoritarian' or punitive. This can then lead to a lowering of trust and an increase in defensiveness – both potentially very detrimental when it comes to getting the best out of people, and therefore both counterproductive in people management terms.

Not following procedures
It is also very important to make sure that we follow procedures to the letter. If we do not, then there is the danger that you could be establishing grounds for an appeal. If it emerges that proper procedures were not followed, then in the vast majority of organizations this constitutes grounds for appeal. Appeals are best avoided because they can be:

- Inconvenient and very time consuming all round;
- Potentially quite stressful for the people involved, including – where applicable – any original complainant or victim of wrongdoing; and
- A source of false hope in those circumstances where the appeal is subsequently rejected.

It is also worthy of note that, if we do not follow procedures precisely, then we may be open to criticisms of discrimination. The argument may be put forward that the reason that proper procedures were not followed was that there was some degree of discrimination towards one or more people involved in the situation. This has the unfortunate potential to lead to very complex, almost nightmarish, situations in terms of allegations and counter-allegations. It is therefore vitally important that we leave no room for error by making sure that we are doing exactly what is required of us under the procedures. A basic commitment to fairness demands this.

Not seeking support
Finally, it has to be recognized that dealing with disciplinary matters can be very demanding, and so it is important that we use our support network wherever we can. Leaving ourselves vulnerable to the pressures involved without adequate support can be a recipe for stress, and that will then put us in a very weak position when it comes to supporting the people who rely on us.

Practice focus 9.1
Karen was a very experienced human resources adviser in a large organization and was regularly called upon to support managers who were involved in disciplinary matters. Her contribution was invaluable because, over the years, she had seen people making all the mistakes that could be made. She was also in a strong position because, while disciplinary matters could be emotionally demanding and nerve-wracking, she was, in a sense, one step removed from the situation because she did not have to be a line manager to the people involved. This made her a really useful resource for managers who had to wrestle with the complexities – especially those who were doing it for the first time. Her experience stood her in good stead for helping managers to look at the situation carefully and calmly, to find the balance between undue delay and undue haste, to keep the channels of communication open and to stick to the procedures

KEY POINT

Disciplinary matters can be highly sensitive, especially if the behaviour deemed unacceptable had proven hurtful to one or more colleagues. It is therefore essential to handle such situations very sensitively, having given them very careful consideration.

Conclusion

If you are lucky, disciplinary matters will rarely, if ever, emerge. It is possible for people managers to go through a whole career without having to deal with such matters, but most people are not that lucky and will, at some point, be faced with one or more disciplinary matters to deal with. There is no reason to panic or to see this as a situation that presents insurmountable difficulties; it is a matter of keeping a clear head, following the appropriate procedures precisely, seeking support where we need it, and drawing on our range of people skills to negotiate our way through a potentially very difficult situation.

Points to ponder

1. In what circumstances would you consider instituting disciplinary proceedings?
2. Why is it important to put concerns in writing where necessary?
3. In what circumstances might an employee have the grounds for an appeal against a disciplinary decision?

Exercise 9

What would be your greatest anxieties if you had to deal with a disciplinary matter? What could you do about these? Who could you go to for support?

CHAPTER 10: DEALING WITH GRIEVANCES

In this chapter you learn about how best to respond when someone takes out a grievance.

Introduction
This is the second of two chapters about 'Fairness at Work'. Grievance procedures exist to ensure that dissatisfied employees have an opportunity to seek redress in relation to an issue that they are not happy about, to prevent an escalation of the problem or – in extreme cases – the departure of the employee. They are there as an important contribution to people management, in so far as they enable staff to have a voice and to insist on being heard in relation to matters that are causing them some degree of concern. Ideally, we should be aiming for a situation in which the existence of grievance procedures gives an important message that staff concerns will be taken seriously, but they are rarely if ever used, as the other mechanisms for supporting staff are working well enough to ensure that staff do not feel the need to pursue a grievance.

This chapter provides an overview of what the common causes of grievances are, explores the nature and purpose of grievance procedures and discusses some key issues that we need to be aware of if we are going to make sure that we deal effectively with any grievance situations that may arise.

What causes grievances?
A grievance is anything with which a person feels so unhappy that they are prepared to raise the matter formally with their employers. There are many different potential or actual causes of grievances, and they can be understood to fall into two main categories. The first of these is unfair or unacceptable treatment and refers to situations in which one or more staff members feel that they have been treated unfairly, without due respect or dignity or in ways that demean them in some way (being talked down to, treated like a child, for example). If people feel that they have been discriminated against in some way, and particularly if they feel they have been victimized, then they are likely to believe that the unfairness involved in this is sufficient to justify raising the issue with their organization as, in effect, a complaint.

As Furnham and Taylor (2004) comment: 'But one does not need to be a sensitive flower to feel unfairly dealt with. It is a very common reaction: in all organizations, at all times, on all levels people feel, from time to time, disgruntled' (p. xvi).

Further examples of unfair or unacceptable treatment would be bullying or harassment, unsupportive line management, what is perceived as an unfair appraisal or job grading, an excessive workload and, along the same lines, excessive working hours. A grievance may arise because of any one of these factors or a combination of them (sadly, it is not uncommon for there to be such combinations – for example, a bullying line manager is unlikely to be supportive). Indeed, it is often the case that staff will tolerate certain dissatisfactions when they occur in isolation, but find it too much when they combine – and it is likely to be at that point that a grievance may be lodged.

The second category can be broken promises. Such promises can be explicit or implied. Examples of such circumstances would be a lack of supervision (where the employee was led to believe that they would receive a certain level of supervisory support and they are not getting it); access to training being denied; and possibly promotion opportunities being denied. Such 'broken promises' can have a very strong negative effect on employees. It gives the message that they are not valued or appreciated, that they are not important as people, but merely as cogs in the machine. If we are to move towards people management based on being truly people focused, then we need to make sure that broken promises is not something that features in our approach to our work. This is because a broken promise gives a very strong message to the effect that: 'we do not value you and we will exploit you as we see fit by making promises to gain your cooperation, but without any real commitment to fulfilling those promises'. Clearly this is not a wise basis for managing people.

Grievance procedures

A key point to emphasize is that, wherever possible, we should work to avoid the need for someone to pursue a grievance (just as organizations should work hard to ensure that they do not receive complaints from customers, clients or patients). However, we also need to be prepared for responding appropriately to grievances if or when they do arise.
As with disciplinary procedures, as discussed in Chapter 9, it is important that we are familiar with the policy and procedures of the organization concerned, as they can vary from setting to setting. However, there are common themes across organizations, and it is quite common for the following three main stages to be followed:

1. *Informal discussion*

This is where the aggrieved person will sit down with either their line manager, another manager or an HR representative to identify concerns and attempt to resolve any difficulties at an early stage. The aim is not to make it difficult for the staff member to pursue their grievance, but, rather, to try and settle the difficulties at an early stage. It is an important way in which the organization says: 'we do not want staff to be unhappy;

we are prepared to listen and, if we feel your concerns are justified, we will take reasonable steps to resolve the matter'.

This is a very important part of the process, because, if people feel that they are not being listened to, that there is no real commitment to addressing their concerns, then the net effect can be that their dissatisfaction is amplified. Consider, for example, a situation where somebody raises a legitimate concern, but they then feel that that concern is not being taken seriously. It is understandable that this can then make them feel even more strongly about the injustice or the inappropriateness of whatever it was that caused them to raise their concerns in the first place. Sadly, this is often what happens in retail settings where customers are unhappy because a purchase proved to be faulty or inadequate and they therefore complain – but the poor response to their complaint makes them feel that they have been 'fobbed off', with the net result that they are even more unhappy. In fact, it is often the case that their initial dissatisfaction pales into insignificance compared with how unhappy they feel with the dismissive response they have received from the organization concerned. It is vitally important that our response to the initial emergence of a grievance does not have the same effect. We therefore have to make sure that we offer informal discussion as soon as we become aware that a member of staff is dissatisfied, and that we tackle such issues carefully and skilfully. The appropriate use of listening skills is therefore crucially important at this stage in the proceedings.

> *Practice focus 10.1*
> Louise was proud of her African roots on her father's side, but she rarely talked about them. One day, in a discussion during a break, her colleague, Ray, made an off-the-cuff comment about Polish immigrants 'taking over' and being given preferential treatment when it comes to housing and benefits. Louise was offended by this, as she regarded it as an ill-informed racist comment. She told Ray that she felt very unhappy at what he had said and was going to 'report' him. He told her that she was being too touchy and that he was talking about Polish people and not black people. Louise decided to take the matter further and spoke to her line manager about the incident and said that she wanted to take out a grievance. Her manager, who was also Ray's manager, listened carefully to what she had to say, acknowledged that it must have been upsetting and told her that she would talk to Ray about the incident. As a result of this, Ray approached Louise and apologized to her. He explained that he had been helped to realize that he had been out of order in what he had said and that he had been insensitive. He also said that he now understood that his views were based on inaccurate and stereotypical views. Louise accepted his apology and went to see

her manager to thank her for her support and to say that she was happy not to pursue a formal grievance.

2. *Preliminary investigation*

This is where there is a limited amount of enquiry into the situation to, in effect, establish whether there are sufficient grounds to undertake a fuller, more thorough investigation. It may well be (and often is) the case that this is sufficient to identify underlying problems and to come up with solutions (or at least ways of alleviating the difficulties) and, in many cases, this is all that is needed to satisfy the person who has raised the grievance.

Once again, listening skills are very important. If the person concerned feels that they have not been listened to, then we run the risk of escalating the situation considerably by amplifying their discontent and strengthening their resolve to get justice. A key part of effective listening is empathy, the ability to put ourselves in the other person's shoes, to understand the situation from their point of view (we shall return to this point below).

3. *Full investigation*

However, it is often the case that a preliminary investigation is not sufficient, particularly where situations are complex or where there are various dimensions to the problem. This is then likely to require a fuller, more thorough investigation of what has happened. The problem with this is that the time that it can take to undertake a proper investigation can be counterproductive, in so far as the ongoing tensions and dissatisfactions can grow during this time. It is therefore important to try and resolve difficulties, if not at the first stage of informal discussion, then as far as reasonably possible at the second stage of preliminary investigation.

Figure 10.1 Common grievance stages

Key issues

Having outlined the overall process of responding to grievance issues, we can now move on to explore some key issues associated with making sure that we handle such situations as effectively and positively as we can. Of course, this is not an exhaustive list, but it should be sufficient to show that grievance issues merit careful consideration and we are taking significant and unnecessary risks if we do not pay them the attention they deserve.

Acting sooner rather than later
Wherever possible it is wise to nip problems in the bud, to try and make sure that they do not become amplified or fester in some way. Where people feel that it has become necessary to raise a grievance, then clearly they are unhappy with at least certain aspects of the way the organization is treating them. The sooner such discontent can be addressed, the better for all concerned.

An early response to concerns gives a message that the member of staff concerned is valued and that the organization takes seriously any concerns that might arise. By contrast, if there is no prompt response, the opposite message is likely to be signalled: 'you are not important and nor are any concerns you might have'. For this reason, it is very unwise to delay responding to concerns (for example, by adopting the ostrich approach discussed in Chapter 9), as it not only misses an opportunity to be supportive, but also comes across as decidedly unsupportive.

Of course, people managers tend to be very busy people, with a wide range of demands being made upon us, and so it is very easy for potential grievances to slip further down our to do list than they should. We should therefore be wary of allowing this to happen, as it can lead to a vicious circle: by not nipping concerns in the bud, we create further problems for ourselves further down the line and possibly lose some credibility and respect in the eyes of the staff member concerned (and possibly others who are aware of what had been happening). These additional problems can then clog up our diary (and the space in our head), leaving us with less time and space to respond to people's concerns in the early stages. This, then, is an important workload management issue (see Chapter 6), and so we need to be aware of it, if it applies to us, so that we can take steps to change how we deal with such situations.

The importance of listening
The need to be able to listen effectively has already been mentioned. It is essential to listen carefully at all stages, as not doing so will give a very unsupportive message to staff and undermine our credibility as leaders. The example I gave earlier of how it feels to make a complaint and not receive an adequate response (perhaps a standard letter from the company concerned or a letter which shows that they have not really listened to what we were actually telling them) shows how this can actually make us feel more aggrieved or more angry than the initial problem which led to our initial complaint. This scenario is worth re-emphasizing, as the same logic can be seen to apply to grievances. If we give the impression, even unintentionally, that we are not listening and not taking the situation

seriously, then we run the very real risk of making the situation much, much worse. It is therefore important to adopt an empathic approach to the situation – that is, to try to see the situation from their point of view and appreciate how it feels to them. If we fail to do this, we are taking a very significant and unnecessary risk. I have been involved as a consultant and/or mediator in a number of situations where feelings have reached fever pitch because a relatively minor matter has been badly handled, leading to a spiral of discontent, anger and even hatred – all because someone who had a legitimate grievance was not listened to and, when they complained about not being listened to, they were still not listened to (see the discussion below of the dangers of defensiveness).

Keeping things informal where possible
We should keep the situation informal whenever we possibly can, as formal procedures can bring considerable extra pressures for all concerned, especially – as suggested above – if those procedures take a long time to be completed. In some circumstances the grievance will be so serious that it will be necessary to adopt a formal approach straight away. However, in many cases, the matter can be resolved informally provided that we are responsive to people's concerns and have a genuine commitment to making a positive difference.

Formal procedures can be potentially stressful, especially if elements of the grievance are contested (for example, where someone is complaining about someone else's inappropriate behaviour who denies any wrongdoing) and can cause a great deal of ill feeling. Anything we can reasonably do to keep matters informal can therefore be very worthwhile. However, it is important that we are careful and sensitive about how we handle such matters. If we are not, then we run the risk that an aggrieved person will feel that we are blocking them from justice by trying to keep what should be a formal matter quite informal (see Practice focus 9.2, for example). This need for balance exemplifies the importance of critically reflective practice. We have to weigh up each situation we are dealing with and handle it appropriately, rather than just blindly follow general guidelines without checking that they are actually suitable for the specific set of circumstances we find ourselves in.

Not being defensive
Grievance situations can be quite fraught and demanding, especially some of the more complex ones or those that have become quite entangled over time. Sometime such grievances include (or at least imply) criticism of ourselves or our colleagues, and that can be hard to deal with – especially if we feel that the criticism is not justified or is disproportionate. We therefore have to be very careful in such situations to ensure that we do not become defensive. We have to remember that, as people managers, we have to work towards getting the best out of our staff. Responding defensively to their concerns

places our own issues at centre stage when it is our job to address *their* concerns. While it is understandable that we will have our own concerns, if we allow these to displace our support for our staff, it is likely to be perceived very badly not only by the member of staff concerned, but also by any other colleagues who may be aware of what is happening. This is not to say that our own concerns or feelings have no place, but we do have to make sure that we do not allow them to get in the way of good practice as people managers.

It is also important to recognize that there can be aspects of defensiveness that are part of an organization's culture and are not just individual responses on the part of certain people managers. As Argyris (1999) comments:

> An organizational defense is a policy, practice, or action that prevents the participants (at any level of any organization) from experiencing embarrassment or threat and at the same time, prevents them from discovering the causes of the embarrassment or threat. Organizational defenses (which include groups, intergroups, and interpersonal relationships) are therefore anti-learning and overprotective.
>
> (pp. xiii-xiv)

They may also prevent us from dealing effectively with grievance situations or learning the often valuable lessons that can arise when staff are unhappy with how they have been treated.

Tuning in to organizational politics
Organizations are complex places with intricate power dynamics that can be very influential in shaping cultures and individual behaviour and interactions. A key part of this is organizational politics ('office politics' as it is often called). Vigoda (2003) makes an important point when he argues that:

> politics in organizations is as crucial as doing the job itself and is as important as politics outside organizations. It has a massive impact on our well-being as employees, managers and stakeholders in organizations. I would even venture to say that increasing one's knowledge in the field often spells the difference between staying with an organization or leaving it, being promoted or being left behind, or winning or losing in competitive situations.
>
> (p. ix)

Successful people managers are generally those who have, alongside their other knowledge, skills and values, a good sense of the political. They are able to read between the lines and tune in to subtle processes and interactions that can make such a big difference in terms of what happens within the organization. It involves knowing who are powerful players are (and these will not necessarily be the people who hold formal power; the idea of the 'power behind the throne' is a very relevant one here) and what the channels of power are (official and unofficial). See the discussion of the 'organizational operator' in Thompson (2018b).

Grievance issues often relate to organizational politics, and so it is worth being sensitive to how these matters manifest themselves in the organization concerned. We are not expected to be experts in this field, but if we naively stumble on without any awareness of the subtle dynamics of organization politics, we place ourselves at a significant disadvantage when it comes to grievances in particular and people management in general.

> *Practice focus 10.2*
> Martin was incensed when he learned that he had been unsuccessful in his application for promotion and that his ex-colleague, Gavin, had got the job. He was aware that he had more experience than Gavin as well as more qualifications. He therefore decided to lodge a grievance, as he felt that the selection process had been unfair. He knew that Gavin 'put himself about', in the sense that he spoke to all the right people, made all the right noises and 'played the game'. However, Martin knew that his own level of performance was much higher than Gavin's and that this was widely known. He felt it was wrong for decisions about promotion to be made on the basis of criteria other than those directly related to work. He knew it was going to be difficult to prove his point as office politics are so shadowy and difficult to pin down, but he felt so dissatisfied with the way he had been treated that he felt he had to make a stand – and pursuing a formal grievance was how he intended to do it.

Handling feelings

Grievances occur when people are unhappy, frustrated or disgruntled, and so it should not be surprising to learn that strong emotions can be to the fore. It is therefore important that we are able to respond appropriately to the emotions being expressed – in a sense, to use our emotional intelligence (Howe, 2008), which involves keeping our own feelings in check. Smith and Smith (2008) offer helpful guidance in this regard:

> Without being too precious, we need to express in our actions a concern with appropriate boundaries. One obvious aspect of this is to remain in touch with ourselves and our role. If we know where we stand, we can be with another in ways that are experienced as safe and grounded. We can provide a reference

point, a firm place in moments of flux. Another aspect is to contain our emotions. If we are all over the place then it is highly unlikely that we will be able to be what is needed. This does not mean that we are some emotionless automaton. That would also be unhelpful and probably experienced as inauthentic. We need to engage with the situation with both our hearts and minds, to show concern but at the same time to be thinking about what is happening so that people may entertain their thoughts and feelings and later work on them.

(pp. 89-90)

KEY POINT

The use of the term, 'inauthentic' is significant, as being able to respond appropriately and constructively to the feelings dimension of our work is a fundamental part of authenticity, the A of Staying CALM. It also reflects the C, for Connection, of CALM, as the richness (or otherwise) of human contact can determine whether or not emotions are well handled.

Communicating

In Chapter 9 the point was made that, in dealing with disciplinary matters, it is essential to keep the channels of communication open. We can now note that the same applies to grievance situations, as a failure to communicate effectively can make the situation much more tense and fraught and therefore much worse than it needs to be.

Learning from the experience

It is also important to try to ensure that we learn from the experience. It is very rarely, if ever, the case that people make a grievance without an understandable sense of dissatisfaction. It may well be that the grievance is not proven, in which case this means that it is not accepted by the investigation that the person concerned is correct in what they are alleging. However, the dissatisfaction associated with the whole process can be such that it can be very destructive. It is therefore important that, whenever such a situation arises, we learn from the experience, so that we can be much better equipped to try and prevent such grievances from arising in future. If there is a culture of people taking out grievances, for example, then that is giving a very strong and powerful message that there is something fundamentally wrong that needs to be tackled through good people management and leadership.

Supporting the employee

It would be very unwise to forget that we are still required to support the employee, even if they are complaining, and even if we do feel that their grounds for complaint do not have full validity. There is still a duty of care towards employees, and failing to support them during what is likely to be a difficult situation for them is basically asking for trouble, in a sense. It can seriously undermine our credibility and the trust and respect we need to be effective leaders.

It is also important to seek support for ourselves in responding to grievance situations. Dealing with such matters can be quite demanding, especially if there is implied, or even explicit within the grievance, criticism of some aspect of our practice. There should be adequate support available for us, either through our line manager or through other sources, but it is important that we seek this out and do not wait to be asked.

Conclusion

The frequency of grievances varies from organization to organization. They are very rare in some, but not at all uncommon in others. However, regardless of this, whenever a grievance does occur, it is clearly something that we have to address as skilfully and sensitively as we can. If we do not, then as I have suggested earlier, we run a very significant risk of alienating one or more members of staff. Indeed, we could alienate a whole team or staff group if it is perceived that what they see as a genuine grievance was not handled well. It is therefore important to see a grievance as a challenge of leadership, a test of whether we have the skills and commitment to be able to deal with people in a genuinely human way and have the good grace to listen to what is concerning them. And, even if we do not agree with their concerns, we need to have the commitment to a human approach to people management, so that we are none the less able to support staff in these difficult times.

Points to ponder

1. Why is an informal discussion stage important as part of handling grievances?
2. What might the consequences be of becoming defensive in response to a grievance?
3. Why is important to 'tune in' to people's feelings when they are taking out a grievance?

Exercise 10

What do you see as the most important steps to take to (i) prevent grievances from occurring; and (ii) deal with them appropriately if or when they do arise?

PART II: ACHIEVING BEST OUTCOMES

Introduction

Part I was concerned primarily with the basics of getting the job done. Part II now seeks to go beyond this to look at what is needed to attempt to achieve the best possible outcomes. This Part therefore emphasizes the role of leaders, whether managers or HR professionals, in helping to fulfil their potential and achieve optimal standards of work. However, the topics covered here should not be seen as optional extras for those who want to 'go the extra mile' and excel. Aiming simply to 'get by' risks undermining our whole people management endeavour. If staff get the impression that people managers are not genuinely interested in helping them to do the best they can and are simply settling for getting through the day, then it is likely that this will have an adverse effect on their morale and thus their motivation. While we have to be realistic and recognize that it is not always possible to achieve optimal outcomes, we also need to be aware that not even trying to do our best, individually and collectively, can be very counterproductive indeed.

We should also recognize that the idea of *Staying CALM*, as discussed in the Introduction, applies no less to the areas covered here than it did to those featured in Part I. In fact, we begin Part II with a discussion of Leadership, the L of CALM. This is because leadership is a fundamental basis for ensuring that we are all clear about what we are doing, why we are doing it and where it is taking us to. Without that clarity it is highly unlikely that people will be able to achieve optimal outcomes.

CHAPTER 11: LEADERSHIP

In this chapter you will learn how to develop your capabilities as a leader.

Introduction

Leadership is a central part of people management, which is why I have included it as the L of the *Staying CALM* model that underpins the whole manual, and, indeed, my whole approach to people management. Its importance rests on the fact that leadership is an essential basis of getting the best out of people. Staff will not perform to their best or achieve maximum job satisfaction if there is no sense of direction, no clarity about what the team, staff group or overall organization is trying to do.

One of the key elements of leadership is therefore the establishing of clarity about goals and direction and the creation of an atmosphere of trust, respect and security that is necessary to help people achieve these goals. As Northouse (2010) puts it: 'Leadership is a process whereby an individual influences a group of individuals to achieve a common goal' (p. 3).

An effective leader is someone who understands how organizations work, someone who can tune in to the way cultures influence staff and be able to influence or shape the culture in a positive direction – creating a situation in which people *want* to do their best and do not have to be pressurized into doing so. It is not simply a matter of being a 'strong' manager. The traditional 'command and control' approach to management does not involve recognizing that we are dealing with *people* – complex beings who do not achieve their best by simply responding to instructions like mindless automata. Telling people what to do may well get the basics of the job done, but it is certainly not going to help us achieve the optimal outcomes that a more enlightened approach to working with people is capable of producing.

Contrary to popular belief, leaders are made not born, in the sense that leadership is based on knowledge, skills and values that can be learned. It is not simply a case of you are either a leader or you are not. People who have no idea about leading can learn the basics; people who are mediocre leaders can become good leaders; and good leaders can become excellent leaders. This does not mean that anyone can be an excellent leader, as different people have different learning abilities, different levels of motivation and different life experiences to draw upon. However, it does mean that we should not be defeatist by assuming that leadership knowledge, skills and values cannot be developed over time.

Similarly, if we are not to exclude potential leaders from our purview, then we need to acknowledge that there is an unhelpful stereotype of a leader as a 'hero'. Much of the traditional literature paints a picture of leadership which has very strong associations with very masculine characters, usually white, who have been involved in heroic deeds of bravery and endurance – military figures, expedition leaders and so on. It is therefore important to be clear, from the outset of this chapter, that we need a more sophisticated understanding of leadership that moves away from such unhelpful stereotypes and which adopts a more inclusive model of leadership that is consistent with a commitment to valuing diversity.

It is also important to recognize that, within a workplace context, it is not only managers who can become leaders. Human resource professionals have a leadership role, in the sense that they have a part to play in shaping the culture of the organization and the extent to which it is a people-focused environment (see the discussion of strategic HRM in the Introduction). It is also worth remembering that, as long ago as 1924, Mary Parker Follett argued that it is the task of leaders to produce leaders, to encourage all staff to be involved in setting the direction of the work and ensuring that goals are achieved.

This chapter explores different aspects of what is involved in good leadership in order to provide a foundation for further learning. It begins by exploring the importance of vision and values and ends by emphasizing the significance of self-leadership and re-emphasizing the value of *Staying CALM*.

Vision and values
The term 'vision' refers to having an idea of where you are trying to get to, what this organization (or your part within in it: your team or section) will look like in, say, three years' time? How will you get to that point? What changes need to take place to make that vision a reality? But, there is more to vision than simply a set of aims. It also refers to the values that will drive us towards that vision.

Values are those things that we hold dear, literally what we value. They usually take the form of principles or beliefs that guide our actions. For example, if we have equality as one of our values, we will feel unhappy when we encounter a situation where someone is being treated unfairly simply because they are different in some way. Because values are such a strong influence on behaviour, then we need to include the significance of values in our consideration of the organization's vision.

So, what type of team or working environment do we want to establish? What do we see as important, indeed necessary to achieve the success that our team or group of staff are motivated to fulfil? These are all questions that help to shape a vision, a picture of where we are trying to get to. Unfortunately, many organizations have adopted a very simplistic approach to such matters by developing a formal 'mission statement' to serve as the basis of their vision, but with little clarity about how it can be achieved. This is especially the case when the mission statement is quite grandiose and far removed from the reality of the organization concerned, where such a discrepancy is likely to alienate staff. If there is no real connection between the vision and the steps needed to achieve it, there is not much point in having the vision, as it will not be influencing people in the direction of achieving the desired outcomes. It will not be meaningful (see Chapter 20).

If there is no vision grounded in reality, then there will be no sense of moving forward towards desired goals. There will then be little by way of motivation to encourage people to move forward. Work teams that lack any sense of vision can easily become stagnant and have no sense of direction or purpose (an important element of spirituality, which will also be discussed in Chapter 20). By contrast, a team of staff who have a clear sense of direction can be much more effective in achieving its goals and, in the process, creating a productive working environment that can help promote a high level of morale.

But, even where we have a clear and realistic vision, we also have to have the values that will facilitate realizing that vision. Values are an important part of leadership because they are also a key part of what motivates people. If people are not committed to a particular set of values, then there will be little or nothing to drive them forward. For example, in an organization geared towards health promotion, if staff are not committed to promoting health, then there are likely to be considerable obstacles to achieving optimal outcomes. Kouzes and Posner (2017) recognize the importance of values when they argue that values are empowering. We are, they say, much more in control of our own lives when we're clear about our personal values. With clarity about our values, we do not have to rely on direction from people in authority (giving us greater scope for creativity, job satisfaction and learning).

It is therefore important that leaders are able to be clear about organizational values and help staff groups to develop their own sense of values within that broader framework. What are the principles and beliefs that they hold dear that will enable them to feel a strong sense of commitment to making the vision a reality?
In a nutshell, this aspect of effective leadership is premised on *aligning* vision and values, making sure – as far as possible – that what we are trying to achieve it and the motivation to achieve it are consistent with one another.

Communication and clarity
Having a vision and a set of values is of little help unless they are communicated clearly and consistently over time to the people concerned. Many organizations have made the

mistake of having a vision that has little or no impact on the organization because it is not communicated on a regular basis. If the vision is not translated into reality (or 'operationalized', to use the technical term), then it will not have any practical value as a driver of behaviour. A good leader is somebody who has the communication skills to be able to ensure that people are clear at all times, what the vision is and the values that drive it, and what needs to happen to make that vision a reality and, in effect, to realize those values.

It should be recalled that, in Chapter 2, I made the point that we cannot not communicate. That is, we are always communicating something – through our body language, for example. There is therefore on onus on us, as people managers, to ensure that what we are communicating is consistent with the vision and values. For example, if we want to emphasize the importance of teamwork as a fundamental value that will help us achieve our shared vision, then we should make sure that what we say and what we do are not in any way divisive or disruptive of teamwork (showing favouritism, for example). Jackson (2000) captures this point well when he argues that:

> Talking about visions and values is not enough. Leaders live them. They never miss an opportunity to relate their decisions to the visions and values. Decisions are then made consistent with those guiding ideals.
>
> (p. 29)

Any leader is likely to encounter a whole range of potential obstacles to effective communication and clarity, but the expectation is that we are able to develop these skills and insights to enable us to work effectively in an organizational context in getting the message across. This takes us back to the point I made earlier that a good leader is somebody who has a good understanding of how organizations work in general, somebody who is tuned in to organizational life, as it were.

Key Point

A good leader is somebody who understands the role of organizational culture and is able to use their skills to shape that culture in a positive direction in line with the strategic vision, building on the positives and addressing the negatives.

Argyris, a highly respected author in the organizational learning field, makes apt comment when he makes the point that:

> Schein defines leadership as "the attitude and motivation to examine and manage culture" (p. 374). He regards the organization as the group, and analyses

organizational culture as a pattern of basic assumptions shared by the group, acquired by solving problems of adaptation and integration, working "well enough to be considered valid and, therefore, to be taught to new members as the correct way to perceive, think, and feel in relation to those problems." In organizational learning, basic assumptions shift in the heads of the group members. The job of a learning leader is to promote such shifts by helping the organization's member's to "achieve some degree of insight and develop motivation to change" (p. 390).

(1999, p. 5)

In *People Skills* I make the point that it is pointless trying to fight a culture, as the influence of organizational cultures is stronger than the influence of any single individual. This is because cultures are based on habits, routinized responses that involve little or no conscious thought, and these are very powerful influences on not only our behaviour, but also our thoughts and feelings. If as leaders, we are unhappy with some aspect of a culture, then we need to try and change that aspect (break the habits in some way, for example), rather than simply go against it and naively expect to be a stronger influence than an ingrained set of habits and ways of thinking. As Northouse (2010) rightly claims: 'Leaders change the way people think about what is possible' (p. 11).

Practice focus 11.1
Nick was a manager who like to be busy and would involve himself in all sorts of projects. He prided himself in his commitment to his work and the fact that he went beyond just the basics of what was expected of him. While this commitment was commendable and an asset to his employers, it had a downside. Nick would often find himself rushing about, going from meeting to meeting, commitment to commitment, and he clearly enjoyed the 'buzz' that this gave him. However, it meant that he was prone to becoming very self-absorbed and concentrating on his own issues. He could therefore lose sight of his role as a leader and would fail to communicate. People who relied on him often felt let down by him because he seemed to be rushing around all the time and appeared to have no time for them or for their collective endeavours. So, in failing to communicate properly, he was not only not fulfilling his managerial responsibilities, he was also failing to communicate the vision and values that would pull the team together and motivate them to move forward with confidence and commitment.

Teamwork and tension relief
It is unfortunately the case that, these days, so many organizations emphasize the importance of teamwork and yet enter into counterproductive ways of working by

offering individual rewards and promotions which have the effect of emphasizing the significance of *individual* effort, rather than team or collective effort. An effective leader is somebody who is able to pull people together and get them rowing in the right direction as it were. In doing this, a leader is able to draw on the vision and values to give people a collective sense of responsibility, a feeling that it is important to support one another (see Chapter 14 on teamwork).

A good leader who is successful in promoting effective teamwork will also therefore be able to address issues of tension relief. Any workplace will produce tensions, either from time to time or on a constant basis, and a team is a good way for dealing with those tensions – a good place, for example, to ventilate concerns and to get moral and emotional support in dealing with them. If tensions are not to be allowed to escalate, to create additional conflicts and problems, then there needs to be good teamwork in place to address these concerns constructively and nip them in the bud. Once again, then, a good leader is somebody who has the skills to develop effective teamwork, rather than just have a group of individual employees who are motivated only by their individual concerns.

A major source of tension in the workplace is conflict (to be discussed in more detail in Chapter 25). Leaders therefore need to be prepared to address conflict issues as and when they arise, rather than just hope that they will go away. Conflict is an inevitable part of the workplace, and so a reluctance to deal with the challenges it presents can be highly problematic. Just as a good, successful relationship between two partners is not characterized by a *lack* of conflict, but by the ability of the two people to manage conflicts constructively as and when it arises, a good, successful team is not conflict free – rather, it is a collection of people who deals effectively with their conflicts. The leader can be a key figure in facilitating this – for example, by making sure that people acknowledge conflicts and talk about them, rather than try and brush them under the carpet.

Motivation and morale
Teamwork is a key part of motivation and morale, as are vision and values, but these are not the only elements of motivation. A good leader is able to tap into who is motivated by what and to promote positive motivation where possible (for example, by identifying obstacles to motivation and addressing these constructively where possible). As we will see in Chapter 15, motivation is not simply an individual matter, it also has a broader social dimension. There is therefore an important role for leaders to help create a positive atmosphere where staff feel supported and valued – creating the right 'feel' in the team or staff group.

Morale, as we have already noted, is one of the most significant aspects of motivational life, in the sense that low morale can be extremely poisonous and can do considerable damage to our people management efforts. A good leader is therefore somebody who tunes into morale and has the knowledge, skills and confidence to be able to create the circumstances necessary for high morale, even when times are very challenging. In fact, it is often the case that handling challenging situations well is what earns the leader the trust, respect and credibility that are so essential as a foundation for effective leadership. Such testing times provide an opportunity for skilful leaders to bring people together and focus on their shared vision and values.

What is also important in terms of motivation and morale is the ability of the leader to promote staff well-being. The comments of Kelloway *et al.* (2008) reinforce this point:

> The suggestion that leaders have an impact on employees' well-being is neither novel nor particularly startling. Research documenting the effects of leadership on employee well-being has been available for over 30 years (Day & Hamblin, 1964) and the conclusions of this research would not surprise any adult who has held a job for any length of time (Gilbreath, 2004). Poor leadership is associated with increased levels of employee stress (Offerman & Hellman, 1996; Richman *et al.* 1992), alienation (Ashforth 1994, 1997) and may provoke counter-productive behaviors such as retaliation (Townsend, Phillips & Elkins, 2000). What may be surprising is just how extensive are the effects of leadership on individuals' well-being.
>
> (p. 25)

Without a genuine commitment to well-being, morale with suffer significantly, with a highly likely negative knock-on effect on motivation. Leadership in particular and people management in general therefore need to be premised on a commitment to promoting workplace well-being, which is why Part III is devoted to that very topic.

What connects these four elements is the organizational culture and context. Indeed, leadership can be understood as a process that involves shaping the organizational culture in a positive direction so that the work context is supportive and empowering. Culture is a very powerful influence on people, and so it is essential that leaders play their part in making sure that the culture is a help rather than a hindrance when it comes to getting the best out of staff.

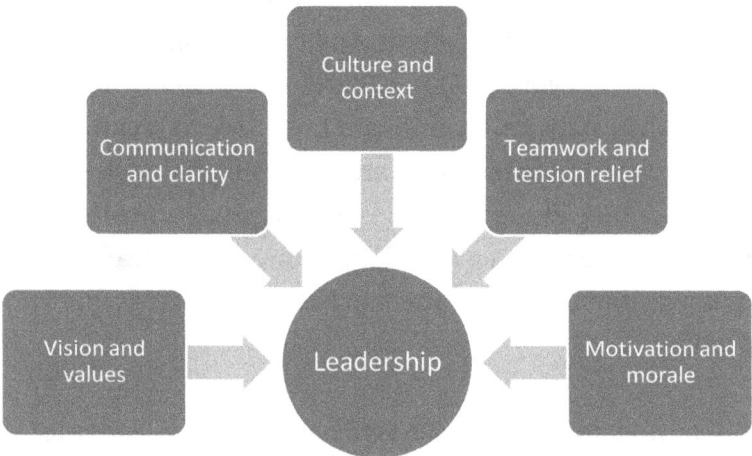

Figure 11.1 The main components of leadership

Self-leadership

There is little point in trying to lead others if we are not able to lead ourselves effectively (Gilbert, 2005). That is, if we are to help others to be clear about their goals and how to achieve them, then we need to be clear about what our own goals are and how we are planning on achieving them, what our values are and how they are shaping our thoughts, feelings and actions. If we are drifting aimlessly through our lives and our careers, we will understandably struggle when it comes to facilitating the coming together of a group of staff and developing a shared vision and values.

 It is very helpful to make your goals explicit and write them down. You are more likely to remember them and they will feel 'more real' if you do so. Having a vague and unfocused approach to goal setting is likely to hold you back.

The idea of self-leadership raises a number of important issues about the degree of self-awareness we have and how we may use that awareness to motivate ourselves and to have clear goals for ourselves. If we are to earn the trust, respect and credibility that we have already noted to be key elements of leadership, and if we are to be able to generate the atmosphere of security that people expect from a good leader, then we have to have a strong basis of self-leadership.

In Chapter 6, I mentioned the importance of self-management, of being organized and disciplined in terms of how we manage our workload and the other demands upon us in our everyday lives. We can now take this a step further by emphasizing that self-management needs to be supplemented by self-leadership. Just as organizations need both management (keeping the wheels turning) and leadership (making sure they are turning in the right direction and with everyone 'on board'). Northouse (2010) offers helpful comment in stating that:

> Kotter (1990, pp. 7-8) contended that both management and leadership are essential if an organization is to prosper. For example, if an organization has strong management without leadership, the outcome can be stifling and bureaucratic. Conversely, if an organization has strong leadership without management, the outcome can be meaningless or misdirected change for change's sake. To be effective, organizations need to nourish both competent management and skilled leadership.
>
> (pp. 10-11)

The same can be seen to apply to individual people managers. If we have good self-management but no self-leadership, then we will be efficient (well organized), but not necessarily effective (achieving our desired outcomes) if we are not sure what it is that we are trying to achieve or where we are trying to get to. By the same token, if we are clear about where we are heading, but we are not well organized and focused in how we can go about arriving at our desired destination, then the chances of being successful will be significantly reduced.

> *Practice focus 11.2*
> Jen was a senior human resources adviser in a large organization. She was delighted to be invited to be part of a strategic review committee that had been set up to try and deal with some of the problems the organization had been having. She was even more delighted that she seemed well suited to the work of the committee and felt very at home in dealing with broad matters of strategy which involved trying to clarify the vision and values the organization was working to and mapping out what needed to happen to make them real. She recognized that moving in this direction might be a very good career move, and so she put her name down for a strategic management course. She found the course very helpful for the most part, but what really captured her imagination was the idea of self-leadership that the trainer had spoken about. It made Jen realize that, while she had really taken to the structured and focused approach of strategic planning, she had not been particularly good at sorting out her own personal 'strategy' – her own vision of what she wanted to do with her life and career. This recognition made her decide to look more closely at her own life and what she wanted out of it.

Staying CALM
The idea of *Staying CALM* can be seen to apply to all of the chapters of this manual, but as I have already noted, it is very relevant to this chapter, as leadership is what constitutes

the L of *CALM*. However, we can see that the other aspects of *CALM* (the C, A and M) are also very relevant. Let us consider each of them in turn.

C: connection
How we relate to people is, as we have already noted, a key part of people management. A good people manager does not just think individual terms but has a more holistic understanding that includes seeing the bigger picture and the connections across the different elements, including the connections people have with one another. This can be seen to be particularly applicable to leadership. This is because effective leaders need to be able to relate well to others, to form trusting bonds and a foundation of respect, credibility and security.

A key part of this is diversity, as there can be tensions involved in how people from different backgrounds relate to one another – for example, in terms of differences in language use and other forms of communication across cultures (Jandt, 2015). It is therefore important that leaders are tuned in to such matters and are suitably equipped for dealing with them sensitively and skilfully.

Gender is also an important dimension of this, as it has to be recognized that there are significant differences between people which often follow gender patterns. For example, Doka and Martin (2010) show that there are differences in how people grieve that follow broad gender patterns. More specifically in relation to the workplace, Northouse (2010) points out that:

> Leadership emergence may also be affected by gender-biased perceptions. In a study of 40 mixed-sex college groups, Watson and Hoffman (2004) found that women who were urged to persuade their task groups to adopt high-quality decisions succeeded with the same frequency as men with identical instructions. Although women were rated significantly lower than comparable men were on leadership. Furthermore, these influential women were also rated as significantly less likable than comparably influential men were. These results suggest that there continue to be barriers to women's emergence as leaders in some settings.
>
> (p. 6)

Adopting a 'gender-blind' approach (that is, one that ignores the significance of gender) to how people in the workplace relate to one another can therefore be seen to be a dangerous one, as it risks missing some key power dynamics that can have a major effect on how people relate to one another and how they face the challenges of their work, including the challenges of working towards a shared vision based on shared values.

Authenticity

Much of the success of leadership depends on our ability to relate to people and to 'get them on board' as part of a shared endeavour. To do this we need to have a genuine rapport with them that is based on honesty and integrity (long-recognized characteristics of effective leaders – Gilbert, 2005). Trying to manipulate, cajole or pressurize people into doing what we want them to do for the sake of the team and the organization is not really what leadership is about. Our dealings with other people therefore need to be based on authenticity, with no deceptions, tricks, hollow gestures or game playing (all of which are sadly not uncommon in modern workplaces – see Furnham and Taylor, 2004).

Meaning

Authenticity is also an important basis for meaning. If work is to be meaningful for people, then we need to make sure, as far as possible, that they feel at home in the workplace, feeling valued, supported and secure, rather than feeling manipulated, exploited or disposable (Uchitelle, 2007).

Leadership will not bring out the best in people unless it succeeds in creating a narrative (that is, a framework of meaning) that makes sense to them and to which they can comfortably relate. Leaders have a central role in constructing that narrative, in telling the story of what it means to work in this particular setting. It can be a positive, empowering narrative that is supportive, nurturing and energizing or it can be a negative one that is mistrustful, undermining and thus counterproductive.

Conclusion

This brief chapter should be sufficient to give an overview of what is involved in leadership and paint at least a beginning picture of what people managers need to do if they are to establish a firm basis of leadership. Leadership is a key part of people management in general, and so this is a topic to which we will return in later chapters. However, for now, it is to be hoped that the chapter has given you a better understanding of why leadership is such a central plank of effective people management and also given you plenty of food for thought about how you can develop your own leadership potential.

Points to ponder
1. What is the role of vision in leadership?
2. What problems could poor or non-existent teamwork lead to?
3. What is involved in self-leadership?

Exercise 11

Which people do you regard as good leaders (whether personally known to you or in public life)? What is it that makes them good leaders? What can you learn from this?

CHAPTER 12: MANAGING CHANGE

In this chapter you will learn how to avoid some of the common problems associated with change management.

Introduction

Sadly, the area of change management is one that is beset with a tendency towards oversimplification – for example, the commonly expressed (but inaccurate) idea that 'change is the only constant'. A dynamic interplay between change and continuity has always been a feature of human experience, and that in itself has not changed. That is, while change will inevitably happen, we should not allow that to distract us from the fact that much also remains the same.

If we focus exclusively on the changes, then we are getting a very distorted picture of the situation that we are dealing with, and that can be dangerously misleading. This can have the unhelpful effect of unsettling people and creating anxiety. This is turn can lead to resistance to change and even sabotage, making change a problem to be worried about rather than a normal and potentially very positive part of working life (and, indeed, of life itself). Instead of allowing a battleground to be established between those who promote change (sometimes for their own benefit and not necessarily the organization's) and those who resist change (sometimes simply because it is change). A more helpful and productive approach is to *manage* change, to accept that some degree of change is inevitable and desirable, but to make sure that the positives of any change are to the fore and any negatives are kept to a minimum.

KEY POINT

The fact that we now face immense and rapid change does not mean that much does not remain constant. We do a great disservice to important continuities in working life if we make the mistake of seeing only change. This mistake can be particularly significant in terms of morale. If people feel that there is a great degree of insecurity because of so much change and because they do not recognize the continuities as a result of this distorted emphasis, then the net result can be a problem with morale, often a very significant problem.

This chapter therefore tries to present a more sophisticated understanding of managing change. It involves recognizing that change is neutral, in the sense that it can be either positive or negative, depending on the circumstances – including how skilfully or otherwise changes are managed. It is therefore not something to be championed for its own sake, but nor is it something to be resisted just because it is change. The question of how it is managed is a question of leadership, in so far as change that is understood in terms of how it helps to achieve the vision and how it is consistent with the values is more likely to be accepted and more likely to be positive. By contrast, change that is imposed without any clarity about how or why such change was necessary and what benefits it will bring is likely to be perceived – and experienced – negatively. Managing change is therefore very much a challenge of leadership, and so this chapter follows on logically from the previous one.

Sources of change

There are various sources of change that we can readily identify. Consider, for example, the following main areas:

- *The external environment.* There can be changes in the market that can make a significant impact on how commercial organizations operate. For example, if a particular product or service is no longer needed because of wider changes, this can have major consequences for organizations that need to be responsive to market demand. There are also changes in the law to consider which will apply to all organizations, whether in the private, public or voluntary sectors. For example, when the Equality Act 2010 was implemented, it introduced new categories of discrimination which meant that, if organizations were to ensure that they are not guilty of unfair discrimination, then they needed to review their policies and practices to ensure that they were compliant with the new law. Sometimes changes brought about by the law are fairly minor, but sometimes they can be on a much greater scale.
- *The internal environment.* Over time there will be changes in strategy, policy and procedures, often in response to changes in the external environment, but sometimes due to changes within the organization itself (for example, as a result of key personnel leaving or new opportunities arising). Such changes can have negative roots (being brought about as a result of complaints, for example), but can none the less have positive outcomes if handled well – that is, if they are dealt with as valuable opportunities to improve services rather than a defensive reaction to one or more criticisms. Indeed, the idea that any organization or group of staff is beyond criticism can be an unhelpful myth that has become part of many a workplace culture. All organizations and staff groups will have strengths and weaknesses, and will all therefore have potential lessons to learn as well as assets to be built up and appreciated.
- *Technology.* The accelerating rate of technological change brings problems as well as benefits. While some people fully embrace the significant benefits that improved technology can bring, it would be naïve not to recognize that there are also tensions and difficulties that arise partly as a result of technology never

being a hundred per cent reliable and partly because of the demands of new learning curves associated with the introduction of new technology. Technology can be a significant nuisance when it does not work as it should (and, sadly, that is often the case), but even where it does work well and brings significant benefits, there can also be a price to pay above and beyond the financial costs. For example, some people's value to the organization can diminish if their skills are no longer needed because of technological developments. Similarly, some people may struggle to learn the new skills needed to use the new technology to maximum effect.

- *Personnel.* Even in the most stable of organizations, people will move on from time-to-time and, at the other extreme, there are some organizations where the turnover of staff is quite immense (see Chapter 8 on staff departures and Chapter 16 on staff retention). Most organizations, of course, will be somewhere in between these two extremes, but there is none the less an important message here in terms of recognizing that changeover in personnel can bring about significant changes. For example, a new person in a particular post may have an identical job description to their predecessor, but may well do the job very differently indeed, with consequent implications for various other people in the organization. Where a new employee is in a leadership position, the change can be even more far reaching – especially if the new leader wants to stamp their own identity on their new setting.

This is not an exhaustive list, and we should also be aware that these four potential sources of change can also interact and produce interesting – and sometimes challenging – combinations. We can therefore see that there are plenty of opportunities for change to arise, and so it should not be surprising that change is seen as such a strong feature of contemporary working life.

The impact of change
I mentioned above that change is often oversimplified, and one example of this is the common assumption that change is, by its very nature, progress. It seems that relatively little attention is paid to the fact that changes can – and often do – make situations worse, rather than better. The fact that so many change initiatives are unsuccessful (Kotter, 2006) is something that many organizations, in their eagerness to embrace change, fail to recognize and therefore pay a high price for it. So, while some degree of change is inevitable, it is not inevitable that change initiatives will be for the best.

Change also has the potential to be quite stressful (Thompson, 2019b), and this can then prevent the benefits of the change being recognized or capitalized upon. If change is not handled well, it can push people over the line from a high but manageable level of pressure into one that is unmanageable and therefore stressful (see Chapter 21). There are therefore significant challenges involved in making sure that change is well handled and that its primary focus is a positive one. In particular, it is important to ensure that we are not initiating change simply for change's sake. While some people use the slogan of 'If it ain't bust, don't fix it' to resist any form of change, there is none the less a strong element of truth in the idea that changing a successful arrangement can mean that success now becomes elusive.

It also has to be recognized that change can have unintended consequences (or to use the technical term, 'counterfinalities'). This means that, while the push in a particular direction may be a positive, sensible and wise one, there can at times be negative results that flow from this because of variables that the people concerned were not aware of or did not pay adequate attention to. It is therefore important, as Pugh (1986) has long emphasized, not only to think *about* change, but also to think it *through* – to map out what the likely knock-on effects are likely to be and weigh up whether the positives outweigh the negatives (we will return to this point below). This also gives the opportunity to plan how to maximize those positives and avoid or minimize the negatives. If we do not think change through, the result can be a worsening of the situation rather than an improvement.

> *Practice focus 12.1*
> Kim was the manager of a youth work project that had been set up in a deprived, high-crime area. Its main aim was to engage young people in constructive activities in an effort to reduce crime levels. The scheme seemed to be working well and had a number of experienced, well-qualified and highly competent staff. However, when a decision was made at a senior level that the focus should be exclusively on activities and should not include counselling (as there was already a counselling service for young people available nearby), two of the most experienced project staff left. One was a qualified counsellor and the other was doing a part-time counselling course at the time. They did not want to lose what they saw as one of the most important and most satisfying aspects of the job and so they moved on. The change had therefore brought about some very negative consequences, with key staff leaving and the morale of the remaining staff being quite adversely affected. To make matters worse, the change brought no positive changes, as the local counselling service was already oversubscribed and could offer little by way of extra services. Clearly, the person or committee that had initiated the change had not thought through the possible consequences.

Also important in terms of the impact of change is the need to recognize that organizations will have existing 'fault lines' (like the fault lines in the Earth's crust that make earthquakes much more likely in some areas than others). They can include existing fault lines of conflict or discrimination that can be intensified by change situations. For example, if there is already a tension between one group of staff and another, the additional pressures of change can intensify that pressure significantly and may have very adverse consequences. The costs to the organization – human and financial – of such negative consequences can in many circumstances far outweigh the hoped-for benefits that stimulated the change in the first place.

We therefore need to recognize that, while change can be very positive and has the potential to produce significant improvement, this is not always the case, and we would be naïve if we did not recognize that there can be significant negative outcomes associated with change, especially badly managed change. This brings us back to the challenge of leadership, as a well-led team or group of staff is likely to be more responsive to change where it brings positives and more effective in articulating their concerns where negative outcomes are envisaged. Indeed, it could be argued that the ability to capitalize on positive change and to prevent negative change and/or to minimize its impact is the hallmark of a team or staff group who are functioning well as an integrated unit.

Principles of effective change management

What follows is not a definitive list of principles, but it should be a good starting point for painting a picture of how change needs to be managed very carefully and how it needs to be undertaken as part of critically reflective practice, rather than simply driven through in an uncritical or unthinking way. As Miller and Katz (2002) point out: 'Every organization is different. A rigid formula for change cannot be applied successfully' (p. 135).

Given that change can do harm as well as good, we should be able to recognize that risk is a key issue for us to consider. Chapter 22 discusses issues of risk assessment and management in relation to health and safety, but we should also note that the lessons to be learned about risk also apply to the management of change. If we approach risky situations without weighing them up carefully and managing them sensitively and skilfully, we could well find ourselves paying a high price for our failings.

1. *Clarify the reasons for change.* We have known for some considerable time that imposed change is the least successful type of change. If people have a good understanding of why change needs to take place, they are much less likely to resist it. This relates to the M of *Staying CALM*, the importance of people finding meaning in their work. If they can see no good reason for enduring the inconvenience of change, then they are likely to see it as an imposition, a problem

to be solved, rather than a set of opportunities to be embraced. The C and A elements of *CALM* are also relevant. C, for Connection, applies because effective change initiatives are characterized by good communication and trusting relationships (Covey, 2008). A for Authenticity also has an important role to play in so far as change initiatives based on manipulation, deception or cajoling are far more likely to produce an attitude of resistance (and even sabotage of the change in some cases) than one of cooperation and commitment.

2. *Listen to objections and take them seriously.* It is a significant mistake to try and brush under the carpet any objections that people may make. This is for two reasons: first of all, they may be raising valid objections that we can learn from; and second, even if their objections are not valid, not listening to them will only make the tension worse and therefore encourage further resistance to the change. What can be much more helpful is to try and encourage the development of a culture of 'we are in this together'. This again takes us back to leadership. A good leader is someone who is approachable and prepared to listen to what people have to say. It is therefore essential not to adopt a judgemental attitude and assume that anyone who is objecting to change is necessarily being 'awkward' or 'difficult'. There are many cases on record where the people managers concerned would have been very wise to listen to the objections being made, rather than pressing on regardless and then realizing, once it is too late, that the objectors had a valid point. It is also important to recognize that, if we do not listen to objections, then we will alienate those people who are objecting and this could lead them to make sure that the change does not work just to prove their point. We will have created an entrenched conflict situation where this was not necessary.

3. *Where possible, set an appropriate pace for change.* If change takes too long to work its way through, people can become demoralized and disillusioned by it but, similarly, if the pace of change is too fast, people can feel overwhelmed and are left feeling insecure, therefore resenting the change. There is no magic formula for working out what the appropriate change is. It all depends on monitoring the situation closely, keeping the channels of communication open and responding sensitively to any concerns or issues that arise. This is where reflective practice comes in – having the skills to be able to reflect on the situation and manage it skilfully, rather than just look for a simple, mechanistic solution.

4. *Think the change through.* This is a principle from the work of Pugh (1986) who argues that many organizations make the mistake of thinking about the change, but without actually thinking it through, working out what the actual consequences will be of specific changes. As I mentioned earlier, failing to map out the consequences of a proposed or inevitable change can be highly problematic. Ideally this should be done in a group context, where possible

including the people directly affected by the change, as we may not pick up on something important that others may well be able to highlight.

5. *Identify potential problems and work on them together.* What is important is for people promoting change to recognize that it is naïve in the extreme to expect that any change initiative will be entirely trouble free, with no problems or difficulties whatsoever. What is more helpful is to be realistic, to appreciate that problems will arise, but to involve people in the process of tackling those problems, so that they develop a sense of ownership for responding to the challenges of the changes involved. Where people feel excluded from change processes they are far more likely to view the change negatively. If, by contrast, they are part of a process of identifying problems and potential solutions, they are more likely to take ownership of the change. However, it is important that this inclusion is genuine and not just tokenistic (reflecting the importance of the A, for Authenticity, of *Staying CALM*).

6. *Seek to capitalize on the change, rather than just survive it.* Change can bring problems, as we have already noted, but there will also be opportunities for improvement, and so, where a change is inevitable, it can be important to encourage a positive approach to it in order to try and make the most of the opportunities presented. Again, including people in the process is a key part of this, as is listening to objections, as discussed earlier. However, ideally, the work needs to start before this. The best leaders will have established a culture where people discuss such matters openly and feel confident in rising collectively to all the challenges the team, staff group, division or organization faces.

7. *Roll with resistance.* This is a term derived from the work of Miller and Rollnick (2002) who developed the theory of motivational interviewing. The basic idea is that it is important to recognize that there will be resistance and that this is not necessarily a problem or a sign that anything is wrong. However, what we have to do is learn to deal with such resistance sensitively and effectively. Simply fobbing people off is likely to make the situation worse. We need to have the skills and confidence to be able to work with resistance and, as suggested above, objections can sometimes be useful as they identify flaws in our thinking or in other people's plans and assumptions.

8. *Encourage innovation from within to reduce the likelihood of imposed change from without.* What this means is that, if people are encouraged to be innovative and creative in their work, then there is a much lower likelihood that there will be a necessity for change coming from the wider organization. A group of staff who are flexible, adaptable and innovative in their approach to their work is likely to have far more control over how things are managed, whereas a group of staff who just play it safe and go through the motions of following official procedures are

unlikely to produce optimal outcomes, and are therefore more prone to having change initiatives imposed on them from outside.

9. *In a time of change, do not lose sight of the continuities.* This takes us back to my comments, in the introduction to this chapter, to the effect that there is a sad and worrying tendency for people to focus on change and lose sight of the bigger picture which also includes continuities. We neglect those continuities at our peril, in so far as we may neglect important aspects of the situation or of our work while we are preoccupied with the change elements. The reality is that working life is a mixture of change and continuity. If we expect there to be complete continuity without change, then we are being naïve, but if we see only the changes and take no account of the continuities, then we risk letting people down by contributing to a situation where people may feel overwhelmed and demoralized by what they see as nothing but change. Providing the balance that helps us keep both change and continuity in perspective is an important role for people managers, whether line managers of human resource professionals.

10. *Recognize and respond to the grief involved in change.* People make an emotional commitment to their workplace ('cathexis' is the technical term), and so when there are significant changes in that workplace, they can have a feeling of grief because what they invested their emotional energy in does not exist in its known form any more. This is an aspect of organizational life that is sadly often neglected. However, again it is something that deserves considerable attention, as the emotional impact of a major change – in terms of a sense of grief – can be very significant, with very broad-ranging consequences (Thompson, 2009). Being able to respond sensitively, in an informed way, to the emotions associated with such grief responses can be seen to be a fundamental part of the ability to create a sense of security that is a key part of being an effective leader.

Practice focus 12.2
Lynn was part of a very effective team that was disbanded as a result of a major 'reconfiguration' exercise across the whole of her organization. She was very sad about this as it had been a great team, very effective and with a lovely, supportive atmosphere that everybody appreciated. She was reasonably happy in her new setting, but it just wasn't the same. Her level of motivation had gone down considerably and she constantly felt sad, sometimes angry and often very unsettled. She had not thought of this as part of a grief response, an aspect of how she was grieving the team that she had put her heart and soul into over a number of years. However, when she met up with two of her ex-colleagues for a coffee one Saturday morning and discovered that they had been having very similar feelings, it dawned on her that it was indeed a grief reaction they were experiencing – they

were mourning for something that had had a great deal of emotional significance for them.

1. Clarify the reasons for change.

2. Listen to objections and take them seriously.

3. Where possible, set an appropriate pace for change.

4. Think the change through.

5. Identify potential problems and work on them together.

6. Seek to capitalize on the change, rather than just survive it.

7. Roll with resistance.

8. Encourage innovation from within.

9. In a time of change, do not lose sight of the continuities.

10. Recognize and respond to the grief involved in change.

Figure 12.1 The principles of change management

 A common mistake is to see grief as a reaction to death, whereas in reality it is much broader than this – it is a our reaction to any significant loss. Be careful to avoid falling in to this trap, as it can mean that you miss signficant grief reactions in response to changes.

Conclusion

I began this chapter by saying that change management is unfortunately a topic characterized by a great deal of oversimplification. Yet another oversimplification in this regard is the oft-quoted idea that 'people don't like change'. Of course, this is far from the truth; it is only certain types of change that people do not like or changes managed in particular ways (without consultation or regard for the impact it has on people's work and their well-being). There would be few people, for example, who would object to changes in their salary in an upward direction on the grounds that they 'do not like change'.

A more accurate and sophisticated understanding of managing change would tell us that people do not like:

- Having change imposed on them without any clarity about why it is necessary or why it is felt to be beneficial.
- Not being listened to, feeling undervalued because their concerns are not being taken seriously.
- Being messed about. All change will bring a degree of inconvenience, but if there is a high level of inconvenience and this is compounded by a sense that the people who are creating the inconvenience are being insensitive towards staff, then the resentment that this can produce can be of quite significant proportions.
- Losing faith (or having their lack of faith reinforced) in what they come to perceive as bad management or poor leadership.

As we have noted, a high proportion of change efforts fail, often with highly damaging consequences, and so it is vitally important that we do our best to manage change effectively. It is to be hoped that this chapter has set us in the right direction in terms of learning more about the challenges involved and provided a foundation for further learning about the complexities of change.

Points to ponder
1. Why is it important to clarify the reasons for change?
2. What benefits arise from emphasizing the continuities during a period of change?
3. What role does grief play in relation to change?

Exercise 12
Consider a positive organizational change that you have gone through. What made it positive? What might have made it less positive if it had been handled differently? Now consider a negative organizational change you have experienced. What made it so negative? What could have made it less negative if it had been done differently? What can be learned from considering these experiences in this way?

CHAPTER 13: INDUSTRIAL RELATIONS

In this chapter you will learn how to develop positive industrial relations and avoid unnecessary strife.

Introduction
We have seen major changes in the world of work in recent decades, not least of which has been a shift away from the traditional idea of trade unionism towards the concept of human resource management (HRM). Industrial relations and collective bargaining issues have therefore been a key part of these changes. While trade unions continue to play an important role in contemporary working life, much of the function of collective bargaining has been watered down. This chapter is concerned with looking at the current situation, recognizing that the changes that have taken place do not alter the fact that there is a fundamental tension between the organization and its employees, individually and collectively. We know from the work of the cooperative movement, for example, that such tensions can be managed effectively to a large extent. Our concern here, then, is to explore some of the basic aspects of how the tension between the interests of an organization and the interests of its employees can be managed constructively. In effect, this is what industrial relations is all about.

We begin by exploring the nature of industrial relations (or employment relations, as it is also often called) in order to establish a baseline of understanding. From this we move on to consider the key role of what has come to be known as the 'psychological contract'. I then relate this to the social and political contracts that we should not ignore if we are to have an adequate understanding of industrial relations to the extent that we are reasonably well informed enough to address the issues such matters will generate.

The nature of industrial relations
The term 'industrial relations' can be understood to mean both an aspect of organizational life (the way in which relations between managers and employees are managed) and an academic area of study or theoretical perspective on the relationship between employers and employees (see Colling and Terry, 2010a). It is mainly in the former sense that I am using the term in this chapter, but the latter sense will also be relevant, as we shall see below.

In the Introduction I made the point that there is a fundamental conflict between employers and employees, a basic tension between two sets of conflicting interests. In a sense, the whole of people management revolves around this point, in so far as both line managers and human resources professionals have a key role to play in making sure that this tension is a creative one and that the conflicts do not reach a level where they are destructive and potentially harmful to both 'sides'. If the interests of employers and employees dovetailed perfectly, there would be little call for the number of managers and HR professionals we currently have.

We shall note in Chapter 25 that effective conflict management is an essential part of being a successful people manager. The focus in that chapter is on interpersonal or team-based conflict. Here, in the context of industrial relations, our concern is more broadly with the significance of collective conflicts, primarily those tensions that arise between employers and employees, whether as a result of the very nature of the employment relationship in general or the specific circumstances that may arise in particular situations or settings.

The fact that there are such tensions is not necessarily a problem. In fact, if handled well, such conflicts can be productive for all concerned (allowing employers to get the best return on their investment in their staff – their 'human resources' – and enabling employees to develop fulfilling and rewarding jobs and careers) if satisfactory resolution can be achieved in relation to specific points of contention. This is not simply a matter of compromising, but rather a more complex process of principled negotiation (see Chapter 19 of *People Skills*).

Brown (2010) emphasizes the significance of negotiation in the workplace:

> Negotiation permeates the relationship between employer and workers. For all but the most transitory of jobs, both sides have some degree of discretion over what they give to the relationship, and what they take from it. Whether it is the employer's discretion over discipline, pay, or working arrangements, or the worker's discretion over effort levels, cooperation, or customer relations, there is the potential for bargaining. Employment is, by its nature, an open and usually long-term transaction.
>
> (p. 255)

Industrial relations is therefore a subject concerned with how relations between employers and employees are managed at a macro or collective level (hence the term 'collective bargaining'). It involves looking at how a firm foundation of cooperation can be laid down to enable a productive working environment to develop.

From a theoretical point of view, the now traditional approach of HRM has tended to view employer-employee tensions as fundamentally a matter of management control. As Colling and Terry (2010b) note:

> Paradoxically, the strength and vitality of the original field is now backlit by the potentially narrow and impoverished nature of alternative perspectives such as HRM, which can reduce workers to one of several *resources* to be blended in production and take the concerns of *management* as the first and sometimes exclusive point of departure in such processes.
>
> (p. 4)

This echoes the point I made in the Introduction that people are indeed resources in the workplace, but we are distinctively *human* resources, and so any approach that recognizes the *resources* part of HR but not the *human* is likely to encounter significant difficulties, not least staff feeling alienated, manipulated and therefore not valued or respected. Organizations are highly unlikely to get the best out of their staff in such circumstances and will therefore fail in their people management endeavours.

The passage from Colling and Terry also highlights the tendency of much of the HRM literature to adopt an employer perspective, and this can easily give the impression that, where there are industrial relations problems, it is the staff side that are the problem (making unreasonable demands, being uncooperative and so on). A more enlightened, people-focused approach will enable us to see that this is a gross oversimplification of a complex topic. To resolve a conflict we need to understand the situation from both parties' point of view and, from this more holistic perspective, look for constructive ways forward that will bring both sides together, rather than take the side of the more powerful group and risk making the divisions even greater and more tense.

Industrial relations (or IR for short) is a theoretical approach to employer-employee relations that avoids the mistake of giving primacy to the interests or perspective of employers and focuses instead on how conflicts and tensions can be understood more holistically and thus more constructively. This involves looking at the role of the various people involved and what contribution – helpful or otherwise – they are making to effective employment relations. As Dean and Liff (2010) put it:

> Thus the essence of an IR analysis of work and employment relations is a multi-actor, multi-disciplinary, multi-level approach concerned, crucially, with varied and competing interests and goals (Clarke *et al.* 2008)
>
> (p. 423)

KEY POINT

As people managers faced with industrial relations challenges, we should not automatically assume that the employer perspective is the correct or only one, as to do so would be to oversimplify a complex situation and risk making it worse by alienating staff. People managers – whether line managers or HR professionals, are well placed to look at the situation from a broader perspective and explore ways forward that will be of value and benefit to employers and employees alike, to the organization and to its staff.

> *Practice focus 13.1*
> Janie was a human resources adviser in a large general hospital. She was asked to intervene when a new shift rota was proposed for the nursing staff as part of a 'flexible working' initiative. The majority of nurses felt that their good will was being exploited and that there was little flexibility for them. They therefore saw this as a potential deterioration in their quality of working life from which they would get no benefit (they also doubted that the hospital would get any benefit from the proposed change, as the current system seemed to work perfectly well anyway). They therefore involved their union who quickly communicated to the hospital management that they would not stand for any diminution in staff conditions of service. Janie was aware from previous discussions with senior managers that some of them had some degree of antipathy towards unions and would make comments like: 'I'm not letting the unions tell us how we should run our hospital'. So she anticipated some potentially difficult negotiations if this matter could not be nipped in the bud. She therefore arranged individual appointments to see the appropriate senior manager and the union branch officer. Fortunately she was able to use her mediation skills to negotiate a way forward that both parties were happy with and thereby avoided a potentially rough ride for all concerned.

The psychological contract

This is a longstanding concept that refers to the unwritten agreement that tends to develop between employers and employees. It is a significant way of managing underlying tensions between competing interests between the management side and the staff side of an organization. It has played a very important part in enabling organizations to function. The sort of unwritten rules of how employers and employees relate to each other have become well established. Historically the trade union movement has played an important part in developing the basis of working relationships between employers and employees.

Simms and Charlwood (2010) remind us that: 'The primary function of trade unions is to represent the interest of their members', but then go on to point out that this is not necessarily a simple or straightforward matter: 'Beneath this relatively simple statement lies a raft of complex, and sometimes contradictory, ideas' (p. 125). As there has been a shift away from trade unionism and the collective strength of the workforce through this, employees have been more exposed to being at the mercy of the good will (or otherwise) of employers and the HR professionals who represent them. This has led some people to be concerned that, in recent years, changes in working life have meant that the notion of the psychological contract is breaking down.

It is relatively easy in any workplace to find examples of how the contract continues to exist, and so it has clearly not broken down altogether. However, it is also not difficult to find examples of how some organizations at least have sought to take advantage of the relative vulnerability of the workforce (because of the weakening of trade union influence and thus the power of the unions to protect their members from exploitation or unfair treatment) to capitalize on the situation – see for example the work of Stein (2007) and Ehrenreich (2005). These workplace changes (downsizing, delayering, temporary contracts and so on – see Schnall *et al.*, 2017) have not so much destroyed the psychological contact as thrown it into sharp relief, and thereby shown just how important it is as a basis for making sure that tensions between employer interests and employee interests are managed effectively, rather than allowed to escalate into hostility. Armstrong (2020) characterizes the psychological contract in terms of:

- how employees are treated in terms of fairness, equity and consistency;
- security of employment
- scope to demonstrate competence;
- career expectations and the opportunity to develop skills;
- involvement and influence;
- trust in the management of the organization to keep their promises.

From the employer's perspective, the psychological contract covers such elements as competence, effort, compliance, commitment and loyalty.

It can be very helpful for people managers to be aware of the psychological contract and remember just how important it is that this contract is not broken in any significant way. Respecting this set of unwritten agreements can be just as important as respecting formal agreements as enshrined in policies and other such documents.

In Chapter 10 we looked at how we need to respond to individual grievances (or prevent them from arising in the first place). There is a strong parallel between what I included in that chapter in relation to individual or interpersonal matters and what now concerns us in his chapter in relation to collective agreements and concerns. While even the best organizations will occasionally countenance a grievance from a disgruntled staff member, we should also recognize that collective grievances are not restricted to a minority of poorly managed organizations. As Furnham and Taylor (2004) comment:

> In the nineteenth century, the desperate, abused factory employee burnt down the factory in frustrated rage. In the twentieth century there was a huge growth in institutions and procedures that attempted to cope with grievances, inequalities and so on. Trade unions, workers' councils, arbitration services and human resource specialists – all attempted to resolve conflicts before they got out of hand. In the twenty-first century, the workplace is more complex and many workers more sophisticated. Some of the ways of dealing with grievances now seem inflexible, out-of-date and discredited. But the need for them has not reduced.
>
> (p. xvii)

What it boils down to is the fact that skilled people managers can make sure that the inevitable employer-employee tensions are effectively managed by seeking win-win outcomes rather than simply taking the side of the employer and risking alienating staff who are, after all, the organization's most important resource. This can play a major role in helping to prevent industrial strife, and can also be very helpful in managing any such situations if they should arise at any point.

While there is considerable debate about the current status of the psychological contract, we cannot doubt its importance, and so people managers need to know that there is a fine and sensitive relationship between employers and employees that has to be managed effectively and constructively if industrial relations are not to deteriorate or break down altogether, as in situations where strike action or other industrial action occurs. An essential part of this is trust, as discussed in the Introduction. Without at least some degree of trust, satisfactory working relations will be very difficult, if not impossible, to achieve, while optimal working relations will need quite a substantial foundation of trust in both directions. In this respect, when it comes to industrial relations, people managers are, in effect, trust builders. This will require all four elements of *Staying CALM*:

- *Connection*. Building trust requires skill in rapport building and a commitment to being inclusive in our work with people. If we are seen as unable to form a proper working relationship with others, then there will be little trust generated, whereas an ability to 'connect' with people (through listening and empathy, for example) is likely to be a key factor in building trust.

- *Authenticity*. This is crucial at all times, but especially in times of potential or actual conflict, where even a hint of disingenuousness can be enough to destroy trust or prevent it from being developed in the first place. Trust can take a long time to develop, but can be destroyed in seconds. Deception, manipulation or cajoling give people a message that we have only our own interest at heart, and that we see them as just a means to an end (an I-it relationship rather than I-Thou, as discussed in the Introduction). This is clearly no basis on which to build trust.
- *Leadership*. The ability to pull people together and focus on shared goals is a key part of leadership, and is invaluable in an industrial relations context. It is commonly assumed that this pulling people together activity relates solely to those people who report to us in the organizational hierarchy. However, there is no reasons why leadership skills cannot be used more broadly to bring together potentially warring factions from across an organization, including both employers and employees.
- *Meaning*. This involves trying to understand how people involved are 'reading' the situation, what it means to them – what is the narrative or story that is helping them make sense of the situation. How might we want to influence that narrative to reduce conflict and build trust? The first step must be to show that we understand that narrative, that we have 'tuned in' to what their understanding of the situation is and how it is affecting them.

The social contract

While the notion of the psychological contract has had considerable influence in the literature relating to human resources and the workplace more broadly, the notion of the social contract is one that has tended to feature a great deal in sociology and other social science disciplines, but less so in literature relating directly to the workplace. The idea of the social contract is that, for people to live in relative harmony together there have to be certain unwritten rules, certain conventions that allow people to interact without conflicts overspilling and undermining the very nature of the cooperative endeavour that we know as a society.

We can therefore see that the idea of the social contract is parallel in some ways with the idea of the psychological contract in the workplace. Society is characterized by certain conflicts, but it is also strongly characterized by various ways in which such conflicts are more or less effectively managed for the most part. A simple example of this would be basic manners. People being polite to each other in culturally defined ways is a significant means by which conflicts and tensions are kept within manageable limits for the most part.

While the focus of the social contract is very broad in terms of society as a whole, we can see how much of its significance also applies specifically to the workplace. There needs to be a good understanding on the part of people managers of what the unwritten rules are that enable people to work effectively together in a spirit of shared endeavour. This is another important aspect of leadership (as discussed in Chapter 11) in terms of the importance of a leader understanding how organizations work and how cultures develop and can be shaped in a positive direction.

An interesting development in recent years in terms of the social contract has been the growth of interest in corporate social responsibility (CSR), with more and more organizations taking their wider responsibilities more seriously (Crane *et al.* 2009). This includes making charitable donations to community projects or other organizations that are committed to social amelioration, as well as being strongly tuned in to environmental concerns. In terms of this latter aspect of CSR, it could be argued that this is mainly a cost-cutting exercise, as reducing energy consumption and minimizing waste has financial benefits for the organizations concerned. However, while there certainly may be a strong element of truth in this, we should be wary of oversimplifying a complex aspect of organizational life.

The political contract
This refers to how society operates at a political level. The Government and other state institutions can be very influential in the workplace in terms of setting legal requirements, regulation and so on. A change of government or policy changes by an existing government can have far-reaching implications for organizations across all sectors, not just for public bodies. A good people manager will need to be aware of this wider political context so that they are able to (i) avoid any difficulties arising from non-compliance with statutory requirements; (ii) anticipate any potential problems arising from this wider political context and be ahead of the game in trying to prevent such difficulties or keep their impact to a minimum; and (iii) be able to explore options for capitalizing on any positive aspects of this political contract.

While the political contract can apply at a broad societal level – nationally and internationally – we should not lose sight that politics is also a key part of organizational life. As Fulop and Linstead (2009a) explain:

> Power and organizational politics are indisputable parts of every social relationship imaginable, and are at the heart of organization. Everyone has to deal with or will be affected by power and politics in their organizations.
>
> (p. 278)

We would therefore be naïve not to take account of how such matters operate in organizations. This will include taking account of such important power dynamics as those associated with gender and race/ethnicity, as well as other many other sociopolitical divisions (Thompson, 2018b). As I have argued earlier, a good leader is someone who understands at least the basics of how organizations work, and understanding 'office politics' and related matters is no exception to this. As Vigoda (2003) rightly argues: 'A central component of organizational politics is therefore, the skill, ability and desire to make use of influence in order to promote goals (Ferris *et al.* 1989, 1989a)' (p. 16). These are clearly part of what leadership is all about, as we saw in Chapter 11.

A people manager who focuses narrowly on just getting the job done without an sense of what they are doing being part of a wider enterprise is likely to be ill-equipped to be an effective leader. Leaders have the ability to develop the broad vision that will enable that all-important overview of a situation to be developed.

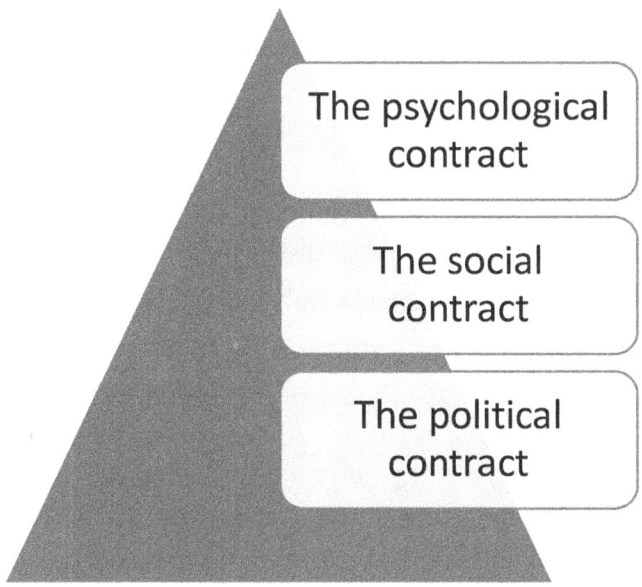

Figure 13.1 Implicit contracts underpinning industrial relations

The implications for people managers
Many people managers will not be involved directly in collective bargaining negotiations but all people managers, none the less, need to be familiar with the relevant policy or policies in the organization concerned. These are often referred to as 'employee relations' or 'collective bargaining'.

 It is also important that people managers should learn to see unions as potential allies in promoting well-being and effective people-focused organizations, and not necessarily as enemies to be wary of or problems to be solved.

Unfortunately, many managers have a stereotypical view of unions and therefore expect to have nothing but difficulties in their interactions with them, whereas more enlightened managers have recognized that a common interest in staff well-being can be highly fruitful for both the organization and for the unions, as staff benefit considerably from an enhanced level of interest in workplace well-being (see Part III for a fuller discussion of the importance of workplace well-being).

What is also important is to be able to recognize the key role of negotiation skills and the commitment to seeking win-win outcomes. Industrial relations is not simply a battleground between the interests of the organization and the interests of staff. The reality is far more complex than that. What can be extremely helpful is for managers to bear this in mind, and to work towards establishing positive industrial relations that everyone can benefit from.

> *Practice focus 13.2*
> Carl was delighted to be appointed as a team manager, although he was wary about the team he was joining, as he knew that Simone, a senior union steward, was in that team and she had a reputation as a strong feminist. To Carl this spelled trouble, and so he was a bit anxious about taking over as the team manager. However, he was very relieved to find that his concerns were misguided. Simone was indeed a strong feminist and heavily involved in union work, but this was because she had a strong commitment to equality and fairness and was very adept at analysing complex situations and helping people find positive ways forward. She also had very well-developed social and interpersonal skills that made her popular with the people she worked with. Carl soon realized that these were major assets for a team member to have, and would also be useful if any other team member – or indeed, the team as a whole – needed union support. He also realized that he had let himself down by relying on stereotypical assumptions about union officials and feminists. He had allowed his judgement to be coloured by prejudice. The positive side of this was that he felt he had learned his lesson and would be more careful in making assumptions.

Conclusion

The world of work has changed in so many different ways, many of them highly significant. The industrial relations scene is certainly part of this landscape of major change. The position now is far less clear cut than it was, say, twenty years ago. Different organizations now have different ways of tackling industrial relations, but, whichever option is adopted, the challenge remains the same: to try and make industrial relations (as the concrete manifestation of the underlying tension between employees and employers) as constructive a phenomenon as possible.

It is to be hoped that this chapter has helped to provide a good basic understanding that will: (i) offer scope for developing a fuller understanding over time; and (ii) provide a good basis for developing the practice skills we need to perform our people management duties in the context of industrial relations.

Points to ponder
1. What do you understand by the 'psychological contract'?
2. Why is effective conflict management important?
3. What role does 'office politics' play in terms of industrial relations?

Exercise 13
What skills do you feel you need in order to carry out your industrial relations duties effectively? What do you see as your strong points to build *on* and your not so strong points to build *up*?

CHAPTER 14: TEAM DEVELOPMENT

In this chapter you will learn about the importance of teamwork and how to develop an effective team.

Introduction

Despite the simplistic cliché that 'there is no I in team', the reality is that teams are collections of individuals (I's), and there will be no real teamwork if individual needs are not met, if they are sacrificed, as it were, to the overall collective interest. Indeed, what makes for an effective team is for people to work together in such a way that everyone feels fulfilled by the collaboration. It is not a case of suppressing individual needs, but rather of incorporating them into the wider picture of collective needs, with some degree of trade off involved – successfully managing the tensions and conflicts involved, rather than naively assuming there will not be any. We have to remember that each 'I' is a person, a human being, and so the 'no I in team' mentality runs counter to the idea of a people-focused approach to organizational life.

Team development is therefore much more complex than is often given credit. Unless we understand this, there is a danger that our efforts to develop teamwork will be counterproductive, and could even be oppressive, leaving members of a group of staff feeling that they are not valued as people in their own right, only as members of a team, as cogs in a machine, as it were. However, if we go for the opposite extreme and focus narrowly on individual needs, then there will be no sense of the collective endeavour which is the hallmark of good teamwork. The challenge for the people manager, therefore, is to be able to establish the healthy and constructive balance between these two extremes: to harness individual contributions in a spirit of collectivism, but without restricting the individuals so much that they feel that they are no longer individuals, or persons in their own right. This is an 'organic' model of teamwork, recognizing that, while the overall emphasis needs to be on the collective endeavour, this is achieved not by individuals attempting to be faceless clones, but rather by team members making their own distinctive contribution (just as the organs of the body do), where each is important for what they uniquely bring. This is consistent with a commitment to valuing diversity (as discussed in Chapter 1), in so far as it recognizes that it is the 'unity in diversity' of good teamwork that produces positive results, not a simplistic idea that team members should abandon their individuality in order to be just cogs in the machine like everyone else. As Miller and Katz (2002) explain:

> Strategies that focus on minimizing conflicts and other possible negative consequences of bringing different kinds of people together – are nothing more than status-quo strategies that maintain diversity in a box. To leverage diversity – to yield greater engagement, interaction, stimulation, and exploration of a wider range of possible solutions – disagreements and conflicts must be addressed.
>
> (p. 97)

This chapter therefore explores some of the key issues relating to team development in order to provide a platform for line managers and HR professionals to be well equipped to play their part in the development of effective teamwork. We begin by focusing on the importance of managing relationships, before considering two other sets of key issues, managing conflict and leadership.

Managing relationships

The idea of managing leadership brings us back to the C of *Staying CALM*, namely the importance of Connection (and the related concept of connectedness which we will discuss in Chapter 20). It is important to recognize that people will work best if they have a sense of connection to other people, that they are not just isolated individuals with no sense of team identity. A people manager committed to promoting teamwork is therefore charged with the task of doing whatever they reasonably can to promote good working relations, so that people pull together in an attempt to achieve common goals.

Fulop and Linstead (2009) place a great emphasis on the idea of managing relationships. Quite rightly, they stress that management involves recognizing the relationships that exist within the workplace and trying to make these as positive and constructive as possible:

> Management is a relational, differential activity, involving criteria that shift and environments that change at different rates. Because management is a relational activity, managers have to deal with multiple realities, roles and identities, and multiple loyalties of individuals. It is the recognition that individuals have multiple realities, roles, identities and loyalties that is so central to managing diversity in organizations. Whether it involves dealing with the natural environment, with other colleagues, with customers/clients and competitors, with communities, networks or alliances, the managing of 'relationships' will be paramount.
>
> (p. 19)

We can therefore see that developing teamwork is part of this. Teamwork involves creating a culture where relationships are:

- *Supportive* Team members can either support or undermine each other, and so a culture that encourages mutual support is far more likely to make a positive contribution to the team being successful in achieving their goals. There are various steps that people managers can take to facilitate this, not least by leading by example – that is, by effectively modelling appropriate supportive behaviours. The concept of reciprocity is important here. If people feel that they are valued and cared for, then they are more likely to value and care for their colleagues – they will want to give support as well as receive it (see Boorman, 2008, for a discussion of the importance of support).
- *Nurturing* Even the most experienced and confident team members can benefit at times from a degree of nurturing. This is especially the case when there are unusual circumstances – for example, when emotional issues are to the fore, perhaps as a result of one or more losses (Thompson, 2009) or where there has been a significant failure or disappointment ('all that work putting an excellent bid together and we still didn't get the contract'). Such situations call for a degree of emotional intelligence on the part of the people manager – the ability to respond sensitively and skilfully to emotional matters.
- *Empowering* In an earlier work on power and empowerment (Thompson, 2007) I drew on Rowlands's (1998) work on 'power from within' (a type of spiritual power that often comes to the fore at times of crisis or adversity) and 'power with' (the power gained from collective responses to situations. A supportive and nurturing culture can be empowering by using power with (the power of teams) to support the development of power from within – for example, by strengthening resolve, providing a degree of reassurance and even security brought about by a strong ethos of 'we are in this together'.

This type of culture can be achieved in a number of ways, and so we now turn to a consideration of some of the main features of what it takes to shape the type of working environment that will allow team development efforts to flourish.

Clear goals
A (reasonable degree of) consensus about why the team exists and what it is trying to achieve is a fundamental part of teamwork. This takes us back to the idea of leadership and the importance of having a shared vision. It is this sense of shared goals that will pull people together and motivate them to achieve positive outcomes. Indeed, Parker (2009) argues that one of the strongest determinants of success in terms of teamwork is clear performance expectations. That is, where members of a team are clear about what is expected of them, they are much more likely to achieve precisely that and become an effective team in the process.

KEY POINT

Without clarity about goals, there is a very real danger that individuals will pull in separate directions and thereby fail to gain any sense of overall team coherence. They may well get in each other's way when it comes to making progress if they are not clear about what direction they need to go in, about what the team is trying to achieve in terms of desired outcomes.

This means that there needs to be explicit discussion about what the team's goals are, as it cannot be safely assumed that everyone will be 'singing from the same hymn sheet'. At times my consultancy work in relation to team development issues has revealed huge discrepancies between what some team members understood the team's goals to be and the perspective of other team members on the desired outcomes they were working towards. They had not been consciously aware of these discrepancies until my intervention focused on these issues. They had simply felt uneasy with one another and could not understand why this was and what was preventing them from gelling as a team. Making goals explicit is therefore an important step in the direction of improving team functioning.

A shared understanding of how those goals are to be achieved and how members will know that they have been achieved (in other words, what success will look like)
The idea of systematic practice is very relevant here and it is one that is discussed in my *People Skills* book. It refers to the need to have clarity about not only what we are trying to achieve, but also how we are going to achieve it and, indeed, how we will know when we have achieved it.

In terms of clarity about how we are to achieve our goals, this is a question of strategy. It requires us to answer the question: Now that we are clear about what our goals are, what is our strategy for achieving them? This strategy is, in effect a plan. The intention is that it should make it explicit what steps we need to take to move forward in the direction of achieving our goals. This is vitally important as it is possible (and, indeed, not uncommon) for there to be considerable consensus about what the team's goals are, but considerable differences in perspective when it comes to ideas about how best to achieve those goals. So, once again, we have to make matters explicit and not assume that everyone will agree on how to achieve the outcomes we need to work towards. Of course, it is not essential that everyone works in the same way towards achieving the goals. There can generally be at least some degree of flexibility which allows some team members to adopt a different approach from others (we are back to the importance and value of diversity), but there needs to be clarity about this if the team is not to falter because the existence of shared goals (a shared vision of where the team is trying to get to) is compromised by differing plans for achieving those goals that are not mutually compatible. For example, if there is agreement that a multidisciplinary mental health team is trying to reduce the number of hospital admissions, but different team members (a nurse and a social worker, for example) are adopting different methods of doing this in working with the same client, the resulting inconsistency could be very confusing for the client and lead them to mistrust both workers and therefore not engage in the process of work being undertaken – thereby leaving them more vulnerable to a hospital admission.

There is also the potential for discrepancy and inconsistency when it comes to looking at how we will know when we have achieved what we set out to do. For one thing, this reinforces the need to have explicit goals. How can we know whether or not we have achieved our goals if we have not clarified what they were in the first place? For another thing, it helps us to understand that we need to be quite precise about what we are trying to achieve, as a vague, woolly approach to such matters can be very counterproductive. For example, if a team agrees that one of their goals is to 'provide better service', then the imprecision in this leaves a great deal of scope for team members to be at odds over whether any improvement gained was enough to justify claiming that this particular goal was attained. While I would not go so far as to say that goals should always be measurable (as some of the most important things in people management are not measurable), but there should certainly be some agreement about how it will be decided whether a goal has been achieved or not.

This framework of systematic practice (What are you trying to achieve? How are you going to achieve it? How will you know when you have achieved it? – Thompson, 2021b) can clearly provide a useful basis for team goal setting.

The importance of open channels of communication as a basis of trust and mutual support
If communication is distorted or partial, then there is likely to be little sense of security in the team, little trust, little credibility towards the leader and therefore a very weak basis for high performance, whether individually or collectively as a team. Hidden agendas, cliques and secrets are likely to create in groups and out groups and therefore a divided team with no overall common identity.

People mangers can be seen to have three sets of responsibilities in this regard. First, we need to make sure that we are communicating effectively. It is very easy for line managers and HR professionals to get very busy and lose sight of the important role of communication. Such a lack of communication breeds mistrust, suspicion and insecurity, each of which can have a very adverse effect on morale in its own right, but can be particularly destructive in combination. The respect and credibility that leaders need will be in short supply if communication dries up – and, of course, being busy is no excuse for not communicating properly, as poor communication is likely to lead to additional hassles that are then likely to make us even busier, potentially leading to a very harmful vicious circle.

Second, leaders need to be communicating the vision and values, constantly giving team members a clear message that 'we are in this together'. If communication is poor in general, then it is likely that the communication of vision and values will be poor too. Third, it is not only our own communication that we should be concerned with. We should also make sure that team members are communicating appropriately too and not holding important things back. This is partly a cultural matter, in so far as it involves creating a culture where people feel it is safe to speak openly and that they will not be penalized in some way for saying things that some people may find unpalatable (provided that what they say is said tactfully, sensitively and supportively in a constructive spirit and not an attack on one or more others). In particular, we need to ensure that people are not forming cliques or subgroups in which they express their views openly – whether positive or negative – while having little or nothing to say in the main team environment.

It is also partly a matter for one-to-one communication (through supervision, coaching or mentoring, for example). If there are any concerns about an individual team member's communication (or lack thereof), this can be usefully addressed in a constructive manner through one-to-one support. What should not happen, however, is that poor or non-existent communication comes to be tolerated. If poor or distorted communication becomes part of the culture, then the potential for optimal outcomes for the team is severely diminished.

A focus on fairness

As we noted in Chapter 1, the emphasis on equality and diversity in contemporary workplaces is justified by the importance of fairness as a personal and organizational value. If people feel that there is a lack of fairness, then this is likely to hamper the collective development of a team identity and that all-important sense of 'we're in this together'. Unfairness can cause resentment, ill-feeling, tension, conflict and even sabotage. It can also undermine the respect, trust and credibility that leaders need to be successful if the leader is perceived to be allowing unfairness to take place.

One particular aspect of this is a commitment to gender equality. Much of the traditional literature on team development has little or nothing to say about the gender dimension of organizational life in general or of teamwork in particular – indeed, the examples given are often of all-male teams (in a sports, military or senior management context). A people manager who sees the world through a single gender perspective is, of course, being blind to some very significant issues, not least the power dynamics involved and the potential for discrimination and exclusion (see Chapter 30).

The idea of a good people manager being able to manage relationships is therefore very relevant indeed to the idea of team development. Fulop *et al.* (2009) make the important point that:

> Management is often presented as the management of things, which includes resources (and people are treated as human resources). This reification (literally 'thing-making') reinforces the artificial separation between the component disciplines through which management is taught.
>
> (p. 19)

As I emphasized in the Introduction, managing people is – or at least should be – at the heart of all management, as we are not going to get very far if we do not take the people we rely on with us. Managing people involves managing relationships between people to a certain extent, and that is certainly very much the case when it comes to developing teamwork.

> *Practice focus 14.1*
> Tina was a very experienced manager who had earned a well-deserved reputation for being an excellent supervisor. Her supervisees came out of supervision sessions feeling valued and supported and highly motivated to do their very best, drawing on the helpful guidance Tina had given them. Supervision was clearly Tina's forte. However, what was not such a strong point was her ability to work with groups of people. She managed one-to-one relationships very skilfully and effectively, but she felt far less confident in managing relationships between staff or across groups of staff. She therefore tended to leave the team to manage itself to a large extent and focused her efforts on trying to influence each member's practice in a positive direction through individual supervision sessions. When it came to her appraisal, her line manager, Yasmine, was not only able to highlight her strengths as a supervisor, but also to help her realize that there were steps she could take to improve her team development skills. Tina felt a little uncomfortable about this at first, but Yasmine was skilful enough to frame it as a positive learning development to embark upon rather than as a criticism of a skills deficit.

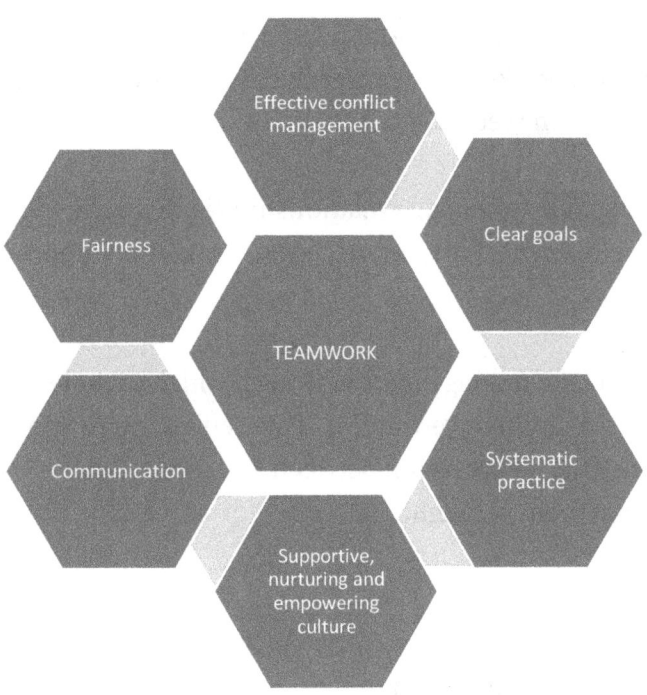

Figure 14.1 Teamwork

Managing conflict

First of all it is important to recognize that conflict is inevitable in teams as in life more generally, and this then brings us back to the notion of managing relationships. We will explore managing conflict in more detail in Chapter 25, but for now it is important to recognize that a good team is not one that is conflict free, but rather one that is successful in managing the inevitable conflicts that arise in the workplace (and indeed in any collective endeavour).

Parker (2009) uses the term 'civilised disagreement'. What he means by this is that there will inevitably be disagreement (which he aptly describes as a euphemism for conflict) in any group of people. A team is therefore expected to deal with such disagreements in a civilized way – that is, in a way that is based on respect and dignity, rather than on attacking each other or trying to score points in a competitive spirit – hence the importance of having shared goals and agreed plans for achieving them.

It also has to be recognized that there are positives involved in conflict, and we will explore these in more detail in Chapter 25 but, for present purposes, it is important to be clear that conflict is not something that we would necessarily want to try and eradicate altogether, partly because that would be impossible and partly because that would also eradicates the positives of conflict – for example, the potential for well-managed conflict to allow people to move forward from previously entrenched positions.

The importance of trust, respect and open communication has already been mentioned in earlier chapters of this manual, and we now need to be aware that, when it comes to managing conflict, these are particularly important This is because, without trust, respect and open communication, conflicts can escalate and become highly problematic, causing a considerable amount of harm in general and doing significant damage to teamwork in particular. Consider, for example, a situation where two members of a team have differences that are leading to conflict, but they do not feel it is safe to discuss these in the team because they have little faith in the leader to be able to manage such issues effectively. The result could be that these ill feelings fester and thereby undermine the effectiveness of the team over an extended period of time.

We also need to return once again to the subject matter of Chapter 1, particularly the notion of diversity which involves recognizing that differences are an asset to an organization and not a problem to be solved. Much conflict arises from such differences, and so we are again in the territory of valuing diversity and recognizing that difference is something that brings positives as well as tensions. Team development involves being able to transcend these issues, to create a working environment in which differences are not seen as a problem and, where we pay the price for difference in terms of potential conflicts and tensions, these are managed constructively, rather than allowed to undermine any sense of collective identity. It comes back to my earlier comment about the need for an organic approach – different people can make different contributions in different ways, all for the good of the team and the collective enterprise, provided that these differences are united by an underlying commitment to the same vision of what the team is trying to achieve and how, and the core values on which that endeavour is based.

The importance of leadership

The L of *Staying CALM* has featured heavily in many of the chapters in this manual, such is the importance of leadership when it comes to managing people. I have already referred to Mary Parker Follett's important insight that leaders are people who create other leaders. What we are now focusing on is the idea that a team leader is not somebody who is separate from the team, but rather a person who is integrated within that team and enables members of that team to become leaders in their own right, to become positive influences on the working culture and the effectiveness of the team. This involves developing a set of skills that enable people managers to make a positive contribution to empowerment as a basis of promoting teamwork in this way. Miller and Katz (2002) bemoan the absence of such an emphasis in the education and training of people managers:

> Organizations that routinely provide effective training and education in developing partnerships or teamwork skills are in the minority. Few invest in the

development of leaders who can model and inspire the use of inclusive behaviors. To produce substantive, sustainable behavioral change, an organization must invest in both the acquisition of these new competencies and in an infrastructure that supports their use. Neither alone is sufficient.

(p. 49)

This does not mean that it is not possible to develop empowering approaches to team leadership, but it does mean that we have our work cut out to try and create the sort of working environment where everyone is helped to be a leader in part, in the sense that everyone can make a contribution to clarifying the team's direction and making sure it moves in the right direction.

> *Practice focus 14.2*
> Padraig was brought in as an interim team manager while Jim was on extended sick leave. He was very pleased to have this temporary promotion. However, the job turned out to be more demanding than he had anticipated. The team he had come from was one in which the team manager encouraged everybody to contribute to decision making, and there was a genuine feeling that it was a collective endeavour. The team he joined by contrast, had no real sense of collectivity – and empowerment was certainly nowhere to be seen. Team members kept coming to him asking him for instructions as to what to do next. He realized that he would have to talk to the team about this and try and instil some degree of a sense of empowered teamwork. He did not want to cause problems for Jim, but he did not feel he would be doing the team any favours if he reinforced a pattern of dependency on the team manager. He started to think about what he would need to do to bring about constructive change.

Try to make it clear to all concerned that the responsibility for effective teamwork rests with every member of the team and not just the team leader or manager.

Conclusion

Team development is often at the heart of organizational success. Those organizations that struggle to develop effective teams are likely to struggle to fulfil their potential, while organizations that have in place leaders with the necessary skills and commitment to developing productive teams are in a much stronger position to rise to the challenges that contemporary society places on so many organizations.

Team development is a matter of shaping or reinforcing a culture of cooperation and mutual support where there is a blend of consensus on the one hand and 'civilized' management of conflict where there is disagreement. A key part of this is the development of a clear set of agreed goals – a vision of where the team is trying to get to. As Parker (2009) argues, group identity comes from a shared sense of purpose with clear performance expectations, and not vice versa.

It is to be hoped that this chapter has provided some helpful insights that will take you in the direction of being better equipped to develop the effective teamwork that can make such a difference to people management.

Points to ponder
1. Why is it important for teams to have clarity about goals?
2. What part does trust play in effective teamwork?
3. How might unresolved conflicts stand in the way of effective teamwork?

Exercise 14
Why is it important to develop good teamwork? What price do we pay for not having good teamwork?

CHAPTER 15: MOTIVATING STAFF

In this chapter you will learn how to improve staff motivation.

Introduction

A key part of people management, as we have already noted, is a genuine commitment to trying to get the best out of people. Motivation is therefore a key issue, as clearly the extent to which a person is motivated will have a significant impact on their level of effort and concentration. But what we also need to recognize is that motivation is quite a complex subject, and there is much more to it than most people tend to realize. Because of this, it is dangerous to oversimplify it and to regard it as a straightforward matter of either carrot or stick, persuasion or threat.

Motivation is also closely linked to the question of 'engagement': what is it that makes staff 'engage' with their work and be fully committed to achieving optimal levels of performance? Good people management is, of course, at the heart of creating that sense of engagement: 'Good employment relations is about understanding what motivates and engages employees and what part you play in making the employee-employer interaction positive and productive' (ACAS, 2015).

At its simplest, to be 'motivated' is to be moved to do something, to have something that spurs you forward in carrying out a particular action or achieving a particular goal. However, it is not simply a matter of putting people under pressure to do what we want them to do (I-it) – it is more a case of working with them constructively to ensure that their needs are met (I-Thou), so that they will want to do well, they will want their individual, team and organizational enterprise to be successful.

This chapter seeks to lay the foundations for developing a more sophisticated and more realistic understanding of what is involved in motivation. Perhaps not surprisingly, the theme of leadership once again arises, this time in the form of an emphasis on self-leadership. I begin by exploring traditional perspectives on motivation, then consider self-leadership before finally focusing on the importance of understanding motivation in its broader context.

Traditional perspectives

There has been a literature base developed in relation to motivation which goes back quite some considerable time now, and so it is not a topic that is in any sense new. However, as I will argue more fully below, there are significant limitations to the traditional approaches to leadership. But, before talking about the limitations, first let us look at the insights they bring. There are four key aspects of this topic that I want to comment on and I shall address each in turn.

Motivating factors

It has long been recognized that there are certain things that will motivate people; that will push them forward to achieve their goals. In fact, having clear, explicit goals can be a source of motivation in itself. In this regard, motivating factors are closely associated with desire. When we desire a particular outcome, then our efforts are likely to be strongly geared towards achieving that outcome. In this respect, the challenge for people managers is to create a wide range of motivating factors in the work setting, so that people will want to do their best and achieve optimal results for all concerned.

Linked to this is the importance of values, those things that we hold dear. Values are important in relation to motivation, in so far as our values will spur us to do certain things and desist from doing others. For example, if we value dignity we will be motivated to treat people with respect and to avoid situations where our actions may lead to someone losing face or being humiliated. Values therefore need to be high on our list of motivating factors. Kouzes and Posner (2017) explain that values are a source of motivation, and they help to keep us focused on what we are doing, why we are doing it and what we are trying to achieve. They see values as 'banners' that fly as we struggle and toil. We can refer to them when we need to replenish our energy.

KEY POINT

In considering motivating factors, we need to be careful not to overgeneralize and, in the process oversimplify a complex matter. For example, while promotion and career development may motivate many people, it will not motivate everybody (see Practice focus 15.2 below). What is much more helpful is to talk to people about what motivates them, rather than make assumptions that could be very misleading.

Demotivating factors

Also known as drag factors, these are the other side of the coin. These are the things that will slow people down, make them less motivated to achieve their desired outcomes. Boredom is a common result of there being too many drag factors or too strong a set of drag factors in place. People managers can usefully identify what the demotivating factors are in a particular work setting or for a particular employee and, with that employee (or team of employees) work out strategies for how to keep those demotivating factors to a minimum if not to eradicate them altogether. For example, if someone feels ill-equipped to deal with a particular aspect of their job, then the anxiety associated with this could be a significant demotivating factor, resulting in their taking far longer to do a particular task than should be necessary. A good people manager can help the person concerned to develop their knowledge, skills and confidence in relation to that task, so that they do not feel so anxious about it and are therefore not demotivated by it.

Sometimes there can be team or organizational demotivating factors in addition to any individual ones that may apply. For example, there may be something about a culture that has a negative effect in terms of motivation. This is commonly the case where cynical, defeatist cultures are allowed to develop in which low morale preponderates and moaning and complaining are the order of the day. I will return to the key concept of morale below.

Hygiene factors
These are aspects of the work situation that will not provide motivation in themselves, but, if they are absent, they can lead to motivation being reduced. The parallel here in terms of hygiene is with efforts to keep a place clean and hygienic which will not make people well, but if there is no adequate attention paid to hygiene, then the result can easily be that people become ill. It is important to recognize that hygiene factors can have a major impact and generally a negative one if they are absent. For example, while having a desk may not motivate people in itself, not having a desk (or whatever other facilities a person needs for their particular job) can be quite a source of dissatisfaction and thus demotivation. This is something that has emerged from various experiments over the years with 'hot desking' arrangements.

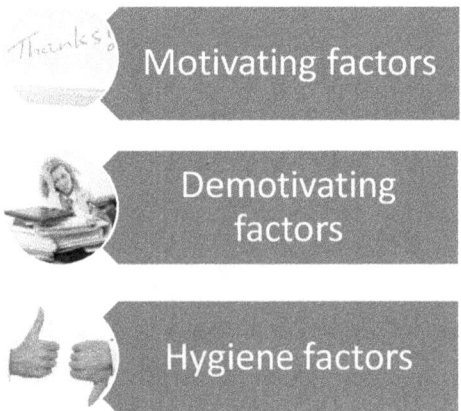

Hygiene factors (or their absence) can also be team or organization based, in so far as they can apply across the board – for example, an organization that does not provide enough parking for its staff, leading to considerable inconvenience for people who have to attend offsite meetings and then cannot find a parking space on their return.

Figure 15.1 Factors affecting motivation

Just as it can be wise for people managers to have a good idea of what the motivating and demotivating factors are, there is also some benefit to be gained from having an understanding of how hygiene factors are affecting people's motivation.

Extrinsic versus intrinsic motivation
This is an important distinction, as it has significant implications for people managers. Extrinsic motivation is the type of motivation that comes from having something delivered from outside – for example, if someone is offered money or other rewards for achieving a particular goal or completing a particular task, then that would be an extrinsic form of motivation. However, if somebody is motivated to achieve a goal or complete a task because they find it satisfying in itself (hence the term 'intrinsic'), then this is what we would refer to as intrinsic motivation. What we have to recognize is that, generally, intrinsic motivation is much stronger, more reliable and longer lasting than extrinsic motivation. If we think of it mechanically, extrinsic motivation is the equivalent of winding up a clockwork toy. It will last for so long, but will gradually unwind, and there will need to be further winding to produce any further action. Intrinsic motivation is, by contrast, a matter of a person not needing to be wound up like a toy because they are able to motivate themselves to move forward to achieve their goals. There should therefore clearly be a strong emphasis on maximizing intrinsic motivation where possible.

Kouzes and Posner (2017) support this view. They discuss the important distinction between extrinsic and intrinsic motivation. External motivation is more likely to create conditions of compliance or defiance. By contrast intrinsic self-motivation produces much better results. There is therefore an important message here: we will do much better as people managers to focus on the intrinsic motivation associated with leadership, rather than the extrinsic motivation associated with traditional command and control approaches to managing staff.

> *Practice focus 15.1*
> Kim was pleased to get the chance to attend a one-day course on motivating staff. Much of the course was disappointing as it just came across as fairly obvious home-grown wisdom and didn't seem to have much by way of a firm basis to it. However, one thing that was very useful from the course, and which Kim really liked, was the idea of a 'motivation audit'. This meant looking at what motivated individual team members, what demotivated them and what the key hygiene factors were. The presenter saw this as something useful to do as part of supervision, coaching or mentoring, as indeed it was, but Kim also saw it as something that could be done collectively with the whole team, perhaps as part of a team meeting or even a team building 'awayday'. This gave Kim a great deal of food for thought and ideas for a number of ways in which such an exercise cold be a very valuable way of trying to boost the motivating factors, reduce the demotivating factors and tune in to what the hygiene factors were to see if anything could be done to improve the situation in relation to them. What had

appeared to be a fairly mediocre course for much of the day, ended up being a very useful source of an excellent, very helpful tool that Kim could put to good use in boosting motivation in the team.

Self-leadership

There is in some ways a spiritual basis to motivation, in the sense that people are likely to be motivated by finding meaning in what they are doing. For example, Pink (2018) argues that it is important to go beyond the idea of carrots and sticks. Certainly, people will be motivated to a certain extent by carrots (that is, positive rewards) and/or sticks (punishments or discouragements for doing things that are seen as undesirable). Pink argues that we need to have a fuller understanding of motivation that incorporates the following three elements:

- *Autonomy.* This refers to the extent to which people are allowed to have a degree of control over what they do. If people are simply following direct instructions and have little or no autonomy, then it is likely that their motivation will be at a very low level. If, however, they are trusted to move forward under their own steam and to take initiative (to be empowered, to use the technical term) then the level of motivation is likely to be significantly higher. This fits well with the idea discussed above of intrinsic motivation – doing things because we want to, because we can see the value of doing so, rather than because we are under instruction to do so.
- *Mastery.* This is also partly a matter of control. If people have the necessary skills and resources to be able to have a full grasp of a situation and to be able to move it forward, then they are much more likely to do that with a higher level of motivation than people who are permitted no such mastery.
- *Purpose.* People can be very strongly motivated by having a sense of purpose, of trying to achieve something. If work is too routinized and lacks any sense of clear purpose, then motivation levels are, of course, likely to be quite low.

Pink's work has been very widely accepted and highly praised for presenting a fuller picture of motivation and thereby moving away from some of the oversimplifications associated with earlier, more traditional, perspectives which have been criticized for being too mechanistic. In a sense, Pink's approach is a spiritual one, in so far as such issues as autonomy, mastery and purpose can be seen as part of spirituality, a topic to be discussed in more detail in Chapter 20.

Pink's approach is also consistent with the idea of self-leadership that was introduced in Chapter 11. Good leaders need to have a degree of self-awareness and self-control that they connect with their awareness of organizational life and, indeed, of people *as people*. Self-leadership enables people managers to have a sound foundation for helping staff to be as motivated as possible. One feature of leadership is that it is based on the idea of *pull*, rather than *push* – that is, while traditional management can be seen to rely on the idea of command and control where the manager issues instructions, contemporary notions of leadership are geared more towards motivating and inspiring people to achieve their goals, hence the idea of pull rather than push. Where there is self-leadership there will therefore be self-motivation, not only on the part of the leader, but also on the part of their followers.

Motivation in context
A very important distinction in terms of organizational culture is that between a culture of commitment (where people are keen for the enterprise to be successful because they feel that they are a valued part of that enterprise) and a culture of compliance (where people are motivated to succeed only to the extent that they feel that they are under an obligation to do so and will 'get into trouble' if they do not). For me, this is a very significant distinction, because effective people managers should be able to promote a culture of commitment and move away from the idea of simple compliance. A key part of this is recognizing the importance of morale. We have already noted that low morale can be a very destructive aspect of organizational life. It can be highly poisonous, affecting not just isolated individuals, but whole teams or even whole organizations. It is therefore vitally important that issues of morale are taken seriously. There is little point trying to motivate individuals, for example, if the overall context is one of low morale.

This brings us back to the key role of leadership once again. If we acknowledge that a leader is someone who has the skills and understanding (and associated confidence) to shape cultures in a positive way, then we should be able to recognize that a culture of low morale is one that a good leader should not be tolerating and should be working very hard to address.

However, motivation is not just a matter of leadership (the L of *Staying Calm*). The other three aspects of CALM are also significant. For example, there is the C of Connection which, as we noted in Chapter 14, is related to teamwork. Teamwork is another important source of motivation through a high level of team morale where that exists. The A of CALM is also important, in so far as the authenticity or genuineness of a manager will be a significant factor in relation to motivation. Staff are not likely to be motivated if they perceive managers or HR professionals as lacking authenticity, of not being genuine in their efforts to seek win-win outcomes for everyone. Finally, of course, in terms of CALM, there is the M for Meaning in *Staying* CALM, and meaning is something that is a major source of motivation. What gives our life in general and our work in particular a sense of meaning or coherence will be important to us. We therefore need to recognize that issues related to motivation are often also related to meaning (see Chapter 20).

Fulop and Linstead (2009) comment on the significance of meaning in relation to gender differences:

> men and women differ in the meanings they attach to the notion of commitment across differing contexts. It seems that there is a gendered aspect to commitment and an emotional dimension to it that is also gendered. In a sobering review of labour trends, and the perceptions that many male managers hold of women employees. Catherin [sic] Hakim (1995) found that women were represented as less career conscious than men, not staying in their jobs for the long haul, being less interested than men in training and promotion, having higher turnover and levels of absenteeism, and unwilling to place work ahead of domestic demands. She found the labour market trends over several decades had not altered these patterns and concluded that, on balance, women tend to be unstable employees (in terms of job tenure and length of time with a particular employer). She acknowledged that many women are found in casual and part-time work, while there is a small group of women who pursue their careers through education and qualifications, although again not necessarily remaining in the workforce as long as their male counterparts.
>
> (pp. 451-2)

In these days of reduced job security and increased reliance on short-term contracts, there may well be further differences that emerge in terms of the meanings that people attach to their working lives (Uchitelle, 2007).

> *Practice focus 15.2*
> Sue was an extremely competent worker who was highly respected by all who came into contact with her. She seemed to achieve very high standards of work without much effort and was always eager to be supportive of her colleagues in whatever way she reasonably could. One day, she was called in for a meeting with the divisional manager. At that meeting he told her of a management vacancy coming up and he encouraged her to apply. He made it clear that there would be open competition for the post, as it was to be advertised internally, but he frankly saw no one in the organization who would be more impressive than she was, so he was very confident she would get it. However, he was very surprised when Sue told him that she was not interested in a management position. She was very happy doing what she did and could fit it into a 9 to 5 framework for the most

part, but she realized that, in a management post, there would be expectations of evening meetings and long hours that just did not fit comfortably with her role as mother and carer for her elderly mother. And, besides, she was not an ambitious person and was not particularly motivated by a promotion. The divisional manager found this very difficult to understand and put her under pressure to reconsider. He told her that he knew of a few people who would be very keen to get that job. Maybe so, she thought, but she was not one of them. She was a bit concerned that she may have unwittingly reinforced the stereotype that women are not cut out for management posts, but she was glad that she had not allowed him to pressurize her into applying for something she basically wasn't motivated to get.

It is a serious mistake to see motivation in isolation without taking account of the wider context. It is as if it is a simple mechanistic process or a characteristic of atomistic individuals. In reality, people are much more complex than that, and so it is important that we have a broader perspective on motivation.

Fulop and Linstead (2009) offer helpful comment in this regard:

> A more sociologically oriented view of motivation suggests that 'needs' emerge and are constituted in social activities and experiences that shape our identities or the 'social self' and give meaning to work. Identities in the work context are not without their limitations and constraints and are socially structured and enacted within the context of different knowledge and power relations. A more critical view of motivation examines how strategies of job redesign, for example, reproduce certain motivational discourses that are embedded in power relations and give rise to particular disciplinary practices, such as techniques of surveillance. Culture and gender are important in how we define ourselves and who we think we are, yet both are often neglected in studies of motivation.
>
> (p. 413)

It should be clear, then, that people managers seeking to understand how to motivate staff need to adopt a broader perspective which incorporates such important issues as morale, gender and culture.

Conclusion

I have run many courses with leaders and other managers over the years around organizational and management issues. The theme of motivating staff is one that has constantly arisen from discussions on such courses. There is clearly, if my experience is to be believed, a major interest in learning how to motivate staff. We are therefore obliged to take seriously the challenges involved. Some of these are specifically about working with individuals who may have their own individual blocks to motivation, but we should not lose sight of the bigger picture which teaches us that culture, morale and leadership – wider aspects of working life – are also very important when it comes to motivation.

People are not puppets who can be manipulated this way and that. They need to be treated with respect. As Furnham and Taylor (2004) explain: 'Managers and those employed in human resources seek to develop staff loyalty, even commitment. They want dedication born of mutual trust, respect and even affection. But loyalty acts both ways: both parties have to give and receive' (p. 1). It is therefore vitally important that we should not lose sight of our own role in creating a culture of high morale and motivation through effective leadership.

Points to ponder
1. What is meant by 'hygiene factors' and why are they important?
2. What is the difference between intrinsic and extrinsic motivation? Which is likely to be more influential?
3. Why is it important to understand motivation holistically?

Exercise 15
What aspects of your working life motivate you? What aspects have the opposite effect? How might you use your understanding of your own motivational factors to help motivate others and create a culture of high morale?

CHAPTER 16: STAFF RETENTION

In this chapter you will learn how to reduce staff turnover by improving staff retention levels.

Introduction

In Chapters 4 and 5 I emphasized the importance of getting the right people in post and getting them started along the right lines. However, we have to recognize that all our efforts in that regard can easily be wasted if people leave prematurely, if their time in post is shortlived. Of course, a certain level of turnover is to be expected in any organization, but if (i) there is a high percentage turnover (what is often referred to as 'churn'); or (ii) some people are leaving not long after starting, then it is telling us that there is something wrong that needs our attention. Surprisingly, and unwisely, many organizations tend to gloss over such matters, as if they are frightened of facing up to the fact that there is something wrong in the organization that is discouraging people from staying (or even actively driving them away) – see Chapter 8 for a discussion of staff departures. Ironically, such a failure to engage with problems may be part of the reason why people are leaving – that is, if they encounter a culture characterized more by problem avoidance than problem solving, they may well lose faith in the organization's ability to provide a secure and positive workbase for them.

This chapter therefore explores the important range of factors that are very relevant when it comes to people managers trying to ensure that there is a high degree of staff retention. I begin by asking the question: why worry? This introduces a discussion of why staff retention is such an important issue for people managers. This in turn leads into a discussion of what steps we can take to reduce staff turnover and an emphasis on the significance of morale.

Why worry?

It is unfortunately the case that some people may take the complacent attitude that retention problems are an inevitable part of working life and therefore nothing to worry about. Such a view is based on the defeatist assumption that they should, in effect be, accepted as normality. However, such a view fails to recognize how much damage staff retention problems can do to an organization in general and to certain aspects of that organization in particular – as well as to individual staff members or groups of staff. More specifically there can be a worrying relationship between morale and retention problems, with each potentially making the other worse – we will return to this point below. It is therefore important to consider what harm a poor retention rate can do to an organization. The following main issues can be identified:

- *The costs of replacement.* Replacing a member of staff who leaves can be a very costly business when we take into account not only the expenditure involved in publicizing a vacancy, shortlisting, interviewing and so on, but also the costs involved in induction and related matters. However, there is not just the financial cost to consider. There is also the lost investment, in the sense that any training that the departing person undertook (including induction) will have been wasted and will have to be repeated for new employees who come to fill the gaps created by people leaving. In some cases where staff have started work on one or more projects, any progress gained may be lost if a new member of staff has to start from scratch because the nature of the projects means they cannot simply pick up where their predecessor left off (for example, where the success of the project involves building up a certain level of trust based on personal credibility – this is not transferable form one employee to another.
- *The impact on the morale of remaining staff.* A high turnover rate is suggesting that there are significant problems. A high proportion of remaining staff are likely to be sufficiently intelligent to work out that this is reflecting underlying problems in the organization. That recognition can in itself be sufficient to lower morale. However, if remaining staff discuss (as they often will) the departure of one or more staff, then the negatives involved in that conversation can reinforce a sense of dissatisfaction with once again the consequence of a lowering of morale with all the destructive and poisonous consequences that brings. This is just one way in which morale is significant in relation to staff retention.
- *The impact on the workload of remaining staff.* Some organizations are fortunate that they have access to temporary (or 'pool') staff who can be called upon to fill vacancies on a temporary basis. Where this situation arises, it adds significantly to the cost of replacement, as discussed above, but in those organizations which do not have access to such cover arrangements (or do not have the funding to pay for them), then this means one of two things: either the work of the departing employee will not get done (with potentially very significant implications for the quality of service and related matters), or there will be an expectation that remaining staff cover for their now departed colleague, thereby potentially significantly adding to their own workload (and thereby risking the development of a vicious circle in which that creates dissatisfaction, which in turn can lead to one or more members of staff leaving).
- *An adverse effect on the reputation of the team and/or organization.* If word gets around (and it often will, of course) that there is a high turnover of staff in a particular work setting, then it will not be long before people put two and two together and come to the conclusion that this is not a good place to work. That can then have a significant impact on recruitment and potentially could lead to

additional retention problems if existing staff, on becoming aware of the poor reputation of the organization that they are now working for, try to find employment with an organization with a better reputation. There will, of course, be other costs associated with a poor reputation. For example, in commercial organizations this could lead to expectations of poor customer service and therefore less interest in buying products or services from that particular company. In public or voluntary sector settings, a poor reputation may discourage potential users of services from seeking help and thereby lead to their problems escalating over time and becoming more difficult for the organizations concerned to deal with at a later date.

- *Loss of talent.* What is also likely to happen is that, in organizations in which there is a high level of staff turnover, then it is likely that the people who are leaving will be the most valuable ones, in the sense that the people who are going to find it easiest to find employment elsewhere will be the most experienced, most highly qualified or most talented employees – they will be the ones who have transferable skills, the confidence to seek new employment opportunities and the intelligence to realize that it is unwise to remain in an organization that fails to prove attractive enough to retain its staff. The sort of churn associated with such situations can therefore be highly costly, in the sense that the overall quality and calibre of the employee base are likely to diminish over time. In the worst-case scenario, an organization which fails to retain its staff will end up employing only the people who are unable to secure employment elsewhere or who are too burnt out to face moving on to an organization which may be more supportive, but which could make fresh demands on them.

There are clearly, then, a number of important reasons why we need to take seriously the issue of staff retention, particularly if we are faced with the situation of a higher than average turnover of staff for the industry or service area concerned. We would be very foolish indeed to neglect this important area of people management, especially as it can undermine or even eradicate the good work we may have done in other areas.

Practice focus 16.1
Lisa was a human resources adviser in a large organization that was divided into two divisions. She was responsible for providing HR services for one of the two divisions. She was also expected to cover for her colleague, Rob, who was responsible for the other division whenever he was on leave or otherwise unavailable. One day, while Rob was on leave, she attended a meeting in his division at which staff turnover rates was one of the items on the agenda. She was surprised to hear that the turnover rate was more than double that of her own division. The report that was presented compared this with the national average

for their type of organization and this made Lisa realize that even her division's rate was higher than the national average. There was considerable concern over this worrying picture. As a result of this Lisa informed the meeting that she would propose to the head of HR that she and Rob should work together to try and get to the bottom of why the turnover rate was so high. Colleagues at the meeting felt that this was a good idea, as they clearly needed to develop a clearer picture of what was going on.

Reducing staff turnover

If we want to keep the turnover rate within reasonable limits, then one of the most important things that we can do is to learn the lessons from each chapter of this manual, in the sense that good management and effective leadership encourage people to stay and to flourish, while poor management and ineffective leadership can often be primary reasons for people moving on.

In my experience over the years, I have noticed distinct patterns in relation to why people tend to leave. These can be particularly pertinent where people are leaving in disturbingly high numbers or with worrying haste. Chief among these are the following.

Not feeling valued

There is a significant literature showing that people who feel that they are not appreciated are less likely to be committed to their organization (see, for example, Robertson and Cooper, 2011). It takes very little, therefore, to work out that such people are more likely to leave than people who feel valued, appreciated and supported in their particular setting. If staff are not given sufficient positive feedback, they are likely to feel taken for granted or even 'used', and this can have a very adverse effect on morale and thus, indirectly, performance and ultimately retention.

Similarly, if staff are not thanked for their efforts, they will soon come to feel that they are just cogs in the machine, a resource but not necessarily a *human* resource (as discussed in the Introduction). It is vitally important, however, that expressions of gratitude and appreciation are *sincere*, and are not being offered mechanistically or tokenistically in a superficial attempt to stave off any dissatisfaction. This brings us back to the A, for Authenticity, of *Staying CALM*: we have to genuinely appreciate the efforts people make on the part of their employers. The M, for Meaning, of *Staying CALM* is also relevant, as it is often the rewards of gratitude and appreciation that give meaning and value to the work we do.

 There is also a need to make sure that we show specific appreciation to individuals to reflect their particular contributions. While comments of the 'Well done everybody, you are all doing a great job' kind have some degree of value, they are not enough on their own. They need to be supplemented by more individually focused ways of acknowledging what each staff member has contributed and achieved (for example, formally through supervision, coaching or mentoring or informally through general everyday interactions).

Unresolved conflicts and tensions

If members of a team or division are working in an atmosphere of tension, then that in itself can be a significant pressure which can subsequently lead to stress in many cases. It can have a very detrimental effect by wearing people down and preventing them from enjoying their work or from feeling comfortable in their work environment. We should not be surprised, then, that unresolved conflicts and tensions can lead to a high turnover rate. Unfortunately, many people adopt a head in the sand attitude towards conflict, naively hoping it will just fade away. As we shall see in Chapter 25, this is quite a risky strategy, as there is a very real danger that unresolved conflicts will do considerable harm to morale, working relations, quality and quantity of work and, of course, staff retention. *Staying CALM* is again relevant here, particularly the C, for Connection (we have to be able to manage conflict effectively if we are to have good working relations and feel part of a supportive team) and the L, for Leadership (leaders are expected to shape cultures in a positive direction, and this will include addressing any issues – including conflicts and tensions – that may be getting in the way of achieving the vision). This latter point is worth exploring in a little more detail.

A lack of faith in organizational leadership

I have already argued that it is important for leaders to be able to establish a sense of security, so that people feel comfortable and relatively safe in what they are doing. Where there is no such sense of security, the result can be feelings of considerable discomfort, disaffection and even alienation. These are the sort of feelings that are likely to encourage people to seek employment elsewhere.

Effective leadership, by contrast, can help to establish a firm basis for high morale and good teamwork, which in turn will generate the sort of feelings that are likely to encourage people to stay, to be committed and to grow and flourish over time. We have already noted the importance of trust, and so, in those work settings where there is a low level of faith in the organization's leadership, trust is likely to be in short supply. If people are expected to work in an atmosphere characterized by a low level of trust, then it should come as no surprise to us that many will be seeking to leave for fresh pastures where trust is more firmly in evidence as a result of higher standards of leadership.

Broken promises and/or feeling exploited
Experience has taught me that it is important not to make promises, especially promises that we cannot keep. The reason for this is that broken promises can do so much damage to morale and to people's sense of commitment. This is because, as we have already noted, trust is a key factor. Without that trust, there will be no sense of security, and without the sense of security, there will be limited commitment. Broken promises can do immense harm to people and organizations alike. It is especially sad, therefore, that some managers have been known to make promises they have no intention of keeping. The folly of this should be fully apparent.

Similarly, if people feel that they are being exploited, that they are not valued for their contribution as people but are seen simply as a means to an end (getting the work done), then their commitment to the organization is likely to be understandably low. This could be an act of omission (people managers who fail to give positive feedback or show appreciation) or an act of commission (game playing as part of a strategy for dealing with a difficult situation – for example, playing one person off against another in order to score points). We have already seen how important it is to give positive feedback and show appreciation. Failing to do this is problematic enough, but where people managers also play manipulative games, the situation can produce a working environment in which there is little or no motivation to remain, and considerable motivation to move on. While I would like to think that such game playing does not go on in modern workplaces, it would be naïve not to recognize that it often does (it can be a key part of bullying, to be discussed in Chapter 24 – see also the discussion below).

Poor induction
I have come across very many situations where people have felt extremely disappointed by their induction – indeed, in many organizations it is the norm for people to receive little or nothing by way of induction. Because of this, they have not been given the message that they are welcome, that they have an important contribution to make and that they are now part of the organization. They can feel isolated and undervalued, and so, for many people, it makes sense that, if they feel that they have joined an organization where things are not going to be working out for them, it is better to move on sooner rather than later. The importance of effective induction in making new recruits feel welcome, clear about what is expected of them and secure was emphasized in Chapter 5, and so the absence of such a good induction can easily be linked with a higher risk of early departure from a post. We should therefore be careful to ensure that induction is

given the attention it deserves if the way an organization handles people entering the organization is, ironically, not to contribute to their early departure.

Bullying and/or harassment
We have already noted the damaging effects of bullying and harassment and clearly one of them can be that staff depart in search of a new post where they will not be open to such unpleasant, painful and detrimental treatment. It can even be the case that people who are not directly affected will be the ones to leave, as they are aware that bullying and/or harassment is going on, but nothing is being done about it, This can lead staff to lose faith in the leadership of the organization (as discussed above). Losing such faith can in itself lead to a sense of insecurity, but this is particularly significant when bullying or harassment are involved because of the element of fear and intimidation associated with them. We will examine the significance of bullying and harassment in more detail in Chapter 24.

Work overload or other sources of stress
A high but manageable workload can be a source of satisfaction, stimulation and motivation, but once people cross that line into what they feel is an unmanageable workload, the result is stress. Again, it is understandable that a high proportion of people in that situation will want to seek other employment opportunities where they hope that they will not be exposed to an excessive level of work. Some will be wise enough to be proactive and look for less pressurized work elsewhere before too much harm is done. However, in some organizations there will be the unfortunate few who leave because the stresses have become so great that they cannot go on. They may resign without another job to go to – a drastic step but one which some people feel obliged to take, such is the harm work-related stress has been doing. Others may seek early retirement on health grounds. We will return to the not insignificant dangers of stress in Chapter 21, but for now, we should note that it can be a major cause of staff turnover (and often, by the same token, an impediment when it comes to recruiting new staff).

Lack of access to training/limited opportunities for learning
If staff feel that they are not being given the training they need to progress in their career or they are being denied opportunities to learn and develop in their day-to-day roles, they are likely to feel frustrated and dissatisfied and will therefore be more likely to leave. This can apply especially to those people who are likely to be the most enthusiastic about learning and maximizing their personal and professional development. What is particularly sad, then, about this cause of early or above-average levels of departure is that it is likely to be the most capable and promising employees who leave for this reason. It is likely to be the staff who have little interest in personal or professional

growth and development who will be content to settle for a limited range of learning opportunities. Getting stuck in a rut as a result of not learning can therefore become the norm and thus be part of what can develop into a non-learning culture (or reinforce an existing one). I will be emphasizing the importance of people managers making learning a priority in Chapter 19, but at this point we can see that obstacles to learning can also be obstacles to staying.

Figure 16.1 Reasons for leaving

Practice focus 16.2
Lisa and Rob developed a questionnaire that was sent out to every employee who had left in the past three months. The survey asked them about their reasons for leaving and for an indication of what steps might have been taken by the organization which would have prevented them from leaving. The people who received the questionnaire were assured of confidentiality and anonymity and were told that their contribution would help to improve the quality of life of their former colleagues who remained in the organization's employment. The return rate was less than ten per cent, but the ones that were returned painted a picture of an organization with a number of people management issues that needed to be addressed. Lisa and Rob felt that they had opened a can of worms. At first, they regretted doing this, as it gave a very unflattering impression of their organization. However, they soon came to realize that it was better to have become aware of these problems and be ready to do something about them, rather than carry on in the darkness.

All of these various issues can be addressed (if not entirely eliminated) by good people management and effective leadership. This review of some of the main reasons for people wanting to depart prematurely highlights a range of challenges that we, as people managers, face. If we can address those challenges, then the problems associated with staff retention are far less likely to arise and be far easier to tackle.

The central role of morale
It should be clear by now that morale is a key issue when it comes to the question of whether staff stay the course and have the opportunity to fulfil their potential or leave and take their potential with them. If we wish to make sure that staff retention does not become a significant problem, then we need to do whatever we reasonably can to keep morale at a high level or at least prevent it from slipping to a destructively low level. Once morale starts to fall it can set off a vicious circle: lower morale means that people perform less well, which in turn can mean that job satisfaction falls, which can then lower morale further. The lower level of performance can lead to criticisms and complaints, which can then also contribute to a lowering of morale.

Staying CALM can help to prevent such a destructive spiral:

- *Connection*. Getting to know staff properly, connecting with them as human beings, listening to their concerns and remembering to focus on the *human* aspect of human resources can all help to form helpful working relations that will help to sustain morale and thereby keep staff departure rates to reasonably low levels.
- *Authenticity*. A lack of sincerity will contribute to a low-trust atmosphere which will, of course fuel low morale and thus increase the likelihood of people leaving. Authenticity and the building of trust should therefore be foundation stones of our people management efforts.
- *Leadership*. As we have seen, leadership involves influencing organizational culture in a positive direction. Shaping a culture of high morale is therefore a key part of effective leadership.
- *Meaning*. If staff do not find their work meaningful, then we cannot expect a high level of morale. In addition, low morale can become the meaning of people's work in some situations – that is, disaffection, resistance and even sabotage can become common because it is through such behaviours that certain individuals make sense of their working lives. They associate work with all the negatives that low morale generates.

Focusing on the lessons of *Staying CALM* will not provide us with any magic solutions, but it will give us an insightful framework that can help us to tackle the problems of low morale are so often at the heart of staff retention difficulties.

Conclusion

It takes little imagination to work out that a key to retaining staff must surely be the importance of well-being (which will be discussed in some detail in Part III). This is a theme that unifies many of the points raised in this chapter. If staff feel that their well-being needs are not being taken seriously, then it is highly likely that they will at least begin to consider the possibility of moving on – and, for many people, a sense that their well-being needs are not high on the people management agenda could well be the reason why they do actually move on. There is therefore a clear need for people managers, whether line managers or HR professionals, to be clear about what needs to be done to ensure that staff retention does not become a significant problem.

This chapter has helped to show that there are various reasons why staff retention can be a problem and has argued that the poisonous nature of low morale is often a key feature of such difficulties. As such it has provided what I hope will be some helpful insights into how our people management knowledge, skills and values can be used to keep staff departure rates within reasonable limits by making our work settings places where people can flourish and will therefore be keen to stay.

Points to ponder
1. What different types of impact does staff turnover have?
2. What do you see as the three most likely reasons a person would leave their post?
3. Why is morale so important?

Exercise 16

What do you see as the three most important things you can do to minimize staff turnover?

CHAPTER 17: CAREER PLANNING

In this chapter you will learn about the importance of career planning as an aspect of making the best use of the human resources available.

Introduction

It is quite common for people to equate the notion of career with promotion, but a good people manager can help staff to develop a much clearer picture of this, to understand that career is about their own development over time whether or not that includes promotion. For example, some people can become excellent practitioners in their particular field and continue to grow and develop over time without leaving their role as a practitioner.

Indeed, it is very much the case that many organizations have suffered as a result of having people who have been excellent practitioners who then become managers and find that they have reached a level that they are not comfortable with (and may therefore struggle to operate effectively at that level). This reflects what is known as the 'Peter principle' (Peter, 1993) which is based on the idea that it is very common for people to be promoted to their level of incompetence. That is, someone may be promoted and cope well at the new level and subsequently be promoted again. However, for many people, there will come a time where they are promoted to a level beyond their capabilities and will therefore not be promoted further. They will therefore stay in a post where they are less than fully competent, hence the notion of being promoted to their level of incompetence. For some people this will happen on their first promotion. We therefore need to recognize that being promoted is not the be all and end all of career development.

The notion of 'career', then, is not something that we should automatically associate with promotion, although promotion can be an important part of it for some people in some circumstances. It can therefore be helpful to support people in developing a broader understanding of career, rather than risk having a frustrated employee who is underperforming and who may become disaffected and have an adverse effect on morale, or who may get stuck on a plateau, with no development or progress and therefore potentially be a candidate for burnout.

It can also be helpful to recognize that the world of work had been changing over the years, and the notion of career is now far more flexible, in so far as the idea of a stable 'job for life' features far less in the modern world of work than was once the case (Schnall *et al.*, 2017; Uchitelle, 2007). The greater flexibility and fluidity of the workplace today means that there are fewer guarantees in terms of longer-term employment, but potentially much more scope for a more creative approach to career development.

This chapter therefore helps to provide a better understanding of how people managers can play a positive role in supporting their staff in relation to career planning. We begin by exploring the notion of the 'Protean career' before examining what has come to be known as 'human talent management' and, finally, looking at what can be done to help staff with their career development.

The Protean career

Proteus was a character in Greek mythology who could change his form at will and was therefore the forerunner to the 'shape shifters' popular with science fiction writers. Osborn-Jones (2004) describes how Hall (1976) coined the term to refer to:

> a process which the person, not the organisation is managing. It consists of all the person's varied experiences in education, training, work in several organisations, changes in occupational field etc. (from Hall, 1976)

(p. 108)

However, over four decades later, we can extend the term to refer to the increasingly flexible career profile that is common today. Given that the notion of 'jobs for life' is no longer a viable one in the contemporary work setting (as a result of an increased number of temporary contracts, more self-employment, greater emphasis on adaptability and transfer of skills), we now have a very different career path expectation from the traditional idea of someone leaving education and beginning on a fairly clear and stable path through their chosen career.

The greater emphasis on adaptability and transfer of skills in contemporary workplaces has produced mixed results. Some people are flourishing in this more fluid work context, while many others are struggling because of the pressures arising from the lack of security involved. This presents an important challenge for people managers. One thing that we need to do is to learn how to be able to recognize which employees are well suited to such a Protean career and can be supported in pursuing one, and which employees are likely to struggle with that type of career and need to be helped to get as much stability as they reasonably can in these very unstable times. This is clearly quite a significant challenge, but the rewards for getting it right can be significant, and, of course the costs for getting it wrong equally so.

Practice focus 17.1
Paul had mixed feelings when his father retired. He was pleased that his father would have more time for relaxing and giving more attention to his beloved garden, but he also felt a little sad that it meant the end of an era as well as the end of what had been a very successful career. Paul's father, James, had studied sociology and criminology for his degree. He then had a job as a social work assistant for two years before being sponsored by the Home Office to return to university to undertake a diploma in social work. Because of his interest and background in criminology he had felt quite comfortable in focusing on probation studies, which was a requirement of the sponsorship. On the successful completion of his diploma he was appointed as a probation officer in his home town. He had remained in that post for just under 12 years when he was promoted to a senior probation officer post in a nearby town. This involved him in managing a small team of probation staff. He subsequently had opportunities for further promotion but was not ambitious and was content to remain in a job he enjoyed and found satisfying and which paid reasonably well. It was from this post that he had now recently retired. Paul was struck by the immense contrast with his own career. He had had a number of low-paid, casual jobs (bar work, for example) and done some travelling before doing a degree in computer science. In the 17 years since he graduated he had had 11 different jobs in different industries and was now considering going part time in his current job and supplementing that with a freelance consultancy role. He had enjoyed the variety of what he had been doing but he did envy the sense of security and belonging that had characterized his father's working life.

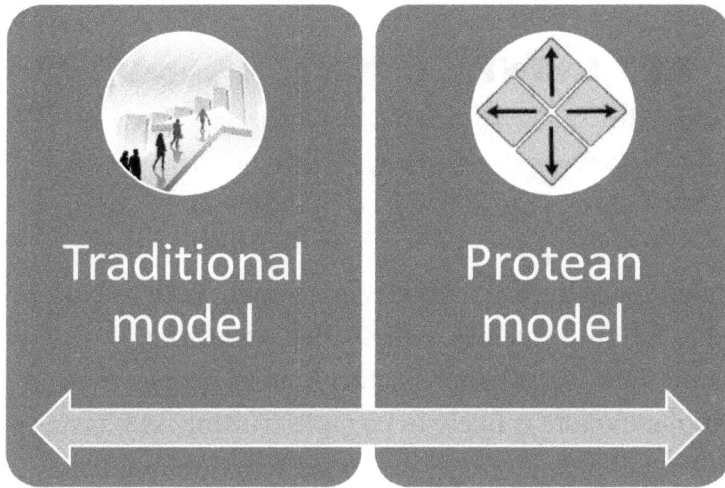

Figure 17.1 Models of career development

Human talent management
From an individual's point of view a career is a pathway through working life, and the challenge involved in career planning is how to make the most of that career. For many people, it is primarily a financial perspective. How can they make as much money as possible from their career? How can they reach the highest salary of which they are capable? In reality, of course, there is much more to career than this. We know that money does not bring happiness necessarily (Bauman, 2005), and it is not uncommon to come across people who are earning significant sums of money, but who are thwarted in their career plans, in the sense that they find it extremely difficult to gain any significant level of job satisfaction and therefore achieve their desired level of well-being. For others, it is status and power that they are seeking, but even here there is no guarantee that achieving success in this regard will give the individuals concerned a satisfying working life and overall career. Indeed, there is a danger that people seeking power and status end up on a treadmill, in the sense that, once they have achieved the status and power they seek, they quickly become hungry for more power and status.

From the organization's perspective, however, career management is not just about individual paths. There is also the overall, collective picture to consider. This aspect of working life has come to be known as human talent management or human capital management (Armstrong, 2021). These terms refer to the fact that an organization can expect that people, as an organization's most important resource, will continue to grow and learn over time and thus to increase in value to the organization (a return on the investment made in staff in effect). What this means is that organizations should have an interest in career planning, rather than see it as a matter simply for the individuals concerned.

KEY POINT

It is about trying to create a culture where the expectation is that people will not simply work towards the next promotion, the next rung on the ladder, but, rather, will seek to maximize their learning and their level of performance in their current job, which may or may not lead to promotion.

Unfortunately, notions of human talent or of human capital management take us back to the systems approach, as discussed in the Introduction, with its dehumanizing tendencies and its proclivity for losing sight of the people factor. A more people-centred approach that recognizes the key human factors is likely to be more fruitful. As I have already emphasized, instead of thinking of people simply as a resource, we should see them as people who are capable of being resourceful – that is, when it comes to HR, we should place more emphasis on the human than on the resources, and that way everybody benefits. To dehumanize people is fundamentally counterproductive, but the idea of win-win outcomes from a career development point of view is none the less a valid and important one. There is therefore considerable mileage in people managers tuning into the significance of career development, not only as a means of supporting individual staff, but also of recognizing that the wider organization has much to benefit from employees who are fulfilling their potential as far as possible and are therefore making the most of their career pathway.

Promoting career development
Some people managers take the view that it is counterproductive to support career development, as it means that staff are, in effect, being helped to increase their chances of moving on to a better job. On the surface this appears to be a reasonable assumption. However, on closer inspection, we can see that there are two reasons why it would be unwise to adopt such a view:

1. As already noted, career development does not have to mean moving onwards and upwards; it can also be a matter of job enrichment – staff getting more out of their existing job by building up their knowledge, skills, values and confidence over time.
2. As a participant on a training course I was running once put it: 'Managers have to ask themselves which they would rather have: staff who are doing a great job and who are learning over time but who will one day leave or people who never learn and who stick around for the long term'.

Given the importance of supporting career development, we need to consider how people managers can be supportive in helping individuals to fulfil their potential along their career path. This can be done in a variety of ways, and we will now consider some of the most prominent ones.

One-to-one support
This can include supervision, coaching and/or mentoring. What these have in common is a process of engaging with an individual in a supportive way that is geared towards, among other things, helping them to maximize their learning and their effectiveness. One-to-one help can be a very powerful means of harnessing an employee's strengths, helping them to turn weaknesses into strengths where possible, boosting their motivation and helping them to develop a clear plan of how they can build up their knowledge, skills, values and confidence.

Unfortunately, many organizations do not invest in one-to-one support. They see it as a luxury they cannot afford, rather than a sound investment that will repay them handsomely over time in terms of a higher level of employee engagement, commitment, loyalty, motivation and performance. They do not see the win-win potential of investing in their staff's career development. A more enlightened approach would focus on the fact that people are likely to do much better, be much more productive and have (and cause) far fewer problems if they are being supported to get the best out of their working life.

Training and learning sets

In Chapter 19, we will explore the importance of training and development, but for now we can note that having the opportunity to be involved in training courses or to be a member of a learning set (to be explained in Chapter 19) brings significant advantages for the employee and for the wider organization. Giving staff the opportunity to reflect on their work, to compare notes with other colleagues, to be exposed to new ideas and approaches and to test out their own ideas in a safe environment can be a major contribution to developing a culture of learning. This can also help staff to identify what they see as their strong points and their particular areas of interest, so that they can form a view about what direction it is best for them to go in. Similarly, they can use the opportunities presented by training and learning sets to identify what areas they feel uncomfortable in and would not want to pursue. This helps to ensure that staff do not find themselves in areas of work where they will feel demotivated and will therefore not achieve their best.

Allocation of work

In some settings there is little opportunity to vary the allocation of work; it is relatively standardized. However, in many other settings there is the possibility to gear the allocation of particular tasks, projects, cases or whatever other form the work may take, to ensure that the employee concerned has the opportunity to broaden their repertoire of skills, to try out new situations and in effect maximize their opportunities for learning and thus for career development. For example, a well-established member of a team may be given the opportunity to supervise one or more junior members of the team so that they are given the opportunity to learn some of the basic skills in preparation for a possible management post at a later date.

However, once again it is not simply a matter of preparing people for promotion. There is also the question of job enrichment to consider. Staff can be helped to explore possibilities of practising certain skills or increasing their knowledge in particular ways so that they are better all round at their job, more confident as a result of their enhanced knowledge and skills base, and with a wide perspective on the workplace and their role within it.

Much can also be gained from staff being allocated work that is at the limits of their current capabilities. By being 'stretched' in this way, they can be given important opportunities for growth and development that will not come from simply doing tasks that they are entirely comfortable with. However, it is important to note that this needs to involve allocating work that stretches their current capabilities a little. If someone is allocated a task that is too far beyond their current capabilities, the result can be that we are setting them up to fail and undermining their confidence in the process – as well as undermining our own credibility as people managers.

Secondment opportunities
This involves the potential for moving from one part of the organization to another to occupy a different role for a set period of time before returning to our original role enriched by the broadening of our experience, exposure to new ideas and working practices and so on. This can include temporary promotions and maternity cover. For example, if a person in section A is looking for an opportunity to broaden their career horizons and a woman in section B is shortly due to go on maternity leave to be replaced by a temporary agency worker, it may be possible to arrange for the person from section A to move temporarily to section B to cover for their pregnant colleague, while the agency worker then slots into the gap left behind in section A. If there is enough time, and it is not too inconvenient, it could even be possible that there is somebody in section C who will slot into the vacancy created in section A and the agency worker then slots into section C.

This sort of musical chairs can be very beneficial to enable people to broaden their experience, learn new skills, be exposed to a wider range of colleagues with potentially different working methods and therefore be a very solid foundation for career development. However, it is important that any such arrangements are well managed and not allowed to descend into chaos, as the disruption that can arise can be very counterproductive in terms of effective people management. When handled well, though, this type of temporary job swap can produce a great deal of learning and help people develop a much clearer picture of what direction they want to take their career in.

Shadowing
This is not possible in all organizations, but can be very helpful in those settings where it is feasible. It involves a member of staff spending some time with a more experienced colleague while they go about their business, so that they can pick up tips and have good insights into that more experienced colleague's job and approach to their work. This again can be a good foundation for career development, in so far as it can broaden an employee's horizons and help them to get a sense of whether the role they have been shadowing is one that may appeal to them in future.
How much time can be realistically invested in shadowing will vary from organization to organization or even from department to department within the same organization, but,

where there is scope for its use, it can be very helpful indeed as a contribution to career development and, indeed, to learning more broadly.

> *Practice focus 17.2*
> Priya was delighted to find out that her employers were introducing a career development scheme. She had long felt that, as a woman and a person of Asian heritage, she had faced two glass ceilings. She was particularly pleased to learn that the scheme included opportunities for staff to receive mentoring support to help them build up their confidence. However, what surprised her was that the information about the scheme explicitly stated that career development was to be understood as something more than just seeking promotion. She had not come across the idea of job enrichment before, but could see that it was a very useful idea, as not everyone can be promoted, but everyone can benefit from getting more out of their job and having the opportunity to put more in. She decided that she would focus on job enrichment to begin with, while she built up her confidence, and then consider after that whether she still wanted to aim for promotion.

So while there is no simple, clear or straightforward way of promoting career development, there are various options that people managers can pursue in terms of trying to be as helpful as they can in supporting the notion of career planning, so that both individual staff members and the wider organization benefit from having a clear focus on the notion of career as optimizing our working life and our developmental pathway, rather than simplistically thinking of it in terms of climbing up the ladder of promotion.

Conclusion

Career planning is often neglected in organizations, despite the fact that there is a price to be paid for not taking enough notice of what is involved in career development. This price includes:

- Existing staff not fulfilling their potential;
- Potential new staff being discouraged from applying for vacancies in the organization;
- Staff leaving to seek better career development opportunities elsewhere;
- Tensions arising because of a sense of frustration at the lack of opportunities to develop; and
- Potential contributions to a culture of low morale because staff feel undervalued and unsupported due to the sense of there being no investment in their future.

 Beware of the tendency for organizations to rely on the simplistic stereotype of career as meaning just promotion and nothing else. If progress is to be made in terms of career planning and development, then there needs to be much fuller understanding of the broader and more flexible notion of career, and this understanding needs to be communicated throughout the organization.

It is to be hoped that this wider conception of career, as presented in this chapter, will help people managers to play an important, constructive role in trying to get the best out of employees by helping them to achieve their best along their career pathway.

Points to ponder
1. What is meant by a Protean career and why is it important?
2. What role do coaching and mentoring have in relation to career planning?
3. How could secondment opportunities be put to good use?

Exercise 17
Do you have a clear idea about your own career plan? What might you need to do to make the most of the opportunities available to you?

CHAPTER 18: MENTORING AND COACHING

In this chapter you will learn how to make mentoring and coaching useful foundations for effective human resources management.

Introduction

Mentoring and coaching are two processes that have much in common, in so far as they both focus on promoting learning and driving performance improvement. There are various definitions and varying distinctions between the two, but as a general rule, coaching tends to be seen as a (relatively) short-term process geared towards specific learning needs, while mentoring tends to refer to a longer-term relationship geared towards learning and development more generally. However, what they have in common is a commitment to using a one-to-one relationship to promote learning. This chapter sketches out the important role that effective mentoring and coaching can play and warns against the dangers of jumping on the bandwagon of fashion and using these two important processes inappropriately.

I begin with an outline of the important concept of the 'learning alliance' and then highlight a number of key issues in relation to how we can make the best of what coaching and mentoring have to offer when it comes to promoting learning.

The learning alliance

This heading is a term drawn from the work of Clutterbuck (1998) who has written extensively on the subject of mentoring and coaching. It is a key term, because it captures nicely what both processes are about: two people coming together to enable the learning of at least one of them and preferably both. Mentoring and coaching can be part of supervision, as discussed in Chapter 3, or can be undertaken as a separate, independent activity by a line manager. However, it does not have to be the line manager; someone else in the organization (somebody from HR, for example) can act as an independent coach or mentor, and we are now seeing the growing use of e-coaching or e-mentoring (with the interaction taking place either just through email or a mixture of email and telephone contact) delivered by independent external providers as well as 'live' services from freelance coaches and mentors.

Coaching is sometimes 'remedial', in the sense that it is used as a means of addressing a learning need or a performance problem identified. It is therefore being used to work on an aspect of performance or learning that has been causing concern. Traditionally, this was the primary focus of coaching, but in recent years, with the growth of interest in coaching and its much more common use in organizations these days, there is a broader focus on learning and development needs that are not simply remedial in their focus. As Schwarz (2006) explains:

> Coaching is not just for problems anymore. Ten years ago, coaching primarily concentrated on people with performance issues. A coach came on board because a leader's personal style had a negative impact on peers and reports, or because his or her skill set was inadequate – conditions that were leading to career derailment. Sometimes, the coach was simply a bulletproof way to communicate bad news about performance before dismissal. Coaching was often viewed pejoratively as something applied to failing leaders or as a last-ditch effort to salvage a career in which the organization had made a long-term investment it didn't want to throw away.
>
> (p. 434)

Coaching is now seen as something that has much broader application in providing a very focused approach to skill development. While training courses can be very helpful in this regard, they are geared to meeting the needs of the group as a whole and cannot be sufficiently tailored to the needs of one specific individual. Coaching, by its very nature, is geared towards addressing the specific issues as they apply to the individual staff member concerned.

Coaching and mentoring can both be very helpful in identifying obstacles to learning and can be of value in establishing a plan for addressing the issues arising from this. The process of either coaching or mentoring can then be usefully put into service to implement the plan or at least part of it. While staff may be invited to comment on their learning needs as part of a training needs analysis survey (which some organizations carry out on an annual basis), many people find it difficult to articulate their learning needs without having the opportunity to discuss the situation with someone who has a good understanding of learning and development. Many line managers are able to offer this type of support through supervision and appraisal processes, but some managers do not feel confident or comfortable in approaching learning needs issues and, sadly, some do not see supporting learning efforts as part of their job. Coaching or mentoring can fill these gaps where necessary, and, where there is already a strong and effective emphasis on learning, act as an important reinforcer of that learning and provide an additional channel for focusing on the implementation of plans to address the learning needs identified.

It is also important to recognize that coaching and mentoring are not a substitute for training and development, but can be very effectively used to draw out the maximum learning from such events. This can be done by, for example, discussing with the attendee what key aspects of learning were gained from the course, consolidating these and relating them specifically to work duties. Some people can be very good at grasping issues at the general level, as discussed on a training course, but none the less struggle to link them to the specifics of their own work practice. Indeed, there can be quite a skill involved in not only being able to understand theoretical issues, but also being able to 'operationalize' them – that is, to make them meaningful in a work context without distorting them.

KEY POINT

The use of coaching and/or mentoring can be very helpful in developing a culture of learning – it helps to give the important message that learning is something that is expected across the organization as a fundamental aspect of working life, rather than something that emerges from time to time and then slips off the radar for a while until there is another training course or other such learning event.

> *Practice focus 18.1*
> When Priya realized that a mentoring programme was part of the new career development scheme, she was keen to apply to be one of the first members of staff to take advantage of it. To begin with the mentoring was being provided by a private company while staff within her own organization were undergoing a mentoring training programme. Priya approached the first mentoring session with gusto and got a great deal out of it. She got a lot of good ideas about how she could develop her knowledge skills just from the first 'get-to know-you' session. She therefore felt very positive about the whole scheme. However, she was disappointed to overhear two of her colleagues talking about their first mentoring sessions and being quite cynical about them. She was quite saddened by their negativity and came to the conclusion that mentoring will only work if people want it to. She was now determined that other she would not allow other people's failure to capitalize on what was on offer to prevent her from being enthusiastic about her own learning.

Overall, then, the notion of 'learning alliance' is a helpful one, as it helps us to realize that people managers have an important role to play in maximizing learning and helping employees to realize their potential as fully as possible. It complements well the more group-oriented learning associated with training courses and the individual learning that can come from reading the relevant professional literature and reflecting on our own practice.

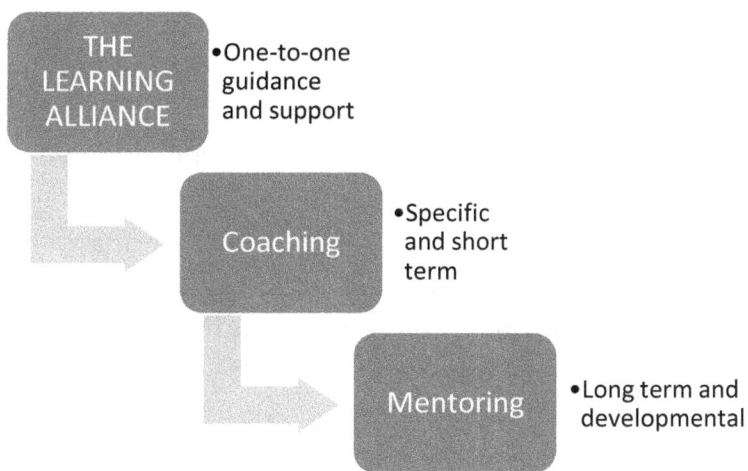

Figure 18.1 The learning alliance

Making a positive difference

Line managers and human resource professionals may well be called upon to provide coaching and/or mentoring. To do this to the best of our ability is likely to require the appropriate training or at least extensive personal study. However, to point you in the right direction, the guidelines below should be helpful. Even where people managers are not expected to provide coaching or mentoring themselves, they may be called upon at times to commission such services. It can therefore be very helpful to have at least a basic understanding of what these processes are all about so that commissioning decisions can be made on an informed basis.

1. *Choose an appropriate venue where you will not be interrupted.* Interruptions can have at least two significant effects. First, they can mean that either or both of the parties involved lose their train of thought, and important ideas can be lost as a result of this. Second, there is also the message that is given by allowing interruptions to take place, namely the negative message that the session is not important, that it has little value or status. Clearly that is not a message that we would want to be giving people. We therefore have to do everything we reasonably can to try to make sure that a suitable venue is made available. The point was made in Chapter 3 in relation to supervision that the venue needs to be conducive to open discussion if it is to provide the right atmosphere for interactions based on trust. The same argument can be seen to apply here in relation to coaching and mentoring – people are unlikely to get the full benefit of the process if the venue distracts from what is going on (or actually prevents anything from going on in the first place).
2. *Be clear about whether the relationship is short-term and geared towards specific learning needs (coaching) or intended to be longer term with a broader*

focus on development more generally (mentoring). If there is a lack of clarity about such matters, then the ensuing confusion can be distracting and can stand in the way of a positive working relationship based on trust and credibility from developing. The point was made earlier that different people adopt different perspectives on the similarities and differences between coaching and mentoring, but, regardless of the semantic subtleties involved, we need to be clear about: (i) what timescale is being offered (there can be a degree of flexibility in this, of course, but a complete lack of clarity can be very problematic in so far as it can prevent a trusting relationship based on transparency from developing); (ii) what type of learning experience is needed (a narrow focus on specific knowledge, skills, values or confidence issues or a broader perspective on overall learning and development. These issues are important, regardless of whether we are intending to provide the service ourselves or commission others to do so.

3. *Establish a positive friendly rapport – not too formal, but without being lax or 'chatty' either.* This is a matter of using our interpersonal skills to be able to get the employee concerned to relax sufficiently to maximize learning, but without relaxing so much that they lose the plot or lose sight of what the purpose of the interaction is. To a certain extent this is a matter of using everyday skills in relating to people, but there is also much to be gained from taking these skills to a more advanced level – for example, by becoming more adept at using nonverbal communication to put people at their ease and create an atmosphere of trust (see *People Skills,* Chapter 13). The time and effort required to take our skills to a more advanced level are likely to be rewarded by a higher level of effectiveness and therefore better results and higher levels of job satisfaction. There can also be a significant rise in confidence on our part if we can achieve this development, and this can be further rewarded by an increase in our credibility and the esteem in which we are held. There is also the issue of self-awareness to consider. If we are tense and unconfident in our role, for example, then we will find it very difficult to help the other person to relax and settle into the role. We may therefore benefit from giving some thought, if we are nervous, to how we can approach sessions in a calmer, more confident frame of mind.

4. *Agree an agenda and do not wander too far from it.* It is very easy for discussions to become unfocused and to lose sight of the key issues that should be addressed in the interaction. A degree of focus is therefore called for. However, we should equally not be afraid to change direction if we feel that this is likely to be fruitful. Once again, it is a matter of balance. There is no need to be rigid for the sake of rigidity. There is scope for a degree of flexibility, provided that we remain focused on the overall process of promoting learning and do not allow the session to descend into a 'chat'. Getting the balance right can be quite a skilled undertaking and may take time to develop, but it is certainly the case that we

should work on achieving that balance. If we do not, then we are risking not only that the session will be of little or no value, but also that our credibility will be harmed in the process – and, as we have already noted, such credibility is an essential part of effective leadership.

5. *Focus on goals, both the goals of your specific sessions together and the wider goals of the learner.* (I use the term 'learner' because, while the terms 'coachee' and 'mentee' are often used, both lack a degree of authenticity, in the sense that they sound artificial.) There is much to be gained from having a clear focus on goals. They can be motivating and help to give a strong sense of purpose (see the discussion of spirituality in Chapter 20). There are specific goals that need to be clarified for each session (and these will influence the agenda setting mentioned in point 4 above). These, in turn, need to be linked to the wider goals of the process itself: why is this coaching or mentoring taking place? What is expected to be achieved by it in general terms? What are the specific outcomes that are sought by engaging in this process? These questions can be helpful in clarifying how the process is intended to be helpful and can minimize the chances of drift occurring and the process becoming too unfocused to be of value.

6. *Focus on double-loop learning.* DeFillippi and Ornstein (2005), drawing on the work of Argyris (1999), explain that:

> Single-loop learning refers to learning that occurs as a direct result of consequences. Double-loop learning adds to the step of interpreting the consequences and deriving learning from this interpretation.
>
> (p. 30)

What this means is that we can not only learn from experience, but also learn from making sense of that experience. For example, if a man learns that many women object to being called 'girls' (single-loop learning), he may be able to deduce form this that there will be other forms of language that may also be unacceptable because they have demeaning connotations (double-loop learning).

 Mentoring and coaching can be of even greater benefit and value if they can help employees to go beyond single-loop learning by developing the insights afforded by double-loop learning.

This can be a daunting task for people managers who do not have a background in training and development, but what it boils down to is developing the analytical skills to draw out the wider lessons from specific experiences. It is therefore perfectly possible (and common) for people without a background in training and development to become very effective at facilitating double-loop learning.

7. *Avoid the danger of cloning.* This refers to the process whereby a coach or mentor loses sight of the overall process of promoting learning and simply uses the sessions as a means of persuading the learner to adopt his or her way of working – what amounts, in effect, to a form of generational transmission: less experienced staff are encouraged to reproduce well-established patterns of behaviour, rather than allowed to develop their own ways of working. This is problematic in at least three ways:

   a. It goes against the ethos of valuing diversity discussed in Chapter 1 by encouraging conformity and thereby presenting difference as a problem to be addressed rather than an asset to be appreciated;
   b. Similarly, it hampers creativity and innovation, potentially blocking important developments in working practices and ways of understanding; and also:
   c. It discourages critically reflective practice, putting staff under pressure to follow unthinkingly in the footsteps of the established staff, rather than drawing on their own knowledge, skills and values and building these up over time.

It is therefore something that should be strongly resisted.

Practice focus 18.2
Richard had been acting as a mentor to new staff for about two years before he had had the opportunity to undergo any mentoring training. He came away from the first day of the training feeling quite unsettled. This was because the course had covered a set of 'pitfalls to avoid', one of which was 'cloning' – that is, the tendency to try and mould people in our own image rather than helping them grow into being the best they can in their own way. He was well aware that, in his line of work, there were no definitive right answers and various ways of tackling the issues that tended to come up, and yet he had allowed himself to develop a mentoring style that was quite restrictive for the people he was mentoring. He could see only too well that he had developed the bad habit of trying to get people to see things his way and therefore do things his way, rather than helping them to find their own way of tackling issues and supporting them

> in doing so. He realized that he would need to change his style of mentoring and was hoping that the course would help him to do that.

This is, of course, not an exhaustive list, but it should be sufficient to give you some helpful pointers, so that you have some clearer insights into what is involved in effective mentoring or coaching. But again, I would want to reiterate the point that it is worth attending relevant training courses if you can and/or reading appropriate literature. Even if your involvement in coaching and/or mentoring is quite limited, the same knowledge, skills and values can also be of value in supervision and in relating to people more broadly (the C, for Connection, of *Staying CALM*). There is therefore much to be gained from investing time and effort in learning about these issues.

Conclusion

There is much to be gained from developing a culture where coaching and mentoring are not only permitted but are positively encouraged or even regarded as necessary components of organizational effectiveness. If people are to achieve their best, then having the opportunity to discuss relevant issues and focus specifically on their own learning and performance enhancement, is very worthwhile. There has been a huge growth in the coaching and mentoring industry in recent years, partly because organizations are beginning to recognize that an investment in learning (or at least this aspect of promoting learning) is a very wise and effective one.

However, while there is much to be gained, we need to recognize that, if the people manager concerned is neglecting their own development, then the whole edifice of coaching and mentoring can collapse. There is therefore considerable benefit to be gained from the self-awareness and self-leadership required to put our own learning on the agenda and, where possible, draw on the benefits of coaching and/or mentoring ourselves. As Rees and McBain (2004) comment:

> The line manager has a critical role in making the organisation a compelling place to work – or indeed the opposite. In the current context of work, the line manager now has a greater responsibility to develop him or herself, and to develop others through coaching and mentoring activities. The line manager is at the fulcrum of turning business and HR strategy into performance. This position implies that the line manager must more than ever understand the HR context and content within the organisation, and be able to identify the key levers that drive individual and team performance.
>
> (p. 250)

Much the same argument can be put forward for HR professionals also to be tuned in to the need for self-development as a basis for helping others to develop.

If we make the mistake of assuming that learning will happen automatically, just through people doing their job or from attending the occasional training course, then we do ourselves, our organization and particularly our employees a major disservice. If, by contrast, we put learning high on the organizational agenda, then, we can put ourselves in a much stronger position to take advantage of the benefits to be gained. The traditional means of promoting learning is through training and development activities, and so it is to this topic that we now turn in Chapter 19.

Points to ponder
1. What is a 'learning alliance' and what value does it bring?
2. Why is the venue for one-to-one sessions important?
3. What is 'double-loop learning' and why is it important to promote it?

Exercise 18
In what ways might you be able to make use of coaching and/or mentoring: (i) for yourself; and (ii) for staff?

CHAPTER 19: TRAINING AND DEVELOPMENT

In this chapter you will learn about the importance of putting learning and development at the heart of organizational success.

Introduction

If, as we have stated in many of the chapters in this manual, we want to get the best out of people, then we need to help them get the best out of themselves. Training and development is a key part of this, but what can people managers do to help employees to get the maximum benefit from the opportunities available? The short answer is: quite a lot, and this is a central part of what this chapter is all about.

I have been involved in delivering training and development for over thirty-five years and have seen enough evidence of its positive impact to be fully convinced of its central role and its benefits. However, I am not so convinced that all organizations make full use of what it has to offer. This is as a result of a tendency not to prepare staff before the event or to draw out the learning after it – often training courses operate in isolation, without adequate links to identified learning needs or the steps needed to put the learning into practice in a concrete way.

This chapter therefore provides an overview of some important issues relating to training and development and emphasizes that the people manager's role is not simply a matter of encouraging staff to attend relevant training events – what is needed if training and development resources are not to be wasted is far more than this. It is divided into four main sections, the first three of which relate chronologically to the process of drawing on what a training or related event has to offer, beginning with what should happen before a training event then moving on to look at some ideas about what can be useful during the event, before discussing the benefits of drawing out the learning after the event to make sure that the lessons learned are integrated into the employee's working practices. The final section discusses the importance of developing a culture of learning.

 Beware of the common mistake of thinking in narrow terms by focusing exclusively on training and paying little or no attention to other important forms and sources of learning.

Before the training event

Ideally, before we even think of sending an employee on a training course, we should (i) establish a clear picture of his or her learning needs through appraisal and/or supervision, and (ii) gain an overview of learning needs across the team, section or whole organization through a learning needs analysis (often called a training needs analysis, but I shall be arguing below that training is only one source of learning).

But, whether or not these have been done, there should be some preparation before a training course, so that the staff member is fully geared up to taking advantage of the learning opportunities available (I have run many courses on valuing diversity, for example, where it has become apparent that several participants had no idea what diversity is or why they were on the course – not a good way of maximizing learning!).

Some people may argue that they are too busy to prepare for training, as it is difficult enough to fit in the training itself. However, this is a time management issue, as a lack of preparation is likely to mean that much of the time invested in training is wasted (see Chapter 2 of *People Skills* for a discussion of time and workload management). Many staff are very good at managing their time and workload pressures, while others can be very disorganized and make poor use of the limited time resources available to them. This can lead to a vicious circle, in the sense that failing to make the best use of time (and energy) can lead to stress, which in turn can mean depleted energy resources and far from optimal use of the time available. We will return to this point in Chapter 21.

> *Practice focus 19.1*
> Ellen and Keith were members of the same team. They both attended the training course on effective communication. Ellen was keen to make the most of the course, so she talked to her supervisor about it before going on the course and thought carefully about what aspects of communication she could do with improving. She was aware of just how important communication was in her job, so she felt that this was time well spent. Keith, by contrast, arrived at the venue on the day of the course without having given the subject matter a second's thought. Ellen quickly engaged with what the course was all about and felt comfortable getting involved in the discussions. Keith took much longer to settle in and struggled at first to see how the course could be of benefit to him. By the end of the day he had come to see how some of the ideas could be useful in his work, but he clearly did not get as much out of the course as Ellen did. His lack of preparation meant that he had not made the best use of the time and effort invested in the day.

During the event
A training course is a social phenomenon, in the sense that its potency stems from its ability to bring people together an enable them to learn from one another as well as from the trainer. Bartel and Garud (2005) reinforce the significance of this when they comment that:

> knowledge results from both individual and collective processes. To this point, Tsoukas (1996: 14) noted, "individual" knowledge is possible precisely because of the social practices within which individuals engage – the two are mutually defined." Hence, social interactions and the sharing of information contribute not only to individual knowledge but also to shared knowledge.
>
> (p. 326)

Given this social, interactive nature of a training event, it is important to encourage participation in discussion and asking questions. It is therefore helpful, if in supervision, for example, the line manager gives a clear message to staff attending training courses that they should not simply sit there quietly, expecting to learn through some magical process based on osmosis. Simply being at a training event will have no benefit whatsoever, unless the participants take the term 'participant' seriously and actually get involved. Of course, some people will be too unconfident to contribute to discussions in the main group and contributions to small-group discussions may be the best that can be hoped for. However, some degree of encouragement and confidence boosting may make all the difference for some participants, as it is often just a case of getting over the initial nervousness about getting involved.

Similarly, it is important to encourage participants to take notes and attempt to link what is being discussed with their own job and setting. Many people will readily sit through, for example, a two-day training course without making a single note and, unless they are fortunate enough to have an exceptional memory, then it is highly likely that they will have forgotten most of what was discussed very quickly, with no proper point of reference to go back to. Some trainers provide extensive handouts, but these are no substitute for the participant producing their own notes which provide their own perspective, with their own priorities and their own links to their practice context (handouts are the equivalent of postcards of a place we have visited on holiday – they can be very useful, but they are not the same as the photographs we ourselves take of those scenes that are of particular interest to us or hold a particular significance for us). Of course, it is not a good idea to encourage people to go to the other extreme and to be constantly scribbling notes. Getting the balance right of being able to make effective notes is quite a skill, and if any members of your team lack that skill, then there can be considerable benefit in helping them to develop it as quickly as possible.

After the event
This is a process of 'operationalizing' the training. It involves identifying what will staff who have attended a training course do differently as a result of having been involved in this learning event? What key ideas will they bear in mind that will shape their practice and/or influence their thinking? Many people will not give such matters any thought,

while others will recognize the importance of doing so, but will struggle to do it for themselves without some degree of support (especially if analytical skills are not a strong point for them). People managers can therefore play an important role in transferring the learning from the training room to the workplace by: (i) making staff aware of the importance of doing so (individually through supervision and collectively through staff meetings, for example); and (ii) helping them to do so if they are unable to do this for themselves.

If we do not do this, there is a danger that the whole training endeavour (accounting for considerable time and expense) will have been wasted, as it will have produced no noticeable change in performance or understanding. As Jackson (2000) comments:

> Many training and development programmes fail to deliver the expected results not because people do not learn but because they return to an organisation that does not reflect and enable the learning they have acquired. People attending learning programmes with new skills, ideas and intentions but then return and run into the treacle of the organisation.
>
> (p. 95)

Below I will be arguing that it is important to work towards developing a culture of learning, and helping staff operationalize their learning by transferring what they have gained in the training room to their work setting can be a key part of this.
It is also important to establish whether the training has highlighted any further learning needs, either directly related to the subject of the course itself or something not so clearly linked, but which has become apparent as a result of some aspect of the training programme followed.

Ideally, a training event should be discussed in supervision so that the ongoing learning can be supported and reinforced through discussion. Similarly, if there is coaching or mentoring being undertaken by the person who has attended the training course, that too would be a good opportunity to maximize the learning. If there is no process of operationalizing the training, then there is a very real danger that discussions that took place on the course will quickly fade from memory and there will be little benefit gained from the time, money and effort invested in the event.

Jackson (2000) comments on the significance of creating opportunities for people to share the learning:

> To avoid continually reinventing the wheel an organisation has to have mechanisms that enable individuals to share what they have learned. Whilst

technology can play a helpful role, the real key to organisational learning is to connect people emotionally as well as rationally.

(p. 139)

This fits well with the C, for Connection of *Staying CALM,* in so far as it can be very helpful for people to learn from each other by discussing training courses and/or other learning experiences (a process often referred to as 'cascading'). However, it needs to be recognized that this is no substitute for people attending a training course for themselves.

> *Practice focus 19.2*
> Ellen wanted to make sure that she built on the learning from the Effective Communication course, so she took the summary of her learning (which all participants had been asked to prepare in the final exercise of the course) into her next supervision session and used the opportunity to get her supervisor's support in taking her learning forward. She had been particularly intrigued by the idea that we 'cannot not communicate', that we are constantly giving off signals of one kind or another. Two weeks later it was Keith's turn for supervision, and so, Jayne, the supervisor was keen to find out what Keith had got out of the course, as she had been very impressed with Ellen's learning. However, Keith had very little to say about the course. He had mislaid his summary of learning and had only a very vague recollection about the idea that we 'cannot not communicate'. Jayne began to wonder whether Ellen and Keith had actually attended the same course, such was the divergence between their experiences!

Promoting a culture of learning

Training is a key part of learning and development, but it should not be the only, or even the primary, source. For example, many organizations use learning sets. This is where a group of people work together for an agreed period of time in order to focus on a particular aspect of their work in order to identify what lessons can be learned and to optimize the learning that can be derived from studying and discussing that particular aspect of the work. As Elkjaer (2005) comments:

> Learning is not restricted to taking place inside individuals' minds but as processes of participation and interaction. In other words, learning takes place among and through other people (Gheradi et al., 1998). Learning is a relational activity, not an individual process of thought. This view changes the locus of the learning process from that of the mind of the individual to the participation patterns from that of the mind of the individual to the participation patterns of individual members of organizations in which learning takes place.

(p. 43)

Learning sets are used extensively in some organizations, occasionally in many and not at all in others. They involve a group of people meeting on a regular basis to explore a set of issues that are of interest to them. This presents considerable opportunity for learning. Some learning sets work to an agreed structure and timetable, while others are more unstructured and free flowing. The idea of learning sets derives from action learning theory (Revans, 1980) which is premised on the view that much valuable learning can be gained by groups of people (staff, managers or a mixture of the two) meeting to discuss their experiences and ask each other questions to help make sense of (and thus learn from) their work. This can be seen as an important part of critically reflective practice (as discussed in the Introduction).

I made the point earlier that training should be seen as the icing on the cake when it comes to learning. Of course, training can play a very important role, but the cake itself should, for the most part, be critically reflective practice. That is, a great deal of learning can be derived from looking closely at our work and the knowledge, skills and values we are drawing upon (in decision making, for example) – as well as learning from the mistakes we will inevitably make from time to time and, just as importantly, learning from what works well. Work settings that have a strong learning culture are likely to support, encourage and reward critically reflective practice, while cultures that lack such an emphasis on learning are more likely to not value it or even actively discourage it ('Stop wasting your time thinking and get on with the job').

Drawing on the work of Clutterbuck (1998), we can identify three levels of what he describes as 'reflective space':

- *Personal*. This refers to the way individuals analyse their experiences and draw out the lessons from the thoughts, feelings and actions involved.
- *Dyadic*. Supervision, mentoring or coaching, or a combination of all three can be very useful in helping practitioners to reflect not just on training courses attended, but also on the overall picture of their workload and what can be learned from it.
- *Group*. Training courses themselves would fall into this category, as would the learning sets discussed above. Sometimes team meetings, where they are working well, can also offer opportunities for group reflective space.

Increasingly now, we are also seeing the significance of online reflective space (Thompson and Thompson, 2023).

There are therefore various ways in which critically reflective practice can be used to maximize the lessons to be learned and take as much benefit as possible from practice in terms of growth, development and performance improvement. It is a mistake to assume that people will automatically learn from experience. It is what we *do with* our experience that is the best teacher, rather than experience itself.

A key part of critically reflective practice is the ability to integrate theory and practice (Thompson, 2017). This involves moving away from the traditional arbitrary separation of theory and practice. Hayes and Walsham (2005) help us to understand that knowledge is not something separated from practice but actually rooted in it:

> knowledge cannot be conceived of as being an entity that can be possessed, codified, organized and shared in the same way that data and information have been in the past. Instead, we have highlighted the importance for both academics and practitioners to view knowledge as being socially embedded and inseparable from practice.
>
> (p. 73)

This passage reinforces the potential value of learning sets, but also highlights the importance of having a culture of learning. The social context of learning is something that needs to be taken seriously, despite the traditional individualist emphasis on learning (the dominant trend in the literature is to focus on the *psychology* of learning, with relatively little emphasis on the *sociology* of learning. If we are to maximize learning within work organizations, we therefore need to pay much closer attention to the social context, including the extent to which there is a learning culture or not.

From my experience of working in or with a wide variety of organizations, I have identified three types of culture in relation to learning:

- *A learning culture.* This refers to organizations (or sections of organizations) where learning is supported, valued, encouraged and occurs largely spontaneously – it is expected that people will learn, and so learning becomes the norm. This is clearly the type of culture to aim for.
- *A non-learning culture.* This refers to work settings where learning is not on the agenda at all. Here the norm is for people to focus on getting the job done, and there is no expectation that they learn and get better at it. The focus is on 'satisficing' – that is, achieving a basically acceptable quality and quantity of work and leaving it at that. Often such cultures are associated with very settled teams where complacency has set in and much of the work is carried out on the basis of

habit and unthinking routines. Such cultures are also strongly associated with high-pressure work situations where people become trapped in a metaphorical hamster wheel in which they are running just to keep up, but actually achieving very little by way of positive results and potentially locking themselves into a vicious circle of stress (see Chapter 21).

- *An anti-learning culture.* This describes cultures where learning is not only undervalued, but actively rejected. Team members who try to develop their knowledge and skills may be mocked and/or accused of obsequiousness; suggestions that some things could be done differently are met with scorn if not actual ridicule. It is as if learning is seen as a threat to the status quo.

It can be helpful if, as people managers, we are clear about what sort of culture we are working within and seek to make the necessary changes to develop a culture of learning.

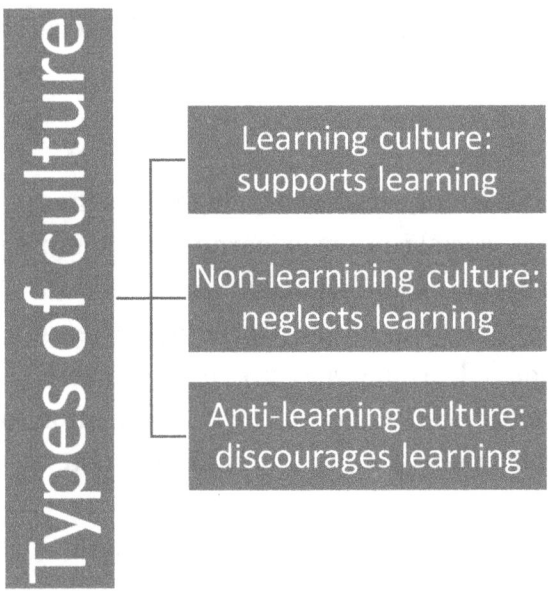

Figure 19.1 Types of culture in relation to learning

One aspect of learning culture that also needs consideration is the role of e-learning, which is now featuring more and more in organizational approaches to learning and development. This can be a very positive development in some ways, as e-learning can be very cost effective. However, it can also be highly problematic if is used tokenistically (if not properly monitored many e-learning programmes can be completed with little effort by uncommitted employees and will therefore produce little or no learning gain). Where possible, e-learning should be part of a 'blended' approach – that is, combined with conventional, group-based training which provides opportunities to consolidate the e-learning and integrate it properly with the specific work demands and learning needs of each employee. Blended learning is based on the recognition that e-learning can be very useful, but it is only one component of an overall learning and development strategy. Similarly, e-learning can be an important part of developing a learning culture, but it will need to be accompanied by other measures if our efforts are to stand any chance of being successful. We can see that there is a two-way relationship between learning culture and e-learning, in the sense that a learning culture is likely to promote the use of e-learning, and e-learning, if used properly, can help to promote a culture of learning.

We are also now seeing the beginnings of virtual reality-based training. The main advantage of this is that the learner becomes immersed in the experience within the virtual reality (VR) headset. In this way, there are no distractions and a strong stimulus to be alert and concentrating. The VR experience is best experienced in short frequent bursts and is therefore a flexible alternative – or supplement – to conventional training.

KEY POINT

Learning technology is expanding at quite a rate. While there is much to be gained from making use of what such facilities offer, we need to be careful to make sure that excitement about the novelty of new approaches does not distract us from the wide variety of learning methods – old and new– that are available to us.

Conclusion

A commitment to training and development should be part of a broader commitment to learning, although it is sadly the case that many organizations adopt a fairly mechanistic approach to training and development (focusing on ticking the boxes of how many people have been trained in a particular area) which will not necessarily contribute to learning, and may actually hamper it (if training is seen as something that is being done for bureaucratic reasons, rather than a reflection of a genuine commitment to the value of learning, staff may become disillusioned and not take the training seriously).

Where training and development activities are taken seriously, they can be of major benefit in terms of raising levels of knowledge and skill, helping people understand the value base of their work more fully and boost their confidence. They can also boost morale, in so far as people can feel that a significant investment is being made in them, with the result that they feel that they are a *human* resource, rather than just a resource. There is therefore much to be gained from people managers having a fuller understanding of the role of training and development and playing their part in making sure that staff make the best use of the opportunities available.

Points to ponder
1. Why is it important for participants to prepare for a training course?
2. What needs to happen to 'operationalize' the training – that is, transfer the learning from the training room to the workplace
3. What are the three levels of reflective space and what role do they play in promoting learning?

Exercise 19
How can you ensure that staff are: (i) aware of training and development opportunities; (ii) fully prepared for any learning events they attend; and (iii) able to transfer the learning from the training room to the workplace? What support or guidance might you need to do this to best effect?

CHAPTER 20: MAKING WORK MEANINGFUL: MEETING SPIRITUAL NEEDS

In this chapter you will learn how meaning, as a central feature of spirituality, has an important role to play in organizations.

Introduction

People commonly associate spirituality with religion, and this is an understandable association, given that for so many people their primary source of spirituality is indeed a religious faith. However, it is important to recognize that spirituality should not simply be equated with religion. This is because there will be very many people who have a spiritual sense of well-being which is not necessarily connected with religion. It is this spiritual sense that is the topic of this chapter. Spirituality is about how we make sense of the world and our place within it, and how we come to understand that there is something greater than ourselves, something *beyond* ourselves in a sense. To look at meeting spiritual needs, we therefore need to be clear about what we mean by spirituality. It involves meaning making, a sense of purpose and direction and connectedness. It is therefore closely linked with the M, for Meaning, of *Staying CALM*, and, as we have already seen, there is a close link between meaning and motivation. Motivation can therefore be understood as a spiritual phenomenon in some respects at least.

If we want to understand people at a level above and beyond the dehumanizing and reductionist approaches so common in the human resources and management theory literature, then we need to understand the spiritual dimension. We need to understand people as meaning-making creatures who are seeking to forge a way forward (that is, to develop a sense of purpose and direction) alongside people who are important to us or who may stand in our way (hence the importance of 'connectedness').

This chapter is therefore concerned with how spiritual factors can be extremely significant in shaping how people experience working life and therefore how they respond to it. This raises important implications for people managers, and it would be very unwise not to pay heed to them. The chapter begins with a discussion of the notion of spiritual intelligence and then moves on to look at various ways in which we can attempt to rise to the challenges of spirituality.

Spiritual intelligence

This is a relatively new term; it is parallel with the idea of *emotional* intelligence. The latter term refers to the ability to 'tune in' to emotional issues, to be able to 'read' emotional signals from others and to manage our own feelings effectively (Howe, 2008).

Similarly, we can understand spiritual intelligence to be the ability to tune in to spiritual matters, to be sensitive to how a person's spiritual needs will be very significant in terms of their well-being in general and their work performance and contribution in particular. A spiritually intelligent person is someone who is able to identify circumstances where a person may need some form of spiritual boost (when they are 'in low spirits', for example) or may need to be given some personal space to 'be themselves'.

KEY POINT

The idea of spiritual intelligence, when applied to the workplace, teaches us that it is important for us to recognize that work needs to be meaningful if people are to fulfil their potential.

Once again there is an important link here with motivation. If people cannot find meaning in their work, they are unlikely to be fully committed. If staff see their job as simply a means of earning a living and have little sense of their work being of importance to them beyond that, then they are going to be operating at a level far below the optimum. Helping people to gain some sense of purpose and direction from their working life can be an important leadership role for people managers. A key part of this is identifying goals to aim for, and so we shall return below to the important issue of goal setting as a dimension of spirituality.

Similarly, commitment can be seen to come, in part at least, from a sense of identity – for example, where people identify with their occupation and/or organization in terms of a sense of it reflecting their chosen vocation or profession. Identity can be closely associated with spirituality, in so far as an important part of spirituality is the need to develop a sense of who we are and how we fit into the wider world. Stein (2007) comments on the significance of work in this regard:

> For most people in Western industrialized (and post-industrial) society, work is part of *who* they are as well as *what* they do. It is far more than a job and a paycheck. Work is a central part of the meaning of one's life.
>
> (p. 56)

For Thompson and Moss (2021), spirituality is a matter of what they call our 'chosen worldview'. A key part of this is connectedness. This is a technical term that emphasizes that we are part of a 'human family', as it were, and that it matters to us a great deal who we are connected to and how. We do not exist in a vacuum, unconnected from other human beings. Indeed, an important part of what makes us human is the fact that we share our lives and our efforts with other human beings. Connectedness is a key part of spirituality and also an important factor in terms of teamwork, as we noted in Chapter 14. Marris (2006) writes about searching for new relationships and attachments:

> However we characterize the growing interest in organizational spirituality and community, it is clear that vast numbers of people, from all, walks of life, are searching for new relationships and attachments and for something more in their individual and collective lives. That this yearning is felt in the workplace is no surprise.
>
> (p. 73)

It is therefore important that we aware of the significance of human relationships and their role in developing a spiritual sense of connectedness, and so we will revisit this issue below.

Zohar and Marshall write of 'SQ', which they see as being parallel with the well-established notion of IQ and the more recently established idea of EQ (emotional quotient) which has been proposed as a measure of emotional intelligence. However, I am not sure how useful it is to try and quantify spirituality, as it is largely self-defeating. In the Introduction I was advocating moving away from pseudoscientific, dehumanizing approaches to people management (see also Stewart, 2009), and the notion of spirituality is helpful in this regard, while SQ is not (see also the critique of the 'commodification' of emotional intelligence – which involves turning a useful concept into a marketing device – in Fineman, 2000).

> *Practice focus 20.1*
> Eurig was not particularly keen on attending the one-day course on spirituality that was being offered by his employers, but he thought it would mean a break from his main work role. However, he was surprised to find that it was a very interesting course and one that raised a number of significant issues not only for his work, but also for his personal life. It made him realize that he had allowed himself to treat his work as just a set of routines and had lost sight of the values that led him to take up this type of work in the first place. It also helped him to understand that he could be more effective in his work if he was more tuned in to how the people he worked with were experiencing their spirituality. He had always thought of spirituality as being basically a matter of religion, but now he understood that religion was just one way in which people could express their spirituality. He had never come away from a training course so fired up and wanting to know more about the subject and so keen to put the ideas into practice.

Rising to the challenges of spirituality

Given the importance of spirituality in shaping people's lives (including their working lives), there is much to be gained for people managers in developing their understanding of spirituality and how it can be brought to bear in our efforts to help people achieve their best. There are various ways in which we can make spirituality a fundamental part of our approach to people management. Some of the steps we can take include the following, although this is a far from comprehensive list.

1. *Do not dehumanize people*

I have already commented on more than one occasion in this text about the unfortunate tendency in literature relating to people management for authors to use language that is dehumanizing and which seems to lose sight of the fact that a person's humanity will be a key part of what shapes his or her behaviour, emotional reactions, level of commitment, and so on. We are therefore making a significant mistake if we allow this strong tendency towards dehumanization to influence how we approach people management.

Thankfully, it is not unduly difficult to avoid dehumanization. What it entails is keeping a clear focus on the fact that people are human before they are a resource. Much of what I have written in this manual is geared towards precisely that, recognizing the need for a people-oriented approach to people management. One useful concept is that of 'empathy', which involves being able to see situations from other people's point of view, being able to 'tune in' to their perspective. This is a skill that can be developed over time and is not just a matter of (relatively fixed) personality. We should therefore not be defeatist about the capacity to develop empathy skills (see the discussion above of emotional intelligence).

It is also important to recognize that dehumanization can occur when people become overloaded. They can feel under so much pressure to get the job done that they lose sight of the bigger picture and the people within it.

1. *Pull rather than push*

In my earlier discussions of leadership, I distinguished between traditional management based on command and control mechanisms (*push*) which involve giving people instructions – a very top-down, parental approach to managing people as opposed to the more enlightened approach of *pull* which involves trying to motivate or even inspire people to do their best. This latter approach is firmly associated with the idea of leadership, and we can see important links between spirituality and leadership, especially in terms of self-leadership, another important topic that we have discussed earlier (Gilbert, 2005).

Effective leadership can help to create a sense of security which enables team members to become more confident; much clearer about their (individual and collective) goals and thus having a stronger sense of purpose and direction; a firmer sense of group or team identity; and a much more pronounced sense of 'we are in this together' (connectedness).

Where there is an absence of leadership, by contrast, there may be little sense of clear identity, little sense of belonging, little or no clarity about purpose or direction and no sense of 'we are in this together'. This can lead to low morale and motivation because people's spiritual needs are not being met. This has implications for stress (see Chapter 21), as people who are spiritually impoverished by their experiences of working life rather than enriched by it are likely to be more prone to falling foul of workplace stress. With a diminished level of spirituality, we are far less likely to be resilient and to be able to bounce back from adversity.

It should be clear, then, that leadership can be a key factor in relation to spirituality and people's efforts to find meaning in their work. Good leadership can be a major help, while its absence can be a very significant hindrance. The L, for Leadership, of *Staying CALM* therefore combines well with the M, for Meaning.

2. *Encourage empowerment and self-leadership*
Wherever possible, we should allow people to make their own decisions and to move forward as they see fit. This is because people are more likely to be committed to what they are doing if they have some degree of control over it (see the discussion below of autonomy and mastery). Of course, there have to be reasonable constraints and safeguards, checks and balances as it were, but the more we can focus on giving people greater control over their working circumstances, the more effective they are likely to be. As we shall note in Chapter 21, control is also an important factor when it comes to keeping stress at bay and keeping pressures within manageable limits.

Again, we encounter the central concept of self-leadership. If we are unable to have the insights required to be good leaders of ourselves, then we are unlikely to have what it takes to be a good leader of others. That is, if we are not clear about our own goals and values and so on, then we will struggle to influence our working environment in a positive direction. By contrast, where people are helped and encouraged to be clear about their purpose and direction, to be self-motivated, self-reliant and reasonably independent, they are more likely to be confident and empowered in what they are doing. They are therefore more likely to be motivated and committed, to learn from their experiences and to want to improve.

In view of the significance of these factors, we need to give some careful thought as to how we can promote empowerment and self-leadership. Primary among the steps we can take must be the elimination of any behaviours on our part that encourage dependency (for example, 'backseat driving', which describes the tendency of many people managers to do the decision making for their staff rather than support them in working things out for themselves where possible and appropriate).

3. *Support people in finding meaning in their work*
The idea, first put forward by Taylor (1947), that people are simply cogs in a machine who are being paid to deliver a certain amount of work over a certain period of time is another example of dehumanization. It fails to recognize the important role of meaning in people's lives. As we have already noted, we will not get the best out of people if we fail to recognize their humanity and treat them simply as a means to an end.

If people do not find their work meaningful, then not only will they not achieve their best, but there is also the danger that their actions will be destructive and counterproductive. Furnham and Taylor (2004) give numerous examples of how employees can be involved in behaviours which are harmful to the organization (ranging from petty theft to major sabotage). Collectively such actions can do immense harm to an organization (and therefore, indirectly, to its employees in the longer term). What they can also do is to lower morale and, as we have already made clear, low morale is a very poisonous and highly destructive workplace phenomenon.

Disaffection can soon set in when people are not finding their work satisfying because they are not able to find meaning in what they are doing. If we genuinely want people to achieve their best, then we need to take very seriously the challenge of helping them find meaning in their work. A key aspect of this will be values, as values are an important part of how we create and sustain meaning in our lives in general and in work in particular. What are the values of your organization and/or profession that can help staff to find their work meaningful and thus potentially satisfying? What are the values of individual team members or the team as a whole? How can these be used to make work more meaningful?

This brings us back to the L, for Leadership, of *Staying CALM*. Leaders are called upon to shape the culture of their particular domain or responsibility in a positive direction. So, an important question to ask is: does the culture support making work meaningful or does it alienate people and make them feel disconnected from their work? Clearly an important task for people managers, in their leadership role, is to promote workplace cultures that encourage engagement and commitment and to challenge aspects of cultures that may alienate staff.

4. *Encourage autonomy, mastery and purpose*
These are concepts discussed by Pink (2018) in his work on motivation (see Chapter 15). By promoting these three features we are helping people to meet their spiritual needs, and this will help to prevent the problems that are associated with an impoverishment of spiritual well-being. It is worth exploring each of them in turn:

- *Autonomy.* Simply being told what to do and being given no responsibility for thinking issues through may well suit some people, but we are likely to find that these are not the people who will be achieving their best. Most people are likely to respond positively to having a degree of autonomy, so that they have the potential to take pride in what they do.
- *Mastery.* This relates partly to the subject of control, as discussed above (and which will also feature in Chapter 21) and partly to the idea of skill development. If we feel that we have some degree of control over what we are doing and we are building up important skills, then we are not only likely to be more confident and effective, but also to have a much more positive attitude towards our work, to feel engaged in it rather than alienated from it.
- *Purpose.* Having clarity about what we are trying to achieve is a recipe for not only greater efficiency and effectiveness, but also for feeling more engaged in what we do. It is for this reason that goal setting is so important, but not just any goals will do. As Pink (2018) argues, satisfaction will depend not only on having goals, but on having the right goals. If, for example, the main goal is money, this can lead to a spiral of dissatisfaction, because there is a danger that the more money we make the more we want. The goals we choose need to be spiritual goals, in the sense that they are consistent with our values, our sense of who we are and the direction we want our lives to go in.

Helping staff to achieve some degree of autonomy, mastery and purpose can therefore be seen as an important role for people managers, and is something that needs to be incorporated into our various roles – supervision, work allocation, induction and so on – rather than a separate activity in its own right.

5. *Facilitate connectedness*

Connectedness, the sense of being part of a broader human community, is a central part of spirituality and also an important feature of the workplace. In some ways this is what makes teamwork such an important part of working life (see Chapter 14). This is why C, for Connection, is a key part of *Staying CALM*. There is therefore much to be gained for people managers by facilitating, in whatever reasonable ways we can, a sense of connection and belonging. Team development is the obvious way to do this, but there are also other steps that can be taken in this direction: clarity about organizational values; an inclusive culture (see Chapter 30); and – perhaps most importantly of all – making staff feel valued, supported and appreciated.

This is not an exhaustive list, but it should be sufficient to give a basic understanding of the range of measures that we can adopt to try and make work a meaningful experience, so that being involved in the world of work is spiritually enriching, rather than harmful to a person's sense of who they are, where they are going with their life and how they fit into the wider world. This links with various other chapters in this course. For example, if people are not treated with dignity (by being bullied perhaps) then that too is likely to run counter to their spiritual needs.

Practice focus 20.2
Steph had worked in a team where it was the norm to have an 'awayday' each year for team-building purposes, and she had always found these events very helpful. In her new team, however, there had been no such tradition, but when she suggested the idea at a team meeting, she received a mixed response. Some people, including the team manager, thought it could be useful to clarify team goals and plans, while others thought it would be just a talking shop and a distraction from the team's main work. Despite this the team manager sought permission from the section head to arrange a team-building day. This turned out to be a very wise move, as the day allowed the team members to reaffirm what the team was all about – its goals, its values and its collective identity. Even those who had been less enthusiastic about the idea had to admit that it had been a very positive and helpful day. Steph said to the team manager that she had found it a spiritually fulfilling day: clarifying purpose and direction, reaffirming the team identity and reinforcing a sense of connectedness. 'Yes', replied the team manager, 'I think we were all enriched by pulling together the way we did.

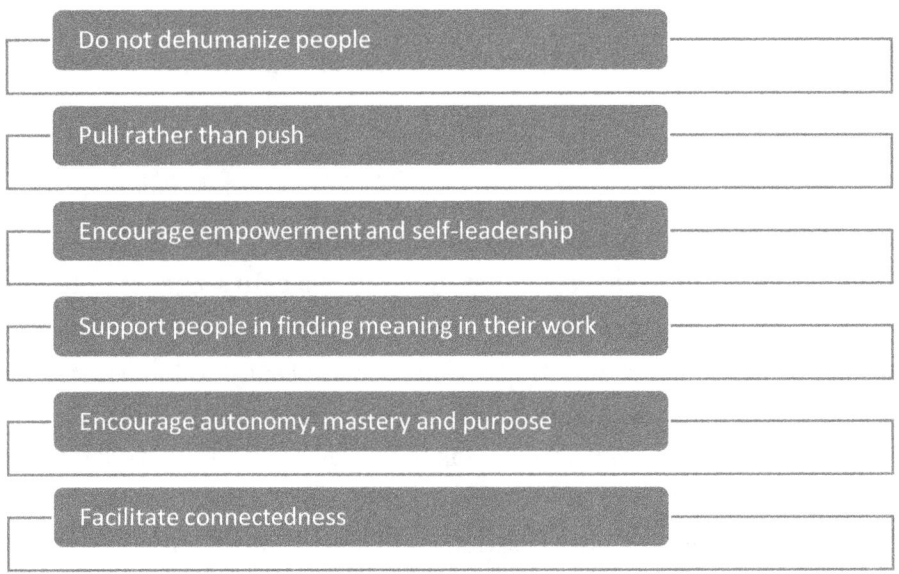

Figure 20.1 Promoting spirituality in the workplace

 Be careful not to underestimate the importance of spirituality. A focus on spirituality can boost morale, well-being, confidence and effectiveness, while a neglect of spiritual needs can contribute to stress, burnout, sickness absence and staff turnover.

Conclusion

It is to be hoped that this discussion has shown that spirituality is a key concept in relation to managing people. However, we also need to recognize that it is often misunderstood, partly because so many people automatically associate it with religion and partly because those who do not associate it with religion do not always appreciate how fundamental spirituality is in shaping a person's sense of who they are and how they fit into the wider world. If we ignore such key issues in our efforts to be good people managers, then we are creating major difficulties for ourselves, and there is a very real danger that we could make the situation worse by actually standing in the way of people meeting their spiritual needs at work.

The focus on spirituality at work is relatively new, but it is now starting to gather momentum as an increasing number of people are recognizing that we cannot simply treat people as cogs in a machine (Allcorn, 2009). To recognize their full humanity means, amongst other things, being clear about the role of spirituality and being at least reasonably well informed about its significance. This chapter has sought to lay a foundation for building up our knowledge of spirituality and the role it plays in helping us all to make sense of our lives by developing a coherent sense of meaning that will help us to guide us through the challenges we face in our lives and those that we face at work in particular.

Points to ponder
1. What is meant by spiritual intelligence and why is it important?
2. What role do empowerment and self-leadership play in producing optimal results?
3. In what ways can 'connectedness' help people find meaning in their work?

Exercise 20
What would you regard as your own spirituality (whether religious or otherwise)? What are the factors that give your life meaning and a sense of purpose and direction? How can you make use of understanding your own spirituality to help others find meaning in their work?

PART III: PROMOTING WELL-BEING

Introduction

We have seen the development in recent years of the significant and justified emphasis on well-being. This is no doubt linked to the growing dissatisfaction with materialism, technology and the pace of modern life (Bauman, 2005). This interest in well-being also applies to the workplace with terms like 'workplace well-being' and 'employee wellness' now being widely used (Bevan and Cooper, 2022).

Well-being is a matter of quality of life. It can be linked to health in various ways, but it should not be equated with it. This is because people can be in very good health, while having a very poor level of well-being, or, conversely, be in relatively ill-health, but still have a high quality of life and therefore well-being. The key principle here is that, if we want employees to achieve their best (so that everyone benefits), we need to address their well-being needs. This means identifying problems that can stand in the way of well-being and developing strategies for solving or alleviating them. Part III therefore discusses a range of workplace problems and potential solutions, recognizing that promoting well-being in this way is an important part of people management for line managers, HR professionals and members of the senior leadership team.

CHAPTER 21: DEALING WITH STRESS

In this chapter you will learn how to recognize, prevent and respond to stress.

Introduction

Stress has come to be recognized as a major problem in the contemporary workplace. There is now a growing body of knowledge which emphasizes how harmful excessive levels of pressure can be. Kinder *et al.* (2008b) point out that:

> The collective cost of stress to US organisations has been estimated at approximately US$ 150 billion a year. In European countries, stress costs the economy an estimated 5-10% of GNP per annum. Studies show that workplace stress was responsible for more long-term sickness absence than any other core factor. With absence come increased workloads, longer working hours, lower morale, increased mistakes and accidents, culminating in reduced productivity.
> (p. 2)

However, it is also sadly a subject that is prone to considerable oversimplification and misunderstanding. This chapter therefore seeks to provide a more accurate understanding of stress and to provide a clear picture of why it is an important topic for people managers to address and to provide a foundation of understanding for beginning to tackle such problems.

We begin by clarifying the important distinction between pressure and stress, then move on to emphasize the importance of support and thereafter pose the key questions of (i) how will we know if someone is stressed?; and (ii) what are our responsibilities? Stress can be extremely destructive for all concerned, and so it is very important that, as people managers, we have a good understanding of stress issues and what we need to do to prevent them from doing so much harm to individuals and organizations.

Pressure and stress

There is an important distinction to be drawn between pressure and stress. Pressure is inevitable, but stress is not. This is because pressure is a neutral term, in the sense that it can be positive or negative. Positive examples of pressure would be situations in which it is at a level where it is stimulating, rewarding, satisfying and motivating. Examples of pressure at levels which produce negative results would be where people feel they are struggling to cope, that work and life more broadly are too difficult for them. It is when pressure gets into these negative areas that we start to use the term stress. Pressure, then, is a neutral term – it can be positive or negative, as I have shown – but stress is always a negative phenomenon. In this sense, it is a problem to be addressed. The idea, then, that 'stress is good for you' reflects an older usage of the term stress, where people distinguished between positive stress and negative stress. The definition of the Health and Safety Executive of stress makes it quite clear that contemporary understandings relate to stress as a problem, a matter of excessive pressure. The UK Health and Safety Executive define stress in the following terms: 'the adverse reaction people have to excessive pressures or other types of demand placed on them'. (https://www.hse.gov.uk/stress/overview.htm)

KEY POINT

It is therefore a mistake to assume that stress is the sign of a weak individual, as everyone will have a limit to how much pressure they can cope with. There is a 'duty of care' on employing organizations to ensure that pressures placed on staff are not excessive and unreasonable. We shall return to this point below.

The emergence of stress depends on a number of factors, including the quality of management support. It is therefore to this question of support that we now turn, as this can make a significant difference in terms of whether pressure crosses the line and becomes stress.

The importance of support

The traditional model of stress is a two-dimensional one in which 'stressors' (the technical term for pressures) and coping methods vie for dominance. Whichever of these two ends up being the stronger will determine whether or not stress is experienced. If coping methods are strong and robust enough to withstand the pressures, stress will not be experienced, but if the pressures overwhelm our coping methods, the result is likely to be stress. Superficially this makes sense, but on closer inspection we soon realize that the problem with this two-dimensional model is that it has the effect of 'blaming the victim'. It individualizes stress and sees it purely as a matter for the individual employee, without recognizing that there is a significant organizational dimension to stress (Thompson, 2019b). If we are not careful, this individualistic (or 'atomistic') approach to stress can result in a vicious circle, because the stigma associated with being seen as a weak, inadequate person who has 'given in' to stress will prevent people from asking for support when they need it. If they do not then receive the support, they are more likely to become stressed, and so the vicious circle begins. If we add the dimension of support to this traditional two-dimensional model to make it a three-dimensional one, we quickly realize that support is indeed a key factor.

Positive, helpful support can make pressures seem more manageable, while poor or non-existent support can accentuate the pressures making them loom large. Similarly with coping methods, positive support can enhance coping methods, whereas poor or non-existent support can undermine coping, especially by undermining confidence. We can therefore see that support has a double effect (positive if present, negative if absent). That is, an absence of support not only fails to improve the situation (by not keeping pressures under control and not boosting existing coping resources), it also tends to make it worse (making pressures loom larger while actually undermining coping methods). It is this doubling effect that can be so significant in fuelling a vicious circle – instead of support making people feel more protected from the harmful effects of stress, its absence (or its poor quality) can make them feel worse. In turn, unsupported staff can feel vulnerable, undervalued and exploited, which can then lead to further stress. Such a vicious circle can be very vicious indeed, in the sense that stress can ruin people's lives and careers (in my work as a consultant I have met many people whose lives have been seriously harmed by the effects of stress and whose career has been ended by it.

Practice focus 21.1
Tina had been reasonably happy in her work and, although it was sometimes a struggle to keep up due to the pressure of work, she had managed to keep on top of things. However, gradually over time her workload increased steadily and she became concerned about whether she would be able to cope. She became quite anxious, which had the effect of reducing her productivity and increasing her error rate. This meant that she was under even more pressure, which in turn made her feel more anxious and therefore less productive. She could feel that the situation was starting to get out of hand, and so she found it difficult to switch off when she was at home, as she was constantly worrying about work matters. This made her feel tired and worn down, which also had the effect of reducing her productivity and increasing her error rate. She felt as though she needed help, but she was too anxious to ask for it, as she feared that she would be labelled as a poor worker, someone who was not strong enough to be able to manage the pressures of the job. Feeling unable to ask for support made her feel trapped, and she started to panic about how much longer she could keep up this level of pressure. The situation was starting to make her feel ill, but she had no idea what she could do to change the situation. She felt as though she had lost control and was very disappointed in herself. She felt as though she had let herself and her team down. This sense of guilt then made her feel even worse and she really could not see any way out of what had become the worst situation she had ever faced in her life.

We therefore need to take the question of support very seriously and this, of course, is where people management becomes a vitally important issue. As people managers we need to be clear about how we can identify stress issues in the first place and what we can and should do to address the concerns associated with stress.

How will I know if someone is stressed?
One of the health and safety obligations on employees is that they need to notify their employers of any factors which may be putting them at undue risk of harm, whether physical risks in the work environment or psychological risks associated with work pressures. This therefore includes stress risks as well as the practical health and safety risks to be discussed in Chapter 24. This means that employees who are stressed (that is, not just under high levels of pressure but under levels of pressure that have become harmful – to health, well-being, competence, relationships and so on) are expected to make this known to their employers.

The technical term for this is 'putting on notice'. That is, an employee is duty bound to put on notice their employer if anything in their environment (including stress factors) is reaching dangerous levels. Therefore, if the system is working effectively, a people manager should know that somebody is stressed because they simply say so. However, this does not take account of two significant factors. One is that the stigma associated with stress can mean that people will very often not raise the issue, as they do not wish to be labelled as weak or inadequate (see Practice focus 21.1). Second, it is very often the case that stress puts people under so much pressure that they lose sight of their responsibilities; they become so engrossed in coping with their excessive pressures that they do not take seriously enough their own health and safety responsibility. It is therefore important that managers are not complacent and leave it to employees to self-report stress, because, in a significant proportion of cases, that simply will not happen.

The ironic fact that stress can actually prevent staff from attending to their own health and safety needs makes it all the more important that, as people managers, we are alert to the dangers of stress. Consequently, it is important for us to be able to tune in to possible indicators of stress. These would include:

- *Changes in behaviour and/or emotional response.* Chief amongst these would be a decline in quality and quantity of work; an increased error rate; someone who is normally calm showing signs of increased irritability; and/or someone whose spirits are normally quite high showing a distinct lowering of mood. However, these and other relevant changes can be very subtle and easily missed if we are not alert to the significance of stress.

- *Signs of distress.* Different people show distress in different ways, of course, but there are enough common themes for the sensitive people manager to be able to identify when somebody is distressed. However, some people can be very stoic and will therefore have developed the skills of hiding signs of distress to a certain extent. Therefore, once again we have to be alert to the possibility of some very subtle indicators that all is not well.
- *Patterns of absence.* Where it becomes apparent that somebody is absent from work more often than it would normally be the case, or there is a significant pattern to the absences (for example, they are absent on specific days when they are called upon to undertake particular difficult tasks), then this may be telling us that there is a stress-related problem beneath the surface.
- *Body language.* Nonverbal communication is generally an important indicator of a person's emotional state and their level of well-being. We therefore have to be sufficiently skilled to be able to read body language effectively, so that we can pick up on anything that seems out of the ordinary, appears to indicate distress, or in any other way is causing alarm bells to ring. We learn the basics of nonverbal communication as part of our upbringing, but there is much to be gained by taking these skills to a more advanced level (Navarro, 2008; Thompson, 2018a).

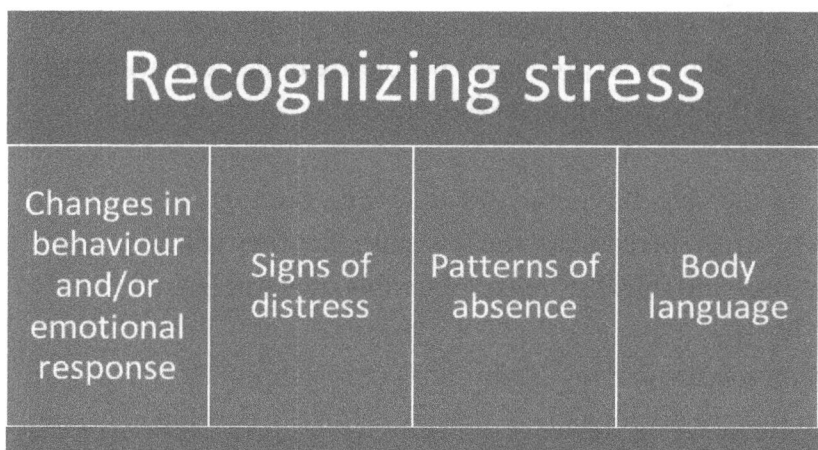

Figure 21.1 Recognizing stress

These are not the only indicators, but should be sufficient to give a picture of the types of signal that people are likely to give off when they are stressed. Of course, it is not simply a matter of reading signals. A good people manager will, where circumstances permit, be in regular discussion with their employees about their work (through supervision, coaching, mentoring, or whatever), and so should have a good idea of whether someone is in a situation where their pressures are excessive.

What are my responsibilities?

As people managers we have a range of responsibilities in relation to stress. The first one is to prevent pressure becoming stress through effective leadership; the appropriate allocation of workload; and, where possible, nipping problems in the bud. This is an important set of duties for people managers to which we need to give close attention. As people managers we also need to take remedial steps when stress becomes apparent. This can include offering support, reducing, stabilizing or controlling workload, making a referral to occupational health and/or confidential counselling services (if the organization concerned has an employee assistance programme offering such opportunities) where appropriate. However, where counselling services do exist, it is important not to see them as a panacea or as an excuse not to adopt other supportive measures.

The UK Health and Safety Executive have developed a set of management standards that can be very useful to provide guidelines for people managers to make sure that they are taking their support duties seriously:

- *Demands* Level and type of workload, patterns of work and the working environment are key factors here. It is important that, as people managers, we are aware of what level of demands (pressures) people are under and whether that is reasonable given their experience, level of education and training, confidence and so on.
- *Control* How much say a person has in the way they carry out their work is also significant. The less control a person has, the less confident they will be about managing their pressures and thus the more vulnerable they will feel – hence making stress more likely.
- *Support* I have already commented on the importance of support. It is therefore extremely important that we do not allow a 'macho' culture to develop in which asking for support is seen as a sign of weakness.
- *Relationships* This reflects the C, for Connection, of *Staying CALM*. This involves making sure, as far as possible, that working relationships are positive and supportive, with conflict managed effectively and any unacceptable behaviours dealt with appropriately.
- *Role* A role is a set of expectations, and there are various ways in which expectations can contribute to stress – for example, when they are unclear, unrealistic and/or conflicting. It is therefore important that we make it clear to

people what is expected of them, keep such expectations within reasonable limits and keep conflicting expectations to a minimum.
- *Change* How change is managed in an organization can be very significant, as poorly managed change can increase pressures substantially. This can mean that even people whose pressures were quite manageable previously are now experiencing stress, and people who were struggling to cope with their previous level of pressure are now in serious difficulties.

(See http://www.hse.gov.uk/stress/standards/index.htm for further details of the management standards approach.)

What can be helpful in ensuring that we address stress issues appropriately so that we are able to meet the challenges involved in the management standards is a three-pronged approach based on the three-dimensional model discussed earlier:

1. *Stressors*. Where is the pressure coming from? What can be done to reduce it to bring it within manageable levels? For example, I have worked with many groups of social workers where much of their work overload has come from receiving poor-quality referrals which then often lead to the social worker wasting valuable time by responding to what turn out to be inappropriate requests (and I suspect that this scenario will apply to many other occupational groups and not just social workers). Clearly, then, in such circumstances, there is much to be gained from being precise about what the sources of pressure are and seeking to do something about stemming them.
2. *Coping methods*. Are these effective? Can they be enhanced? Do new coping methods need to be introduced? Are there any coping methods being used which actually make the situation worse unintentionally? Being clear about what forms of coping are being used and how this situation can be improved in whatever ways possible can potentially make an immense difference when it comes to fending off stress. Often a key part of this is confidence, and so people managers who are skilled in boosting confidence can be particularly helpful in this regard.
3. *Support*. Is the organization doing what it reasonably can in terms of formal support mechanisms? Is there anything that can be done to enhance informal support – for example, through more or better teamwork? Often effective support can be as simple as showing concern and appreciation, emphasizing the human element of human resources. At other times, more complex situations may demand more sophisticated, carefully worked-out forms of support (for example, where the stress may be arising from bullying or discrimination).

Our duties as people managers also include helping to reintegrate staff after a period of absence from work as a result of stress-related illness (see Chapter 23 for a fuller discussion of this topic).

> *Practice focus 21.2*
> Tina had been off sick for almost three months with what was officially diagnosed as 'stress-related debility'. To her colleagues this meant she had had a 'breakdown' because of the stress she was under. They were unsure how to relate to her after this and, consequently, were 'walking on eggshells' and, to a certain extent, keeping their distance from her. Tina was very anxious and unsure about coming back to work, and sensing that her presence was creating tension among the team made her feel even worse. In the first week back she was on 'light duties', but by the second week the work started to build up again. Her supervisor was very friendly towards her and made encouraging comments to her about how good it was to have her back and how much she was valued as a team member. This was helpful in itself, but was not enough on its own. There was no discussion about concrete steps that could be taken to keep the flow of work to manageable levels, no action plan for avoiding the same problems from re-emerging, no real strategy for reintegrating Tina back into her role. This made Tina feel very vulnerable which in turn sapped her confidence, which was already quite low, and increased her anxiety, which was already quite high. The net result of this was that, in the middle of her third week back, her workload started to increase again and she started to panic. By the end of the day was sitting at her desk crying, feeling helpless and totally adrift. The following day she did not return to work. Ten days later, still feeling unable to face returning to work, she tendered her resignation. Her employers were saddened by this, but were also concerned that she may subsequently commence legal proceedings against them (for example, on the grounds of constructive dismissal).

Dewe (2008) provides a helpful guide to making sure we are on track in addressing stress concerns, particularly in terms of avoiding litigation:

- Is the individual subject to undue pressure of work which is:
  - unreasonable by any standard?
  - unreasonable judged in comparison with the workload of others in a similar job? Or
  - due to individual vulnerability, which is known to the employer?
- Has the individual received an injury to health, either physical or psychological, which is directly attributable to stress at work?

- Was this injury reasonably foreseeable by the employer?
- Is this injury directly and mainly attributable to the employer's breach of duty of care, in failing to reduce workplace stress (by providing confidential counselling, redistribution of duties, training etc.)?

(Source: Adapted from Hatton v Sutherland, 2002)

 The best way to avoid litigation is to make sure that workplace well-being is high on the agenda and is taken seriously. This involves making sure that demands on staff are kept within reasonable limits (asking staff to do more than is possible in the circumstances does not benefit anyone) and proper support is provided in dealing with the challenges that the workplace presents to us.

Conclusion

Stress is largely, but not exclusively, a health and safety matter. We will be discussing health and safety issues in Chapter 22, and much of what is covered there in terms of legal requirements will also be relevant to the topic of stress. However, it is important to recognize that stress is not simply a matter of compliance with health and safety regulations. Stress can be an extremely destructive phenomenon. It can wreak havoc in people's lives and can do untold damage to workplaces, particularly if it is allowed to develop into the sort of vicious circle I outlined earlier.

It is important that we realize that stress is not inevitable. There are various ways in which pressures can be kept within manageable limits, and so the topics discussed in many of the other chapters of this manual are also very relevant to keeping pressures within an acceptable range and therefore preventing stress from arising. Consequently, it is important to see stress not as an issue separated from wider people management practice, but rather as an indicator that there is potentially something very seriously awry in terms of people management practices if stress is a significant problem in a particular workplace. Stress can therefore be understood as a form of litmus test of the quality of people management practice in any given organization. Where there is stress (as opposed to pressure, which will occur in any organization, of course), there are warning signs that something is wrong at the human resources level and needs careful attention. Without that careful attention, there is a danger that the situation will get seriously worse. People managers who try and take what they assume to be the easy way out by regarding stress as the sign of a weak individual are taking a very big risk in terms of the adverse consequences that can flow from failing to recognize the social and organizational dimensions of stress as a workplace phenomenon.

Points to ponder
1. What is the difference between pressure and stress and why is it important to make this distinction?
2. In what ways is it possible to know that someone is stressed?
3. What needs to be done to support a member of staff returning from stress-related absence?

Exercise 21
In what ways can you play a part in making sure that staff do not become stressed? What steps can be taken to keep pressures within manageable (and non-harmful) limits?

CHAPTER 22: HEALTH AND SAFETY

In this chapter you will learn about not only meeting health and safety requirements, but also developing a health and safety culture.

Introduction

When it comes to matters of health and safety, organizations have the legal and moral duty to safeguard their employees from undue hazards. It is therefore important for people managers to be aware of such hazards and our responsibilities in respect of them. Duncan *et al.* (2010), commenting on the UK context, highlight the significance of health and safety:

> Every working day, there is on average one death and 361 reported non-fatal injuries to workers. Every year, three quarters of a million people take time off work due to *work-related* illnesses, and as a result, about 30 million work days are lost.
>
> (p. 1, emphasis added)

The workplace is therefore a dangerous place. It presents a number of challenges to us if we are to keep staff (and ourselves) as safe as possible.

Unfortunately, health and safety is a topic prone to extremes, with some people being very lax and complacent, while others may become overcautious, verging on paranoia, and thereby giving health and safety a bad name in the process. This chapter therefore tries to present a more balanced view of health and safety,
so that we can recognize its important in the workplace and to lay down some foundations for developing a fuller understanding of what is involved.

We begin by briefly clarifying the legal basis of health and safety at work before considering what constitutes a hazard and examining some of the key issues relating to, in turn, risk assessment and risk management. Finally, we explore what is involved in developing a culture of health and safety and I emphasize why it is important to do so.

The legal basis of health and safety at work

The UK legal picture with regards to health and safety is a very complex one, with several different acts covering different aspects of the topic. There will also, of course, be different legislation in countries outside the UK. I will therefore not go into detail about specific legal provision, but rather comment on the broad principles and issues.

KEY POINT
At the heart of health and safety legislation is the idea that work inevitably poses certain risks to a person's safety and potentially to their health, but a range of steps can reasonably be taken to keep these risks to a minimum. Legislation places a duty on employing organizations (and their employees) to ensure that such steps are taken as far as reasonably possible.

Where an organization fails to fulfil its legal obligations in this way, it may be open in certain circumstances, to criminal prosecution (as a result of someone being killed due to negligence, for example) and/or civil proceedings whereby injured parties may sue for damages (that is, claim financial compensation). People managers therefore have a responsibility, on behalf of the organization, to make sure that no unnecessary risks are taken and that the risks that do have to be taken are accompanied by appropriate safeguards.

Although legal compliance is clearly an important consideration, I will be arguing below that we need to go beyond this to create and sustain a *culture* of health and safety as part of a commitment to workplace well-being.

What are the hazards?

A central part of promoting health and safety is the ability to recognize hazards and then take the appropriate steps to prevent them from doing harm. In order to try and identify the types of hazards that can lead to significant problems in terms of health and safety, it is useful to divide potential hazards into two categories, physical and psychological. Psychological hazards are linked with, amongst other things, stress, as discussed in Chapter 21, and they are also very relevant in relation to bullying and harassment (Chapter 24), loss, grief and trauma in the workplace (Chapter 27) and mental health problems (Chapter 28). Issues to do with aggression and violence (discussed in Chapter 26) are also significant psychologically, in addition to the physical hazards associated with assault.

Physical hazards can be further subdivided into two categories: general or specific. General hazards are the ones that will apply to more or less any workplace. This involves things like the earthing of electrical equipment, making sure that there are no trailing wires that people can trip over, making sure that wet floors are signposted, and so on. However, there will also be specific hazards, in the sense that some workplaces will present additional dangers due to the specialist nature of that particular setting. For example, some workplaces will use toxic chemicals, in which case there is a need to ensure that proper safeguards are taken to prevent those chemicals from doing significant harm. Similarly, all workplaces carry some risk of aggression or violence, but some will have a much higher risk (police work, for example) and will therefore be a specific concern in certain workplaces. There will also be specific hazards related to specific roles or activities across settings. For example, administrative or secretarial staff can face risks of repetitive strain injury from keyboard use and eye strain from excessive use of computer monitors.

In view of this categorization, it is important that we are aware of what the range of hazards is within our own domain of people management responsibility. Just having a general awareness of the need for vigilance in respect of hazards may not be enough, as not being sufficiently aware of particular hazards in particular circumstances may mean that we are ill prepared to safeguard ourselves and our staff.

The following list of risk factors to consider is far from exhaustive, but it should be sufficient to paint a helpful picture of just how broad the health and safety field is. Each item below is a potential source of danger if not given adequate attention:

- *The work environment:* space; lighting; temperature; ventilation; electrical safety; rest facilities; waste disposal; labelling and signage.
- *Protective equipment (where needed):* guard rails; helmets or other protective clothing; vehicle safety features.
- *Health and hygiene:* toilet and washing facilities; food hygiene; first aid (equipment and suitably trained staff); manual handling/safe methods of lifting; infection control.
- *Fire:* appropriate equipment (extinguishers and/or fire blankets); alarm system; evacuation procedures; appropriate training/briefing re procedures in the event of a fire and how to avoid fires.
- *Well-being*: manageable workloads; dignity at work; protection from aggression and violence; effective conflict resolution; equality and diversity.

My aim, in presenting this list, is to emphasize the importance of recognizing that there are very many potential sources of danger in the workplace and that we therefore need to be alert to the possibility of harm. This is another example of the need for critically reflective practice – having a list to refer to mechanistically is far from adequate; we need to reflect on the situations we encounter and analyse them in terms of potential risk factors. It is for this reason that risk assessment needs to be something ongoing and dynamic, reflecting changes in our working environments, rather than something that can be done once and for all in a static way. It is to this complex issue of risk assessment that we now turn.

Practice focus 22.1
Will was an HR adviser who was given the task of responding to a very critical health and safety inspection. He was asked to speak to the appropriate departmental heads and develop a draft response to the inspector's report. It was basically a process of systematically going through the list of criticisms and, for each one identified, proposing a remedial action to address the particular deficit concerned. In carrying out this task Will was surprised at the variation across departments in terms of attitudes towards, and understanding of, health and safety issues. Some departmental heads seemed to have a good grasp of the issues and felt disappointed that they had been criticized in some respect in the report. Others, by contrast, seemed to regard the matter as a bit of a nuisance and a distraction from 'getting on with the job'. Will had to bite his tongue on more than one occasion, as at times he wanted to say, rather pointedly: 'But making sure everyone is safe is a key part of what the job is all about'. It annoyed him that some people could be so lax about their staff's safety and about potential threats to their health.

Risk assessment

Given that there is such a wide range of potential hazards in the workplace, it is important to ensure that organizations undertake appropriate risk assessments as and when required. In general terms it is no excuse to say that we were not aware of a particular hazard – the expectation is that we should have reviewed the situation carefully to identify likely hazards. It is essential to carry out a risk assessment in relation to our work environment in general and in relation to specific changes or ventures – for example, a school trip, a conference being organized, new equipment being introduced, and so on.

We also need to consider hazards in relation to specific individuals or groups of people. For example, people with disabilities may face additional hazards that non-disabled people are not likely to encounter – consider, for example, a person who is blind or with a significant impairment of sight. Similarly, new or expectant mothers will face risk that other staff will not. In line with our commitment to equality and inclusion (see Chapters 1 and 30), we need to ensure that we identify key risks to *all* employees and not just the majority. It can be very dangerous to think too narrowly about risk issues. Organizations therefore need to be aware of the wide range of risk factors, so that they are in a position to respond as effectively as possible to them and ensure, in the process, that some people's needs for protection from harm are not neglected.

Unfortunately, many organizations seem to think that it is sufficient to draw up a list of the risk factors and simply leave it at that, as if this will somehow make the workplace safer. Of course, the idea of a risk assessment goes far beyond that. The expectation is that, where risks are found to be at an unacceptable level, then appropriate action is taken to address the situation, to bring risks within acceptable limits (see the discussion of risk management below). The very existence of a risk is not necessarily a problem. What matters is how serious the risk is, and that can be seen to apply in at least two main ways: (i) how likely it is that the identified hazard will result in harm; and (ii) how severe any such harm is likely to be.

Of course, no workplace is going to be totally risk free, but there are significant steps that can be taken to ensure that hazards are kept to a minimum, so that people do not face unnecessary risks in their working lives. These steps are precisely what risk management is all about.

Risk management
As we have noted risk situations will change over time, and so risk assessment needs to be a recurring feature of working life, rather than a one-off occurrence. It is therefore fair to say that an important part of risk management needs to be keeping risk on the agenda and ensuring that re-assessment takes place at appropriate intervals or when significant changes occur.

What is also of significance in terms of managing risk is the development of a policy. Of course, a policy in itself will not necessarily make any difference, but it provides a basis of understanding and a framework for staff and managers to work to. In this respect it is a key foundation stone of effective health and safety practice, as a well-written policy will give everyone a clear picture of why health and safety issues are important and worthy of close attention; what is expected of everyone in terms of safeguarding employees and other stakeholders (customers, clients or patients, for example); and what consequences there may be if the policy and related procedures are not adhered to.

Within such a policy there needs to be clarity about recording. It is good practice to keep clear and accurate records of accidents, illnesses or other matters relating to health and safety. An effective policy should be one that gives guidance on what should be recorded and where. This can be of particular importance – indeed, it could be crucial – if there should be any formal proceedings (an employment tribunal, litigation, grievance or disciplinary proceedings) as a result of a health and safety concern or incident. We therefore have to be clear (to ourselves and to our staff) that appropriate recording is essential and not just desirable. The price for not having a clear, accurate and helpful record could be very high indeed in some circumstances.

Training to back this up will also be of value where available. Many organizations provide training at a broad organizational level, while others may offer more specific training to particular staff groups who face a distinctive set of risks – as a result of the use of particular machinery, for example, or perhaps an increased risk of aggression or violence in some quarters. However, it is not uncommon for organizations not to offer training at all and to rely on people learning what they need to as part of their induction. What this variety of provision means, then, is that we need to be aware of what arrangements exist in our organization for learning about health and safety issues, make the best use of what is available and seek to improve the situation where possible.

One thing should be very clear, then: if our organization has a health and safety policy (and it almost certainly will), we will need to be aware of its contents and its implications for us and any people who come within our domain of leadership responsibility. We should also think carefully about how we are going to make sure that the people we are responsible for are aware of what is expected of them and why it is important. Ideally, we should also be looking at how we may possibly improve the policy to make it more effective. This is part of leadership – helping to move things in the right direction rather than just leaving organizational matters to others.

Managing risk effectively also means maintaining the balance mentioned above between being careless and complacent on the one hand and unduly risk averse on the other. This means that health and safety risks need to be constantly on the agenda, but without going to the extreme of allowing a degree of risk paranoia to develop. Maintaining this balance is part of what it means to have a culture of health and safety.

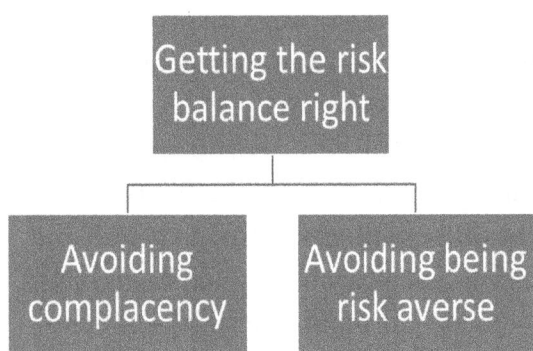

Figure 22.1 Getting the risk balance right

A culture of health and safety
Sadly, many organizations and many people managers tend to regard health and safety as primarily, if not exclusively, a matter of legal compliance. That is, the emphasis is a

defensive one, with the focus being on staying out of trouble: how not to be sued, criticized or complained about.

This defensiveness is fundamentally unhelpful, as it: (i) creates a culture of negativity, presenting health and safety issues as problems to be solved, rather than as opportunities to make the workplace a safer and healthier place (there is a parallel here with equality and diversity issues which, as we noted in Chapter 1, have been prone to being viewed in unnecessarily negative, defensive terms); (ii) marginalizes health and safety as workplace concerns and therefore fails to connect them with the wider (and more positive) workplace well-being agenda; (iii) discourages creativity and innovation with regard to the challenges involved (defensiveness is not a basis for inspiring the imagination!); and (iv) reaffirms an emphasis on systems and procedures and therefore works against the development of genuinely people-oriented workplaces that do justice to (and get the benefits of) the complexities of people, a truly *human* resource.

To move away from a culture of compliance, we need to focus on developing a culture of commitment – a genuine commitment to promoting health and safety for everyone associated with the organization as an aspect of workplace well-being. This brings us back to the A, for Authenticity, of *Staying CALM*. There has to be *authentic* concern for making sure that people stay safe and well, rather than simply a bureaucratic process of ticking boxes to avoid criticism or worse. Where this exists there is a real possibility of developing a culture of health and safety. The word 'culture' is very significant, as it implies that good practice and ongoing concern are the norm, part of everyday routine practices, rather than something that is just given attention from time to time.

Such a culture could develop from (and be sustained by) health and safety:

- Being included in induction, but not in a mechanistic or bureaucratic, compliance-based way;
- Featuring as part of the overall training provision, but again not in a compliance-based way;
- Being discussed in team or staff meetings;
- Being considered when any environmental changes are being planned or implemented;
- Including consideration of psychological risk factors associated with: stress; bullying; conflict; discrimination; grieving; aggression and violence; and other such emotional demands upon us; and

- Incorporating regular, holistic risk assessments that are meaningful and helpful and geared towards genuinely trying to keep everyone safe and well, rather than just defensive tick-box checklists geared towards bureaucratic compliance.

Influencing the development of organizational culture is, as we have already noted, a key part of leadership, and therefore very much in tune with the L of *Staying CALM*. However, the C, for Connection, is also relevant (in so far as health and safety is a *shared* responsibility, shared by employers and employees and therefore something that can bring people together in a spirit of shared endeavour), as is the M, for Meaning (in so far as incorporating a concern for making sure everyone stays safe and well in the dangerous world of the workplace is something that can help make our work experience a more meaningful and fulfilling one).

Literally staying calm is also a wise consideration when it comes to health and safety, as this will help to make sure that we do not follow in the footsteps of some individuals and organizations by overreacting to the inevitable risks of the workplace (but without slipping into dangerous complacency).

Developing a genuine culture of health and safety can be a challenging undertaking, but it is certainly one that repays the time, effort and energy that go into it. It also helps to give a strong, clear and helpful message that well-being issues are being taken seriously in a spirit of developing an authentically people-oriented workplace.

 Beware of the trap of thinking narrowly in terms of legal compliance. Focus more broadly on how you can develop and sustain a *culture* of health and safety.

Practice focus 22.2
Will felt satisfied with the job he had done when he presented his report in response to the health and safety inspection. One thing that had intrigued him was that there was only one department across the whole organization that had not received any criticism from the inspection report. Because he was so curious about why that one department did not feature, he met with the head of that department to ask her about health and safety and her department's approach. He was very glad he did as he learned a great deal from the meeting. He became aware that the department had developed a culture of health and safety based on a commitment to developing a genuinely people-oriented workplace. Caitlin, the head of department, spoke eloquently about how she had instilled a commitment

to well-being in her staff team, as she was a firm believer that failing to take people's well-being needs seriously was a major mistake. To her making sure that staff were safe and well was a foundation stone of a successful department. Will could see that this understanding of health and safety – as a major plank of workplace well-being rather than just a set of regulations to comply with – had produced much better results. He wished he had spoken to Caitlin before completing his report, as he would have wanted to include reference in the report to how much positive difference a culture of health and safety (as part of a culture of well-being) could make.

Conclusion
By way of conclusion, it is worth emphasizing that organizations have what is known technically as 'a duty of care' towards their employees. This means that it is not simply a matter of complying with the legislation in a narrow and precise way. It is just as important that organizations recognize the spirit of the law and, indeed, their ethical responsibilities towards their staff, so that they do not allow unnecessary accidents or other harm which can arise in the workplace. This is why I have emphasized the importance of developing a *culture* of health and well-being.

As we have noted, it has to be recognized that the workplace is a dangerous place, with a high proportion of incidents occurring at work, many of them fatal. Organizations that neglect their health and safety responsibilities are playing a very dangerous game, and so people managers, whether line managers or HR professionals, need to be fully tuned in to their health and safety responsibilities.

Points to ponder
1. In what ways can workplace risks be assessed?
2. What is meant by the 'risk balance' and why is it important to get it right?
3. What do you see as the main elements of a culture of health and safety?

Exercise 22
Why is it important to develop a *culture* of health and safety? What role could you play in developing such a culture?

CHAPTER 23: SICKNESS ABSENCE

In this chapter you will learn how to handle the sensitive matter of sickness absence.

Introduction

There are various reasons why it is important to have a good strategy for managing sickness absence. This can be because of the needs of the organization to be properly staffed and to get value for money in terms of the salary and other costs that are being invested in the employee. But, of course, there are also the needs of the employee concerned to be taken into consideration, their well-being. If sickness absence is not managed effectively, then a bad situation can get worse, sometimes significantly worse. However, there is also the team to consider, in so far as colleagues who are absent on a long-term basis, or who are frequently absent for short periods, can place an undue strain on the rest of the team. There is therefore a strong need for people managers to be sensitive to the challenges associated with managing sickness absence. This can relate to both genuine sickness related to actual physical conditions people are suffering from and what is known colloquially as malingering or swinging the lead – that is, when people are not genuinely ill, but are claiming to be so in order to get unauthorized time off from work. In addition, there is also the more complex area in which there may not be direct physical illness, but where it is not simply a case of malingering either – for example, when someone is stressed or distressed for whatever reason.

There are various causes of sickness absence, but, as Russell (2008) has commented:

> The chief causes of long term absence were stress, anxiety, depression and back pain. The figures remain roughly the same from year to year and don't disclose any real surprises. The main area of change in recent years has been a steady growth in figures relating to stress, anxiety and depression.
>
> (p. 3)

KEY POINT

Given the combined effect of physical and psychological causes of sickness absence, the topic is clearly not something to be taken lightly. Poor handling of situations involving sickness can prove very costly in both financial and human terms.

This chapter provides an overview of the people management responsibilities relating to sickness absence and considers the importance of being aware of relevant policies and procedures.

Our responsibilities

Of course, illness is an inevitable feature of working life, and so people managers need to be clear about the challenges involved and the responsibilities associated with them. In Chapter 22, in relation to health and safety, the concept of duty of care was introduced. This can also be seen to apply towards a member of staff who is ill or otherwise incapacitated and unable to attend work as normal. That duty of care can take various forms, but much of it has to do with good leadership, in the sense of ensuring that people feel valued rather than exploited. However, it is not only the L of *Staying CALM* that applies, but also the A, for Authenticity, in the sense that, if people managers see people who are genuinely ill as a nuisance and an additional problem for them to solve, without any genuine understanding of, or commitment to, their well-being, then their credibility as leaders is likely to be seriously undermined, if not totally destroyed. Good practice in people management is therefore premised on being sensitive to people's difficult situations.

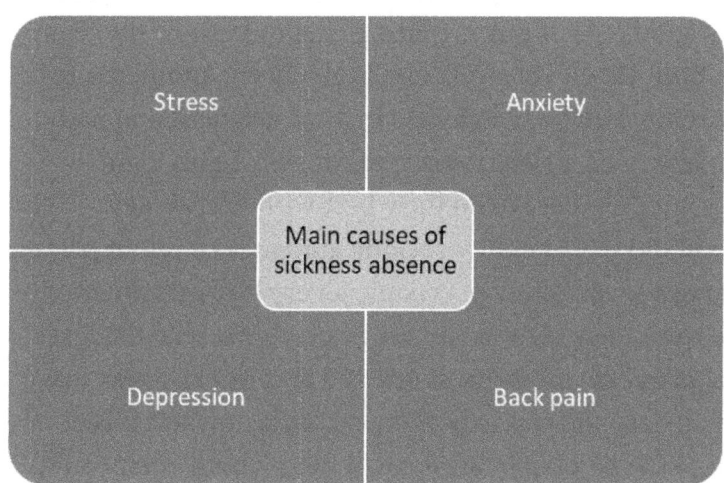

Figure 23.1 The main causes of sickness absence

To be fair to the team and to other organizational stakeholders, it is also important that the duties of the absent colleague are covered to a minimal level at least. In this way it is being ensured that people do not lose out as a result of sickness absence of a colleague – for example, in situations where one person cannot do what they need to do because someone else is off sick and no one covered for them. This can create a 'knock-on' effect of frustration. Person A cannot make progress with their work until Person B has completed their part of the process, but Person B is on sick leave and there is no Person C who is ensuring that this important activity is done to prevent Person A from being able to do what they need to. Of course, in most work settings it would not be possible for all the tasks of an absent colleague to be completed in their absence, but some degree of prioritizing tasks to ensure that the most important get done is a wise move.

Similarly, it is important to make sure that other staff are not overloaded, because one or more colleagues is on sick leave. What can happen in some circumstances, which can be a very difficult and challenging situation to deal with, is that the absence of one colleague puts undue pressure on the rest of the team which can then lead to the sickness absence of another colleague (perhaps due to stress), and then a form of domino effect can occur whereby the increasing pressures on remaining team members can actually increase the number of people who are absent on sick leave at any one time. It is therefore very important that people managers take the necessary steps to prevent the mishandling of sickness absence from producing this very destructive sequence of events.

Practice focus 23.1
Sam was concerned to hear that Tim, one of the most experienced members of the team, had been diagnosed with a brain tumour and would not be back in work for the foreseeable future. The other five members of the team worried about how they would cope without him. Sam encouraged them to do their best without him but did not offer any specific guidance or put in place any plan for how the team could best manage the situation. Next came the news that Olwen, another very experienced member of the team, had been involved in a car accident and had broken her wrist. She was likely to be absent for several weeks. Again, Sam encouraged the remaining team members to do their best without two key members of the team, but still did not offer any specific guidance or put in place a plan for how they could manage what had now become a very difficult situation – four people trying to do the work of six. It was not long before, Marcia, the least experienced member of the team became quite distressed and went on sick leave as a result of the stress and anxiety she was experiencing. This now left three people doing the work of six, with no plan or strategy in place about what could be done differently or what could safely be left until staffing levels were more realistic. The remaining team members were very disappointed at Sam's apparent inaction and failure to 'get hold of' the situation. With trust and credibility at an all-time low, Sam eventually spoke to the team about the need to look carefully at what needed to be done to get through their current immense difficulties. The three team members still left standing wondered whether this was a case of better late than never or too little too late.

One further consideration in relation to absent staff and workload is the need to prevent the potentially quite stressful situation of someone who has been quite ill and is perhaps still quite weak and not fully recovered coming back to work to find a huge backlog, and no arrangements in place to support them with this. Sadly, in my role as a consultant, I have come across this scenario a number of times, and the net result is often a further period of (stress-related) sickness absence, which can then mean an even steeper uphill climb to come back to work next time (see Chapter 21 for a discussion of returning to work after a period of stress-related absence).

Where there are issues relating to long-term sickness, it may be necessary to explore other options. The most extreme option is retirement on health grounds, but, while that should not be a first option, it is something that may need to be considered in some circumstances for some people. A less extreme option is to consider transferring the person concerned to a less demanding job, or one better suited to their diminished capacities, if there is something appropriate available. This is because, while some forms of sickness make it impossible for people to do any work at all, there are some conditions which will allow a certain degree of work to be done, provided that it is not too demanding. This can therefore be one potential solution in the right circumstances. However, it is important to emphasize 'in the right circumstances', as to use this as a general rule for sickness absence could be potentially disastrous, in so far as it could mean people who are too ill or incapacitated to do any work are being expected to contribute to the organization at a lower level than usual, rather than being given the necessary time and space to recover and recuperate.

When it comes to sickness absence, there is also the challenging of addressing dishonesty to take into account. Where there are suspicious absences, or where other information comes to light to suggest that somebody is not genuinely ill, then there is a need for people managers to take this very seriously. This is partly for ethical reasons about not allowing people to take advantage of the organization, and therefore of their colleagues, but partly because there is also the reputational dimension to consider. This is a matter of recognizing that a leader who is perceived as not dealing with such problems will be seen as a weak and inadequate leader and will not inspire the confidence or develop the credibility and sense of security that are important foundations of effective leadership. Someone who is perceived to 'chicken out' of dealing with challenging issues will be afforded little trust or credibility, which in turn will make it more difficult for them to carry out their duties as people managers.

Ultimately, there is no need for people managers to avoid tackling the thorny issue of dishonest absences from work, provided that we have the assertiveness skills to be able to address the issues without being unnecessarily confrontational at one extreme and too lax and 'a pushover' at the other. If the message we are (unintentionally) giving staff through our attitude and approach to such matters is that we will not address any concerns about dishonest absences, then we are contributing to a culture of unauthorized absences by allowing staff to assume that such matters will not be addressed. By contrast, where staff know that suspicious absences (or patterns of absence) will be investigated – fairly but thoroughly – then they will be less likely to 'try it on'. This has the added bonus that those honest staff who would never dream of cheating are likely to have far more faith in, and support for, a leader who does not allow dishonesty to feature in that particular work setting.

In between the two extremes of genuine illness and outright dishonesty or malingering, is the more complex set of circumstances relating to situations where someone is struggling to maintain their attendance at work. This can be for a variety of reasons, not least the following:

- *Caring responsibilities.* This could be in relation to a sick or disabled child or to an elderly or disabled relative who places caring demands on an employee. This could apply on a short-term basis (where someone who has a parent who is currently unwell but who will get better before too long), but could also be a longer-term matter (for example, where someone is caring for someone who is chronically ill and/or severely disabled). In some areas there are carer support schemes that can be helpful, and so it can be useful to know what sort of support is available for people in these circumstances. What can also be helpful is to discuss the situation openly with the staff concerned. Often people in carer roles who are also trying to hold down a job will be under immense pressure, and in such circumstances, it is not unusual for people to try and 'soldier on' stoically, rather than engage in a constructive dialogue about what the possible ways forward are. The introduction of flexible working arrangements in many organizations has allowed some staff with caring responsibilities to be able to manage their work responsibilities without any unauthorized absences.
- *Grieving.* It is often the case, especially in the early stages of recovering from a major loss, that people struggle to deal with their life demands generally, including the work aspects. There is therefore a need to handle such matters very sensitively. We do not need to be experts in the subject of loss and grief, but we do need to have at least a basic understanding of what is happening to grieving colleagues if we are to be able to support them adequately (see Chapter 27). There is a difficult balance to be struck in terms of grieving staff returning to work. On the one hand, it can be harmful and counterproductive to put too much pressure on people too soon (the idea that all that is needed is a few days' compassionate leave to tide grieving staff over until the funeral is out of the way is a dangerously inaccurate one – but sadly not an uncommon one), but on the other, returning to work, establishing as much of a sense of normality as possible and getting the social support of understanding colleagues can also be very helpful at times. We need to be able to talk about such matters with the grieving individual concerned and sensitively gauge their views (Thompson, 2022). A

'walking on eggshells' approach that involves keeping our distance from grieving staff can be highly ineffective and even counterproductive.

- *Conflict.* Sometimes there is so much conflict at work with one or more people that one of the persons concerned finds it difficult to face coming into work. Conflict can make people feel physically ill because of the tensions involved, and this can then be the basis for which a member of staff seeks sick leave. There is therefore considerable mileage in being able to recognize conflict in the early stages and have the courage to 'nip things in the bud', rather than allow them to smoulder or fester (see Chapter 25). If we become aware that someone is missing a lot of work and we are not convinced they are ill, then the fact that they may be avoiding the tensions associated with conflict is certainly something we should consider as a possible reason (or at least a contributory factor alongside other reasons), and therefore something that we would need to address in order to find a solution and a way forward.
- *Addiction problems.* Where people have a dependency problem relating to alcohol or drugs, they may find it difficult to be available for work at the times when they are expected to be. This is an important topic that is discussed in more detail in Chapter 29, but for now we should note that such problems are generally more common than people tend to realize, and so we should be wary of the danger of missing warning signs.
- *Moonlighting.* Some people may have an additional part-time job or another way of earning money (for example, running a small-scale business) – whether or not this is permitted within the terms and conditions of their current employment contract – and this may mean that, at times, there is a clash between their main employment duties and their secondary employment, with the result being that they try to take time off which they are not entitled to by claiming to be ill. If secondary employment is not allowed, then this potentially becomes a disciplinary matter (see Chapter 9). If, however, secondary employment is permitted, then looking at the effective use of flexible working may well be a helpful way forward.
- *Capability.* It may be the case that, in some circumstances, people are absenting themselves from work because they are struggling to meet the demands of their particular job. If they do not have the necessary knowledge, skills or confidence to carry out their duties effectively, they may struggle to get through the working day, and may therefore take every opportunity to be absent from work. Clearly, this is a matter that would need to be addressed through supervision (and possibly through training and/or coaching).

There is clearly, therefore, a wide range of possible reasons for people being absent which do not fall neatly into either the genuine illness or unethical malingering categories. These can be complex and sensitive issues to deal with, and so it is important that we give them our full attention and seek the necessary advice and support where necessary.

Policies and procedures

It is, of course, important to be familiar with the policies and procedures of the organization concerned, as there is considerable variation from place to place. The key elements are likely to be the following:

Reporting procedures

What is expected of people who are not attending work? Who should they report this to? Do they need to do this themselves or is it acceptable for someone to do this on their behalf? These are issues that will vary from organization to organization, policy to policy.

What level of absence triggers a formal response?

In some organizations there is a fixed number. As soon as someone has been absent for X number of days, then the people managers involved are expected to institute the sickness absence procedures. In many other workplaces, there is no fixed number, but the expectation is that managers should be aware of any potential problems and commence the appropriate proceedings when necessary.

Return to work interviews

These are now widely used by a broad range of organizations to help people to reintegrate into the workplace. They are particularly important when an absence has been stress related. The interview can be very useful in terms of identifying where the pressures were coming from and what can be done in terms of coping methods and support to ensure that pressures remain within manageable limits.

The importance of record keeping

There is an obligation to keep appropriate records, especially if deception is suspected, as such information may be necessary in relation to future disciplinary proceedings. This echoes the point made in Chapter 22 about the importance of effective record keeping in relation to health and safety.

The importance of following procedures to the letter

There is a very real danger that, if procedures are not followed strictly, there will be subsequent allegations of discrimination. As Russell (2008) comments:

Tackling absence isn't always straightforward. Absences come in many different forms, may be of varying durations and come about for a variety of reasons. Employers have to develop a range of proportionate responses. There is no one 'right' way of going about it, but any actions you take must always be fair and reasonable. Remember that inappropriate or discriminatory action can lead to expensive legal settlements.

(pp. xviii-xviii)

There is also the importance of dealing with any situations that involve deception. If there is an absence of appropriate records, then it may not be possible to take any formal action to deal with people who are abusing the organization's trust by absenting themselves without good reason.

It is understandable that busy people managers may be tempted to rush when dealing with sickness absence matters and therefore do little or nothing in terms of record keeping. This is likely to prove to be a major mistake if things get more complicated further down the line.

Practice focus 23.2
Kieran had been away from work for over two months as a result of complications following a minor operation. He had become very anxious about what had been happening in his absence and whether he would be able to cope after being out of action for so long. He therefore welcomed the opportunity to have a return to work interview with Marie. She had never done one before, so she prepared very thoroughly for it and sought a lot of advice from more experienced colleagues. This preparation paid off, as the interview went really well. She managed to put Kieran at his ease, even though he was very nervous. For his part Kieran was delighted, as the interview had allowed him not only to talk about his fears and concerns, but also to outline a plan for his return to work, with a gradual build up of responsibilities, rather than being thrown in at the deep end. He felt so much better after the meeting and was now feeling far more confident about his return to work, and he knew that the meeting, because it was so well handled, would make it far more likely that his return would be a successful one.

It is not expected that people managers should be experts in the relevant policies and procedures, but we do have to have at least a basic awareness and be prepared to follow those procedures precisely when we are called upon to do so.

Conclusion

It is important to bear in mind that sickness absence can arise for a range of reasons – genuine sickness, malingering or other matters which could be related to the workplace (conflict or bullying, for example) or outside of it (carer responsibilities). Whatever the cause of the sickness absence, the fact that somebody is not available for work raises significant issues in terms of how people managers need to deal with the situation. The causes of the absence are, though, none the less important, in so far as the reason for the absence will, to a certain extent, determine how we should respond. What we should not do is simply see sickness absence as a general category, without being aware of the subtle differences involved, depending on the type of absence and the different reasons for it. Overall, though, there is a very real challenge for people managers to be able to deal with sickness absence sensitively and constructively.

Points to ponder
1. What are the main causes of sickness absence?
2. Why is it important to have reporting procedures?
3. Why is it essential to follow sickness absence policies to the letter?

Exercise 23
How confident do you feel in dealing with sickness absence matters? What would help you to feel more confident? Who could you rely on for appropriate support?

CHAPTER 24: BULLYING AND HARASSMENT

In this chapter you will learn about the importance of dignity at work by ensuring that bullying and harassment are not tolerated.

Introduction

The notion of 'dignity at work' is one that has become firmly rooted in the modern world of work. It has arisen largely in response to significant concerns about bullying and harassment in the workplace and related problems.

In view of this, effective people management requires us to do everything that we reasonably can to prevent bullying and harassment from occurring in the first place and to respond sensitively and supportively if or when it does arise. This can be seen to be part of our commitment to developing genuinely people-focused organizations. If we neglect this aspect of our duties, we will be failing in our efforts to get the best out of people, as staff who are being bullied or harassed are highly unlikely to achieve their best. In many situations, the existence of these problems will also stop other staff, not directly affected, from achieving their best because of the tensions, ill-feeling and resentment involved.

Bullying and harassment can do immense damage to individuals (and their families), to teams and groups of staff, as well as to the organization as a whole. They are therefore clearly behaviours that we cannot tolerate in a workplace that takes seriously the notion of dignity at work. Einarsen and Hoel (2008) highlight the significance of the problem:

> Studies have indicated that as many as 30% of the working population are exposed to some kind of mistreatment at work (Raynor, Hoel & Cooper, 2002), with more than 10% labelling themselves as victims of bullying (Hoel, Cooper & Faragher, 2001). Bullying is prevalent in both private and public organisations and finds its targets among men and women alike. It occurs on all organizational levels, with female managers as a particular risk group (Hoel *et al.*, 2001). Furthermore, bullying may have overwhelming negative effects on the health and well-being of targets as well as bystanders, causing organisational problems such as absenteeism, turnover and loss of job satisfaction. For targets, exposure to bullying can cause severe emotional reactions such as fear, anxiety, helplessness, depression and trauma, altering their perceptions of the work environment to one of threat and insecurity.
>
> (p. 161)

Given the extent and negative impact of these problems, this chapter explores: (i) what is involved in preventing bullying and harassment from occurring; and (ii) dealing with it appropriately if or when it should arise. We begin by exploring what is meant by bullying and harassment before focusing on what our responsibilities are and, finally, why it is important to work towards a culture of dignity if we do not already have one in place.

What are bullying and harassment?

Bullying and harassment have certain things in common with one another, in so far as they can both be understood as affronts to dignity. They both involve people being treated badly, generally by people more powerful than themselves. Indeed, power is also a common theme linking the two, as both involve the unwitting misuse or deliberate abuse of power. The net result of this is people on the receiving end of such behaviour are demeaned and treated disrespectfully, hence the emphasis on 'dignity at work' (Bolton and Houlihan, 2007).

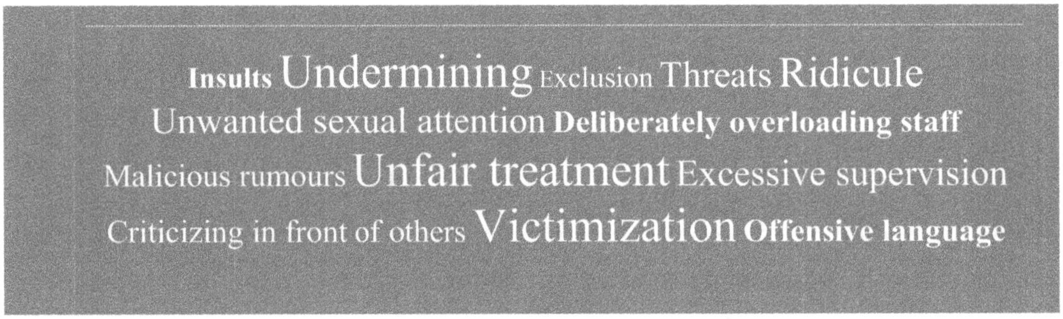

> Insults Undermining Exclusion Threats Ridicule
> Unwanted sexual attention Deliberately overloading staff
> Malicious rumours Unfair treatment Excessive supervision
> Criticizing in front of others Victimization Offensive language

Figure 24.1 Unacceptable behaviours in the workplace

In terms of differences between the two, bullying tends to refer to actions against individuals for mainly individual reasons related to the person and the circumstances, whereas harassment tends to have more of a social dimension to it, in the sense that it is generally members of particular groups that are harassed (for example, sexual, racial or disability harassment).

Bullying and harassment can manifest themselves in various ways. These are illustrated in Figure 24.1, which shows just how many behaviours can be used to demean colleagues and undermine their dignity.

While it is clearly the case that some of these forms of bullying or harassment are clearly visible and unmistakeable, it is also very important to be aware that some other forms of bullying and harassment can be quite subtle and insidious, and therefore far from obvious. Both types are none the less very harmful. We therefore have to have at least a reasonably good understanding of bullying and harassment to be able to detect possible concerns. If we rely on the simplistic assumption that we will easily know bullying and harassment when we see it, we may actually be missing some very subtle (and very destructive) processes that are taking place and thereby failing to protect people from the major harm such processes can do.

> *Practice focus 24.1*
> Denise had worked with a number of managers over the years and had never had any major problems with any of them, although they did vary significantly in terms of how helpful they were to her. However, her current manager, Ray, was proving to be quite a problem for her. Although he never came out and openly criticized her, he seemed to be constantly undermining her. He never gave her any praise or acknowledged how well she was doing or how hard she was working, but he would frequently make comments that made her feel she was inadequate, that she was somehow falling below his expectations. She watched how he related to other staff and noticed a very different pattern. He gave other team members praise and did not seem to undermine them. Why, she wondered, does he seem to treat me differently from everyone else? The only reason she could think of was that she was the only woman in the team. Ray showed no other signs of being overtly sexist, but Denise wondered whether this was at the heart of it. Whatever the underlying reasons, Denise was being very adversely affected by the situation. He confidence had dropped, her enthusiasm for the job was waning and she feared that this decline in her performance would give ray more ammunition to subtly and slyly express his disapproval of her work and of her as a person. What was especially sad about the situation was that she felt so 'hemmed in' by the way he was treating her that she was not sure she would have the will to do anything about the situation – especially as the bullying would not be obvious to other people and she felt she may struggle to convince others of what was going on. She was starting to feel hopeless and helpless, a common experience on the part of people who are being bullied.

What are our responsibilities?

At the very least we need to treat staff with dignity at all times. That is, we need to make sure that we are not open to accusations of being a bully or a harasser in our own right. That, of course, should not be a problem if we are taking on board the messages from the various chapters of this manual, and the manual as a whole, in terms of the importance of a people-centred approach to the workplace. However, it is perfectly possible – and not uncommon – for people mangers to engage in bullying without realizing that they are doing so. For example, in Practice focus 24.1, Ray may well have been totally oblivious to what he was doing in terms of treating Denise less favourably than other staff. The dynamics of bullying can be very subtle as well as very complex. We therefore need to make sure that we are not being defensively complacent and give careful consideration to whether any aspect of our behaviour towards staff could be experienced by them as undermining of their dignity.

Beyond this, it is also important to make it clear to all staff that there is a very strong expectation that they must treat each other with dignity. This involves creating a culture of respect in which unacceptable forms of behaviour are not tolerated. Better still, the culture of respect should be so strong that such incidences do not occur in the first place (see the discussion below of the importance of developing a culture of dignity). One important aspect of this is the use of humour. While there is certainly nothing wrong with humour in itself, of course, we need to be aware that a great deal of bullying takes place through the medium of humour. What is 'just a joke' to one person may be confidence-sapping ridicule that undermines dignity to the person on the receiving end. We therefore need to have a degree of sensitivity towards the potential for humour to cross the line from harmless fun to harmful bullying.

It is also important that people managers are able to manage conflict effectively. This is because, at times, conflict can spill over into bullying or harassment. Where there is a degree of enmity between two or more people in a workplace this can produce some very harmful interactions, with the result that one or more of them engages in bullying tactics. There is therefore a need to have at least the basic skills and confidence required for effective conflict management (see Chapter 25). Conflict is a topic that we can relate to the C, for Connection, of *Staying CALM*. Conflict is a matter of how we relate to one another, and the challenge of managing conflict is to ensure that how we relate to one another is positive and constructive, despite any differences or disagreement between us. Where conflict is not so well handled, the result can be one person using the undermining of another person's dignity as a 'weapon of war'. At times, this can be more than a one-way problem, in the sense that two or more people may be undermining each other's dignity, each abusing their power in relation to their colleague(s).

The culture of the workplace is also important in terms of valuing diversity. If a culture which genuinely does value diversity has developed (or is in the process of being developed), and it is one that is for real and not just a slogan, then that culture can be a helpful significant obstacle to the emergence of any harassment relating to race, gender, disability, and so on. A key part of valuing diversity is valuing people for what they bring, including any differences. Bullying and harassment are often the opposite of this, in so far as they involve picking up on differences and using them against the person concerned (or group of people) in one or more ways.

Where it does become apparent that bullying or harassment is taking place, it is clearly important to provide appropriate support for the people on the receiving end. As we have noted, bullying and harassment can have devastating effects on people. This can be in terms of their well-being, their ability to do their job and even their health. In this respect, bullying and harassment can be seen as an aspect of our health and safety responsibilities as people managers (see Chapter 22), in so far as a great deal of stress is due, in whole or in part, to bullying and harassment.

Where allegations are made, it is essential that these are investigated thoroughly and sensitively. However, it is important that we check the specific procedures of the organization concerned to establish who is expected to carry this out. In some organizations, it will fall to the line manager. In others, the expectation is that this is a role for either a line manager from outside that particular team or division or a representative of the human resources team or department. In yet other organizations, depending on the seriousness of the allegations, an independent investigator with suitable skills and expertise may be brought in. Whichever process is adopted, it is important that the situation is handled very carefully, as a badly handled investigation can exacerbate the situation significantly, potentially upsetting a wide range of people: the alleged bully or harasser, the alleged victim and members of the wider team or organization.

> *Practice focus 24.2*
> When the new dignity at work policy was implemented, the manager who had been appointed to coordinate the scheme was amazed to receive seven allegations of bullying on the very first day – and all the allegations related to the same person, a team manager. It was decided that, given the seriousness of the allegations, it would be wise to commission an independent investigator to try to get to the bottom of the matter and reach a satisfactory conclusion. The investigator interviewed all the current members of the team plus two of the seven complainants who had already left the team. After forming a view of the situation based on these interviews, the investigator then interviewed the team manager and sought her views about the situation and the concerns that had been raised. The picture that emerged was that the team manager had originally had a team of very experienced and highly competent staff. But, steadily over about a year the old team broke up as individuals moved on to other posts, several of them being promoted. Every time an experienced member of staff moved on, they were replaced by a newly qualified worker straight from university. This required the team manager to lower her expectations somewhat and be supportive in helping the new, less experienced member to build up their knowledge, skills and confidence. However, she did not do this, and continued to expect the same quality

and quantity of work as she had received from much more experienced colleagues in the past. This made her very frustrated, and sadly she would then take out her frustrations on the new team member and treat them very disrespectfully, like an angry parent scolding a naughty child. This led to some new staff quickly moving on to other posts, as they felt that they needed more support than they were receiving. Each time a member of staff moved on another newly qualified worker would join the team, and the process would start all over again. In the interview with her, the investigator was able to help her understand that this was not appropriate, and – to her credit – she acknowledged that she had let her own feelings of insecurity about the break up of such a good team get the better of her, and had not been sufficiently sensitive to the needs of newly qualified staff joining an established, but changing, team.

Promoting a culture of dignity

In Chapter 22 I emphasized the importance of trying to develop a culture of health and safety, rather than rely on simply trying to comply with policy and legislation in a spirit of defensiveness. Much the same can be argued in relation to tackling problems of bullying and harassment by making concerted efforts to develop a culture premised on promoting dignity for all.

Developing a new culture is a complex matter that can take a great deal of time and effort, but the distinct benefits should make it worthwhile. The following elements can usefully be included in any culture change efforts.

Equality, diversity and inclusion

If we are taking equality and diversity (as discussed in Chapter 1) and inclusion (to be discussed in Chapter 30) seriously, then we should be making sure that everyone is treated fairly and no one is excluded. This will then give the 'bonus' effect of helping to prevent bullying and harassment. Similarly, not tolerating bullying or harassment is an important contribution to developing and sustaining a culture of equality, diversity and inclusion.

Miller and Katz (2002) provide a helpful picture of how these two aspects of people management can combine effectively in relation to gender equality when they argue that:

> Although many organizations have done a good job of developing formal policies and practices to address overt sexual harassment, the new baseline seeks to identify and eliminate the more subtle forms of harassment. It focuses not only on what *not* to do, but also on creating a new set of inclusive behaviours that enable women and men to partner effectively across genders.
>
> (p. 86)

There is therefore much to be gained from linking a commitment to dignity at work to a commitment to fairness, valuing of difference and inclusion.

Use of language
Unfortunately, issues of language use have tended to be oversimplified, resulting in very superficial 'political correctness' approaches to the topic that do not do justice to the complexities involved (Thompson, 2018a). However, it is important to recognize that language use can be highly significant in shaping not only interactions between people, but also cultural patterns (cultures are sets of habits, taken-for-granted assumptions and unwritten rules, and so language will play a key role in relation to these). In the same way that language use will have contributed to the present culture, so too can it be used to change cultural assumptions. This is not a simple ('PC') matter of banning certain words and preferring others. What is required is a much more sophisticated understanding of how language works and a more sophisticated plan for influencing language use. For example, it can be helpful to have a discussion at a team or staff meeting about the importance of language in safeguarding dignity at work and identifying any forms of language that may need to change in order to promote inclusion and fairness. Prior to this it can be helpful to listen carefully to forms of language commonly used and identify which ones, if any, run counter to the idea of dignity. This understanding can then be fed back to the team or staff group to aid discussion and reflection. It is likely that the forms of language you identify as counterproductive in relation to dignity are those which exclude or marginalize; stereotype; demean or 'put down'; and/or dehumanize.

Constructive disagreement
As we will see in Chapter 25, conflict is an inevitable part of the workplace, but it does not have to be a problem. People can learn how to work effectively together even if they strongly disagree with one another – it is a case of being expected to handle such conflicts in ways that continue to show respect to one another. Disagreeing with someone is, of course, no excuse for treating them disrespectfully.

An important factor here is open communication. People managers can use their leadership skills to develop a culture characterized by open communication. This will help to prevent conflicts from 'going underground' and then surfacing inappropriately at times – for example, when tensions are high.

Positive humour
The point was made earlier that humour can be used to ridicule and thus to bully or harass. However, this is not to say that there is no room for humour, as it can have a very positive effect in terms of teamwork and morale. What is important is to ensure that humour is used positively (to ease tension, to promote a sense of camaraderie, to raise spirits) and

not allowed to cross a line and become destructive. Much humour (often called banter) involves friendly insults, and these can be entirely appropriate provided that (i) the same person or group of people are not being picked on consistently (to the point where it becomes victimization); (ii) it does not become too strong a feature of the workplace (to the point where some people feel very uncomfortable about it); and (iii) there is no element of cruelty involved (boundaries of acceptability have to be recognized – it cannot be an 'anything goes' culture that is justified by an 'it was just a joke' mentality).

Clear expectations
Do staff know what is expected of them in terms of treating one another (and others outside their staff group) with dignity? Are they clear about what the boundaries of acceptability are? To make sure that the answer to both these questions is yes, we may need to discuss the issues at a staff or team meeting or even arrange training. These expectations can also usefully be included in any team philosophy documents or equivalents where they exist (or can be a good reason for developing such a document if one does not already exist).

Explicit values
Many organizations make their values explicit as part of their strategic plan. However, many do not and even those that do may express them at such a level of abstraction that they have little meaning for most staff. Making explicit a team or staff group's values can therefore be a useful exercise in spelling out, for example, a commitment to everyone being treated with dignity.

Effective leadership
I have deliberately left this until last, as it sums up much of the message I have been putting across in this chapter: preventing bullying and harassment will largely depend on having a culture of dignity at work and having such a culture will depend to a large extent on effective leadership – having one or more leaders who are able to influence the culture in a positive direction.

It is important not to be complacent about bullying and harassment. The 'Oh, it wouldn't happen here' attitude is a highly risk one, as these damaging phenomena are much more common than is generally recognized and no organization is immune.

Conclusion
Sadly, but perhaps not surprisingly, there are no easy answers when it comes to the problems associated with bullying and harassment. They can raise very complex and sensitive issues and have at times been described as nightmarish situations to deal with.

Of course, the wisest approach is to prevent bullying and harassment from arising in the first place by creating a culture where people understand that it is essential to treat people with respect and dignity, even people with whom they are in conflict or have little by way of agreement to build on. It is a matter of what Parker (2009) has called 'civilised disagreement'.

Where it has not been possible to prevent such problems from arising, then the next best thing is to nip them in the bud, to be aware of any potential behaviours or reactions that could indicate that bullying or harassment is beginning to emerge and act accordingly. A 'wait and see' policy can be very detrimental, as it can mean that a great deal of harm is being done while we are not responding effectively. If, however, the situation gets beyond the nipping in the bud stage, it is vitally important that we handle it skilfully, sensitively and, above all, constructively. This could well mean getting advice and support for ourselves in certain circumstances, as the demands made upon us in dealing with such potentially fraught situations can be immense. Indeed, recognizing the emotional challenges of responding to bullying and harassment issues should be an important part of our self-care, so that we do not allow ourselves to be overwhelmed by the pressures and tensions involved.

Points to ponder
1. What harm can bullying and/or harassment do the individual and the organization?
2. What is meant by a 'culture of dignity' and why is it important?
3. How can making values explicit help to prevent bullying and harassment?

Exercise 24
How might you recognize signs that a member of staff is being bullied? How might you raise the issue with them? Where could you get advice and support from in dealing with such sensitive matters?

CHAPTER 25: DEALING WITH CONFLICT

In this chapter you will learn how to respond effectively to conflict situations.

Introduction

Conflict, as we have noted, is an inevitable part of life, including working life. While it is generally perceived in negative terms and therefore defined as something to be concerned about, conflict is not necessarily a problem and can be seen to have significant positive elements at times. An effective people manager therefore needs to have a good understanding of at least the basics of conflict in order to be well equipped to avoid, or minimize, the damage that conflict can do and to capitalize on the positives results that it has the potential to bring.

This chapter therefore seeks to provide a grounding in the art of conflict management, focusing on different levels of conflict and looking at both its negative and positive effects, so that, as people managers, we are better placed when it comes to dealing with conflict in the workplace. We begin by looking at four different levels of conflict then move on to explore the negative effects before balancing this out by looking at the positive potential involved. Finally, we look at some guidelines on managing conflict.

Levels of conflict

We can identify at least four main levels of conflict, each of which has significant implications for us. It is worth exploring each of these in turn.

1. *Everyday interactions*. This refers to day-to-day situations where people disagree with one another or somehow get in each other's way, whether literally in physical ways, as in traffic jams and queues, or in a more metaphorical sense when they are perhaps blocking each other's progress because they have different ideas about how to deal with situations, different values or different priorities. It is important to recognize that, while these situations do not necessarily involve any degree of ill-feeling or any form of enmity towards other people, they are still none the less examples of conflict. If we reserve the term conflict for situations that involve some degree of hostility, then we create an unduly negative picture of conflict and see it as an exception to the rule, whereas, in reality, conflict and harmony are both basic fundamental parts of human experience.
2. *Raised tensions*. This refers to situations that have arisen beyond everyday interactions in terms of the level of pressure and where there is clearly an 'edge' to the situation. This can be where disagreements, for example, become more pronounced, and there may be hints of hostility in terms of how people are

dealing with the conflicts involved. It is often at this stage that we need to think about trying to nip situations in the bud, to try and address any concerns before they escalate.

3. *Aggression.* This is where we have reached a level of more than just a hint of hostility, where there is a degree of open hostility, where people are perhaps being rude and disrespectful to each other (or at least one person is to at least one other). This can be a very difficult and tense situation to deal with, and one which reinforces the importance of trying to deal with situations at the Level 2 stage before they get to this more demanding situation.

4. *Violence.* This is where in a sense conflict reaches its ultimate level of destruction, where people are either physically attacking each other or one person is attacking at least one other. This is a very harmful situation when it arises, not only because of the physical injury that can arise from violence, but also because of the negative effect on emotional well-being that can come from being involved in incidents of violence. In extreme circumstances, the result can be a psychological trauma (see Chapter 27).

Key Point

It is important to have an understanding of these four levels so that we can try to ensure that everyday interactions (Level 1) do not go beyond Level 2 of raised tensions into aggression and therefore potentially violence.

Practice focus 25.1
Ahmed knew that Mr Cosgrove had been asking about the outcome of his application, but he had not got round to processing it yet, as he had been very busy. He had told Mr Cosgrove that he would let him know the outcome as soon as a decision had been reached. Despite this, Mr Cosgrove came into the office and asked to see Ahmed. Ahmed, for his part, felt a little annoyed as this interruption just meant that it would take longer to get round to processing the application. However, he agreed to see Mr Cosgrove. He started off by calmly reiterating that he would let him know the outcome of his application as soon as he could, but he couldn't say precisely when that would be. Mr Cosgrove clearly felt that he was being fobbed off and therefore raised his voice and asked why it was taking so long. Ahmed tried to keep calm but his annoyance started to show through in the tone of his voice when he said that he was very busy and the application would have to wait its turn in the queue. This made Mr Cosgrove even more unhappy, and he showed this by raising his voice even more and leaning forward menacingly towards Ahmed. This was a very stark gesture and Ahmed

clearly felt quite threatened and unnerved by it. He suddenly became aware that he might be at risk of violence if he did not handle this situation very carefully.

Figure 25.1 The four levels of conflict

The negative effects of conflict
The point has already been made that conflict can do a lot of harm. It may not be appreciated, though, just how broad ranging this harm can be. Consider the following examples.

Stress
Dealing with situations of conflict particularly when we are directly involved in that conflict can generate a high level of pressure. That pressure, when added to existing demands, can result in stress (as discussed in Chapter 21). Conflict can generate considerable tension, especially for people who are not very experienced, or confident, in dealing with such situations. We shall return to this point below when we discuss the three Cs of conflict management.

Bullying and/or harassment
As we noted in Chapter 24, situations where people do not see eye to eye can degenerate into one person behaving disrespectfully and unethically towards one or more other people involved in the situation. This can lead to further conflict. Conflict can therefore be understood as both the cause and effect of bullying or harassment in such circumstances, and so it is important that we are aware of this relationship in order to be better equipped to manage conflict effectively and prevent – or nip in the bud – any possible bullying or harassment.

Poor teamwork
Effective teamwork should be able to ensure that conflicts at the day-to-day interactions level are dealt with constructively and appropriately, and, in those situations where

issues reach Level 2, they are tackled appropriately by the team in a constructive way. However, where that does not occur, then conflict can be ruinous of a team, leaving people feeling quite poorly disposed to one another within the team context. Teams can be sources of great support, camaraderie, security and motivation when they work well, but they can also be highly problematic where they do not. Bullying and harassing behaviours present quite a challenge to a team, and how well it rises to that challenge can be a significant litmus test to establish how well or otherwise the team is operating as a team (rather than just a set of individuals).

Communication breakdowns

Conflict can so easily create tensions, and those tensions can then lead to people either deliberately not communicating with certain people (because they are at odds with them) or failing to communicate because they were distracted by the conflict and the feelings it generated. Either way, the result can be quite unsatisfactory and potentially quite dangerous, especially if key information is not passed on because of such tensions. There is therefore a very strong need to ensure that, when staff are in conflict situations, they do not cut off communication. Indeed, the more conflict is to the fore, the more important it is to keep the channels of communication open. We need to be aware of this ourselves and make sure staff are too.

Poor performance

It should not come as a surprise to learn that, where there is a great deal of conflict, people are not likely to be performing to the best of their ability. Indeed, performance levels can drop quite significantly and error rates can rise significantly. This can be quite costly for all concerned, as it means that staff are not fulfilling their potential and getting optimal satisfaction; the organization is not getting the best return on its investment; and other stakeholders (customers, clients or patients, for example) are not getting the best level of service either. Poor performance can also lead to a vicious circle that contributes to stress being experienced (see Chapter 21).

Discrimination

Conflict can escalate to the point where people are very negative towards one another or even hostile, and where there are differences between the individuals or groups of people concerned, this can then become a basis for unfair discrimination. When this occurs the idea of valuing diversity is likely to be seriously undermined. By the same token, conflict can occur because of discrimination. A tendency to see social differences as a problem, rather than as an asset, can contribute to considerable conflict where certain individuals or groups see other individuals or groups as inferior or as a threat. Ensuring that staff are properly trained and informed about equality and diversity can therefore make an important contribution to keeping conflict within manageable limits.

Grievances

Where somebody is in conflict with one or more other people, the net result can often be that person taking out a grievance because they feel that they are being badly treated. Perhaps the worst-case scenario is two people in conflict with one another who both take out a grievance against each other. But, even where there is only one grievance being pursued, the additional pressures for the individuals concerned – and for the team as a whole – can be of quite significant proportions. Unfortunately, grievances can also, at times, create further conflicts or exacerbate existing ones (see Chapter 10 for a discussion of the significance of grievances for people managers).

Departures

As an extension of the previous point, it can sometimes be the case that the situation is so bad that people actually leave, because they do not want to remain and be part of a situation characterized by a high degree of conflict and tension. As we noted in Chapter 8, losing staff prematurely can be highly problematic, costly in both financial and human terms, and so this is something that is very much to be avoided if possible.

Low morale

It is quite understandable that, in situations where there is considerable conflict and it is not being addressed, the result will be a lowering of morale. We have already noted how destructive low morale can be, and so there is a high incentive to prevent conflict from having an adverse effect on the morale of a team or staff group – or even a whole organization in some cases. What is particularly significant in this regard is that, while conflict itself can lower morale, it is perhaps the failure of leadership to address conflict that can prove even more detrimental, in so far as the loss of credibility for the leader (and the sense of security and teamwork that good leadership can, and should, bring) can create considerable ill feeling and a sense of disappointment.

Aggression and violence

If conflict is not handled effectively it can escalate to the point where people are attacking each other, either verbally or even physically, and producing, in the process, considerable risk in terms of both physical and psychological harm. As we shall discuss in Chapter 26, aggression and violence can do immense harm in various ways. For example, levels of trust can be reduced considerably as a result of such incidents.

What we also have to recognize is that this long and worrying list of the negative effects of conflict is exacerbated by the fact that any combination of these factors can interrelate to produce an even more damaging situation. For example, an incident of violence may lead someone to leave. It is therefore vitally important that, as people managers, we are aware of the negative effects of conflict, and are therefore fully able to appreciate why it is important to address conflict issues constructively and not shy away from them in the misguided hope that they will simply fade away. Once again, the reputation of the leader is at stake here, in the sense that a leader who is known to be aware of conflict, but is seen to be doing nothing about it, will be perceived in very negative terms, and will not succeed in creating the trust, credibility and sense of security that is associated with effective leadership.

The positive potential of conflict

One of the interesting things about conflict as a workplace phenomenon (and indeed as an aspect of life in general) is that, despite its immensely destructive potential, there is also considerable positive potential involved in conflict. Conflict can have positive consequences in terms of any of the following areas and, indeed, any combination of them.

Clearing up misunderstandings and establishing better communication

In some circumstances, an initial conflict can lead to people trying to move beyond that conflict which then has the positive effect of establishing a stronger basis of understanding. Indeed, there are many situations in which people can at first 'cross swords', but ultimately have a better working relationship as a result. This is often because the people involved have respect for the other person's moral courage in standing up for what they think is right and appropriate.

Improved creativity and innovation

There are many ways in which conflict between people with different approaches can lead to the development of a broader picture of the situation which provides fertile soil for more creative and innovative approaches, rather than people simply staying within their own silos and practising in fairly standardized, routinized ways. What initially starts out as a clash of perspectives can often lead either or both parties to develop broader horizons by taking on board aspects of the other person's view of the situation. This in turn can lead to new ways forward being developed.

Highlighting underlying problems

It is often the case that conflict is not a major problem in its own right, but, rather, a surface manifestation of underlying tensions. This conflict can therefore be useful and positive, in so far as it can give us a clearer picture of underlying problems that need to be addressed. It can therefore be, in a sense, a useful warning system that alerts us to potentially very damaging issues that would perhaps otherwise not have emerged. For example, the fact that two staff are finding it difficult to work together on a particular project may help us to highlight a fundamental incompatibility between their approaches which may need to be addressed.

Boosting confidence
The successful management of conflict situations can have a very positive effect on self-esteem and can enable people to grow and learn in terms of how they manage interpersonal interactions. There is therefore potentially much to be gained from engaging in conflict situations rather than trying to avoid them, as the more experienced we become at handling conflict, the more confident we are likely to become about managing conflict in particular, but also about ourselves in general.

Serving as a basis of learning
Similarly, conflict situations can provide us with opportunities to learn, not just about managing conflict itself, but more broadly about the situations that conflict brings us into. There are many lessons we can learn about negotiation, assertiveness and communication skills, for example, that can be of great value to us in developing our interpersonal skills as people managers.

Earning respect
How someone manages conflict can earn them respect not only from the person or persons they are in conflict with, but also from the wider team or organization. As we have already seen, this is especially the case for leaders who have to rely on respect, credibility and trust in order to be effective as leaders. It is therefore particularly important that, as people managers, we recognize this aspect of the positive potential of conflict and its contribution to our standing as leaders.

Managing conflict
Managing conflict can be a difficult and challenging undertaking and so there are no easy or simple answers to this. What is required is a good basic understanding of how conflict works and a willingness to wrestle with the issues involved as part of critically reflective practice. As part of this I want to emphasize two key aspects of managing conflict and also give a brief introduction to a particular model that can be helpful.
The first important tactic is to make sure that, at all times, we are able to listen and empathize. We have to be able to take on board other people's points of view, and we cannot do that unless we listen and adopt an empathic approach to such situations. Second, we need to be prepared to use mediation where appropriate. This can be done informally on occasions, but at other times it may require the involvement more formally of a qualified mediator. This can result in expense being incurred at times (if there is no suitably qualified person available in house), but the benefits of formal mediation include that it is less likely that someone will leave, and the costs of replacing a member of staff can be far higher than the cost of mediation.

Practice focus 25.2
Ahmed feared that Mr Cosgrove was about to become violent, so he knew he either had to leave the situation urgently or deal with it very sensitively. He decided on the latter. First of all, he apologized for the delay in processing the application and began to explain that they had been having a much higher level of applications than usual. Mr Cosgrove was clearly still angry, but he mellowed a little after this apology. Ahmed went on to say that, to prevent any criticisms of unfairness, he and his colleagues were obliged to deal with applications strictly in the order that they were received and that there were still a few more applications that would need to be processed before a start could be made on his. Mr Cosgrove was not delighted to hear this, but he did start to calm down. This was because, although he did not like the delay, he now understood it better. He turned towards the door and barked: 'If you had told me that in the first place I would not have got so worked up about you keeping me waiting'. Ahmed realized that he had a very good point and decided that, in future, he would try and make it clearer how the system works to prevent this type of incident. He could understand now that he had been looking at the situation from his own point of view (anxiety about the backlog of applications building up at this busy time) and had not appreciated Mr Cosgrove's perspective. That is, he had not shown empathy, and, when he realized that he had also allowed his own annoyance to show through, he could see why Mr Cosgrove had become angry and aggressive.

To bring this discussion of managing conflict to a close, I want to emphasize the importance of recognizing the value of adopting what I call the three Cs of conflict management:

- *Calmness*. This applies in the usual sense of remaining calm, but also in our specific sense of *Staying CALM,* as discussed in the Introduction. Conflict situations can generate a great deal of tension and, if we are not able to remain calm, those tensions can take over and make the situation much more fraught than it needs to be.
- *Confidence*. If we do not have confidence in ourselves, then we cannot expect other people to have confidence in us. We therefore need to approach conflict situations with as much confidence as we can muster. We are unlikely to be effective people managers in general or conflict managers in particular if we have no faith in our own ability.
- *Control*. We need to take control of the situation as far as reasonably possible. This is captured by the idea of conflict being analogous with fire, in the sense that, if fire is controlled and well managed, it can be very positive and

constructive. But, if it is allowed to get out of hand and there is no control involved, then fire can be extremely destructive. The parallel with conflict can therefore be seen as a very helpful one.

 Conflict can generate considerable anxiety which can, at times, contribute to making the situation more tense and therefore more likely to generate conflict. Keeping anxiety levels – our own and other people's is therefore an important part of conflict management.

Conclusion

We have noted that conflict is an everyday occurrence and that it is not necessarily a problem. However, it can easily become a problem if difficulties are allowed to escalate. There is therefore an important responsibility placed on the shoulders of people managers to be tuned in to conflict issues and to be able to address them sensitively and constructively sooner rather than later.

We have also seen that conflict, if managed well, can have positive benefits, and we should be looking towards capitalizing on those benefits whenever we can. Indeed, being a skilled conflict manager can be a major asset when it comes to people management.

Points to ponder

1. What are the four levels of conflict?
2. What do you see as the three most significant consequences of conflict not being managed properly?
3. In what ways can conflict be used positively?

Exercise 25

What anxieties do you have about managing conflict? What can you do to reduce these anxieties so that you are suitably well equipped to deal with conflict when you need to?

CHAPTER 26: HANDLING AGGRESSION

In this chapter you will learn how to respond to situations involving potential or actual aggression.

Introduction

In most organizations aggression or violence are not regular occurrences, while in others they can be a significant feature of working life, or at least the risk of such occurrences can be. However, no organization is entirely free from the potential for aggression to develop and to lead into actual violence. It can therefore be a dangerous assumption to make that such events will never happen, although sadly many organizations do not make any preparation for the possibility (in terms of policies or training, for example). This tendency to neglect such issues can leave organizations ill-prepared for dealing with aggression when it does arise. It is therefore important to be realistic and accept that handling aggression is something that any people manager may be called upon to do at any time. It is not something that is reserved for organizations that regularly encounter aggression (for example, the police). We also need to be aware that aggression and violence can bring about major ill effects that can be very detrimental for an organization and the people working within it.

This chapter provides an overview of some important issues relating to handling aggression, including a discussion of causes of aggression, what we can do to help prevent aggression and how we should respond if aggressive behaviour does arise in our workplace. We also explore some of the main effects of aggression, a topic that helps us to understand why it is important to take these issues seriously and dangerous to be complacent towards them.

Causes of aggression

As noted in Chapter 25, aggression is generally the result of an escalation of conflict from everyday interactions through to raised tensions, to aggression itself and possibly on to violence. Such an escalation can develop slowly over time until a line is crossed and aggression then flares up. Alternatively, the escalation can be quite rapid, depending on the person and on the circumstances. There is no one, definitive cause of aggression, but we can identify a number of key factors. It is worth exploring each of these main ones a little further.

Frustration

We can all find it difficult to deal with frustration at times, but some people find it more difficult than others, particularly if whatever it is that they have become frustrated about is very important to them or very significant in terms of their current circumstances. So, while it would be untrue to say that frustration necessarily leads to aggression, it would be naïve not to realize that there can be a significant link between frustration on the one hand and aggression on the other.

In some situations, it may be the case that the frustration has been building up over time and our involvement becomes the last straw. It can therefore be wise to be aware of potential signs of frustration and for this knowledge to be included in any training or guidance documents.

Losing face
This refers to situations where people feel humiliated, where they are made to feel ashamed in some way. This can be linked to frustration, in the sense that, if somebody becomes frustrated in public view, as it were, then they can also feel that they are losing face, that they are being made to feel small and are thus angered by the experience. This can be a significant source of aggression, or even violence (Baumeister, 2001). It is therefore important that, in our interactions with people, we do not put them in a situation where they lose face and risk feeling humiliated by the way they have been treated.

Feeling threatened
It is generally the case that people will respond to a feeling of threat by trying to get out of the situation, but that is not always the case. Some people, in certain circumstances at least, can respond to feeling threatened with an aggressive reaction, as if they are fighting fire with fire, as it were. In such circumstances, their aggression is being used as a counterattack to try and deal with the feelings of threat that they have. This can then combine with a sense of losing face, in so far as feeling threatened, particularly in front of other people, can also leave them feeling slightly humiliated.

If we are to be successful in preventing aggression, then it is important that we are aware of these common causes of aggressive behaviour. It is also worth noting that these factors can produce aggression by combining and interacting in various ways – that is, they do not just operate in isolation. This adds an extra layer of significance, as the presence of more than one factor can significantly increase the chances of aggression or violence occurring, making it all the more important that we are aware of these various factors and how they can combine.

Key Point

Most, but not all, incidences of aggression are predictable if you know what to look for and you are remaining alert to the potential for such problems to arise

Practice focus 26.1
Maisie had been trying to persuade the team to make a decision about their response to a policy consultation exercise, but they kept raising new aspects of the situation and seemed to be struggling to come up with a coherent response to the proposed new policy. Maisie was finding this quite frustrating, as she knew that the deadline for the response to be made was very soon. 'If we don't get this sorted soon', she said 'we will miss the deadline and then our voice won't be heard at all'. Martin, one of the more experienced and cynical members of the team replied quite brusquely: 'What does it matter to you? You might want to suck up to management if you want to, but that doesn't mean we want to'. Maisie was furious at what she saw as an attack on her integrity, a questioning of her commitment to the team. Although normally a very calm person, this combination of frustration and losing face made her blood boil. For the first Time ever in her career she responded by shouting angrily and being quite abusive to Martin and his cynicism. The team were taken aback by this aggressive response but could see that Martin had been very insensitive and actually quite rude in how he had spoken to her.

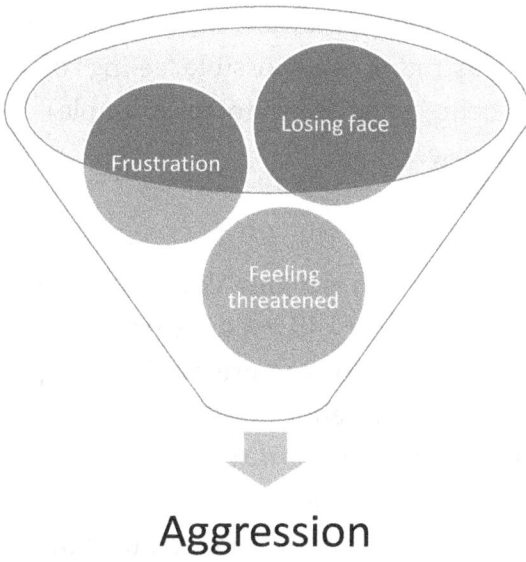

Figure 26.1 Causes of aggression

Preventing aggression
There are various ways in which we can seek to minimize the likelihood of aggressive behaviour arising. One of the most important ways is to develop our conflict management skills, as discussed in Chapter 25. If we are able to use in particular the

three Cs of conflict management – calmness, confidence and control – then we will be in a stronger position to prevent aggressive behaviour from developing (or to prevent initial aggression from escalating).

It can also be helpful to learn to identify potential trigger points. The three major causes of aggression outlined above will be an important part of this, but we need to think more broadly than this, in so far as there will be other events which may well lead to aggression that we need to be aware of. The term 'trigger point' is an important one, as this refers to the sort of event or comment that can trigger a strong reaction.

Similarly, it can be important to learn to recognize warning signs in terms of body language. Nonverbal communication is a powerful vehicle for getting across our feelings. It is therefore very likely that somebody who is on the verge of behaving aggressively will be giving off tell-tale signs (for example, reddening of the face). Where this happens, we need to be alert to the possibilities and be prepared to try and calm the situation down before it gets any worse.

Perhaps one of the most effective ways of preventing aggression is to make sure that, at all Times, we are listening and are empathic. By this I mean that we need to show that we are taking on board the other person's point of view. If they feel they are not being listened to, then that can add to a sense of frustration (and possible feelings of humiliation because they feel that they are being talked down to, for example). Each of these can potentially fuel an aggressive response.

Responding to aggression

Of course, even the most diligent people manager who is highly skilled in preventing aggression cannot guarantee that aggressive behaviour will not arise from Time to Time. It is very often beyond our control, despite our best efforts to prevent it. We therefore have to be alert to the possibility that, despite our best efforts, aggression will arise. In this case we need to be aware of health and safety issues (as discussed in Chapter 22). We have to make sure that we are not putting ourselves or other people at risk of harm through violence. It may therefore be necessary to withdraw from certain situations. For example, some organizations that have a higher than average likelihood of aggression occurring are equipped with alarm systems or other means of trying to safeguard staff from harm. It is therefore important that people managers are aware of what may be in place to assist in the process of responding to difficult situations involving aggression. Our people management response to how incidents of aggression are managed can be very significant. It is linked with the M, for Meaning, of *Staying CALM*. How people make sense of such highly emotive experiences will in large part influence how they react to them. Receiving a strong message of support can therefore be very important in determining whether someone gets over an incident without any major detrimental effects or becomes overwhelmed by the powerful feelings involved. This, then, is another test of whether we are able to develop truly people-oriented organizations.

A crucial part of this can be ensuring that key staff have had appropriate training. By key staff, I mean those who are most likely to be vulnerable to aggressive behaviour. This will vary from organization to organization, but in many settings reception staff, for example, may be the ones who bear the brunt of any dissatisfaction and frustration and could therefore be in the firing line, as it were, in terms of potential or actual aggression. We can also see that it is essential to make sure that staff involved in incidences of aggression and/or violence are suitably supported in the aftermath of such an event. This may amount to simple and straightforward messages of reassurance or could require more in-depth support – for example, in terms of a referral for confidential counselling. If situations involving aggression (and especially violence) are not handled sensitively, then there is a danger that one or more people may experience a traumatic reaction, a topic to be discussed in Chapter 27. The temptation to simply calm down a tense situation and try to get back to normal as soon as possible could therefore be problematic if it leaves someone feeling that their concerns are being glossed over and their feelings are not being acknowledged.

The effects of aggression
Aggression can do a great deal of damage to individuals, teams and whole organizations. It is therefore worth exploring some of the main ways in which we can lose out if we allow aggression to feature in our workplaces without doing whatever we reasonably can to prevent such problems from arising. I shall focus on four particular areas, but we should note that this is far from a comprehensive list.

Stress
In Chapter 21 we noted that, where pressure becomes excessive, it can lead to health-affecting stress which can have major detrimental consequences. Aggression and violence can be major contributors to stress problems. Aggression can lead to increased tensions, a strong sense of insecurity and vulnerability, a reduction in confidence and an overall sense of unhappiness. These, in turn, can lead to physical difficulties, such as: upset stomachs, headaches and an exacerbation of existing health problems (see below). These can then create a vicious circle whereby feeling unwell makes the individual(s) concerned feel even more tense and insecure. This can then have a knock-on effect in terms of relationships, in so far as the additional tensions can put a strain on relationships both at work and in our private lives.

These difficulties can arise from a single incidence of aggression, and so work settings in which staff are regularly exposed to aggression could be potentially much more stressful. Of course, for some people, more frequent exposure to aggressive incidents could give them the knowledge, skills and confidence to tackle them effectively without becoming stressed. However, not everyone will be able to do this, and so some people will be quite vulnerable to stress if they are encountering the challenges of aggression on a frequent basis. Work settings where aggression is a not uncommon occurrence therefore need to be sensitive to the potential for stress and guard against the dangers of complacency by seeing aggression as a normal feature of working life.

Violence (that is, situations that go beyond aggressive behaviour to constitute an actual assault) can be even more of a problem when it comes to stress. In effect, violence is a more intensive experience than aggression, and so its impact can be even greater. Of course, it also has to be recognized that, in the vast majority of cases, violence will be preceded by aggression, and so the negative effects of violence are *in addition to* those of aggression. Violence can also result in psychological trauma as well as potentially physical trauma, and so it is to this topic that we now turn.

Trauma
Chapter 27 is devoted to a discussion of loss, grief and trauma in the workplace, and so the topic of trauma will be discussed in more detail there. However, for now we can note that being exposed to violence can lead to a profound traumatic reaction. This goes far beyond stress (in which our coping methods are *overwhelmed*) to a point where our coping methods are *shattered* (Thompson, 2022). The result can be a devastating one that prevents us from continuing as before, as the example in Practice focus 26.2 illustrates. There can also be knock-on effects for friends, relatives and, of course, colleagues that can be quite significant who may struggle to support someone who is suffering greatly and wrestling with some very powerful emotions.

While it is possible to recover from trauma, especially if appropriate help is given, the negative effects can be long lasting, even permanent. The price that people pay for encountering traumatizing experiences is therefore very high indeed, and so the onus on people managers to protect staff from potentially trauma-inducing violence is very great indeed.

Exacerbation of health problems
Stress has the capacity to make existing health conditions significantly worse, and so aggression can produce the same effects. Being exposed to aggressive behaviour can significantly raise blood pressure, with all the attendant risk factors in terms of stroke and heart attack, for example. Where the aggression spills over into actual violence, then

the result can be even worse – partly because of the physical harm that violence can do (exacerbating an existing back problem, for example) and partly because of the psychological harm associated with such incidents.

Mental health problems can also be worsened considerably by aggression or violence. For example, someone who already has problems with anxiety can become even more anxious, while someone struggling to cope with depression can become even more depressed.

Clearly, then, we can once again see that failing to prevent aggression can result in very harmful consequences, with serious detrimental effects that can go far beyond the workplace and make a major difference to people's private lives.

Departures
In Chapter 8 we explored the significance of staff departures and the negative impact they can have. Aggression and violence can very much be part of that scenario, in so far as they can lead to staff departing in search of a safer or more supportive work setting.

In some cases, an incident of aggression or violence can be the last straw, in the sense that a dissatisfied or disaffected employee was considering leaving and an incident of aggression tilts the balance in that direction. However, in other cases, someone who was previously perfectly happy to remain in their post decided to leave because the incident concerned has spoiled for them what was a reasonably happy working life. This can be especially the case when the person concerned has been traumatized by the incident in question.

Significantly, one key factor that can affect whether or not staff leave after encountering aggression or violence will be the level and quality of support they receive. If the incident undermines a sense of security and leaves people feeling vulnerable, then poor leadership and people management support thereafter can reinforce these negative feelings and thereby propel people towards what they anticipate will be a safer and more supportive work environment. Some people may even give up work altogether.

> *Practice focus 26.2*
> Lynette was reluctant to visit the Kempson family at home, as they had a reputation for being very difficult to deal with. However, she needed to update them on the situation and to explore the next steps with them. When she arrived Mr Kempson was not there, but Mrs Kempson explained that he was due home soon. He arrived about 15 minutes later, and it soon became clear that he had been drinking. He started to get aggressive as soon as he realized Lynette was

there. 'This should all have been sorted by now' he kept saying over and over again. Lynette decided it would be better to withdraw rather than try to do the impossible job of trying to make progress when Mr Kempson was clearly not in a mood for cooperating. She explained that she would come back another day at a more convenient Time. Mr Kempson seemed to accept this at first, but as Lynette walked towards the door he grabbed her from behind by the hair and pulled her to the floor, punching her as she fell. Thankfully, Mrs Kempson came to her aid and Mr Kempson left the room, shouting and swearing and slamming the door behind him. Lynette thanked Mrs Kempson, but left the house straight away as she was in fear of her life. Although she was physically relatively unharmed, the emotional impact of the incident was to be much greater. For weeks afterwards she was tearful most of the Time and easily distressed. She could not face doing home visits any more, even though they were a significant part of her job. She did not take any Time off work, but she was on 'light duties' for almost three months before she eventually came to the conclusion that she would have to transfer to an office-bound job that did not involve direct contact with the public. Fortunately, her employers were very supportive and facilitated this switch, but it meant a significant drop in income for her, and she was still very nervous about potential violence situations in her private life. She hadn't quite become a hermit, but her social circles were now considerably restricted because of her fear.

It is essential to make sure that victims of aggression and/or violence are not made to feel that the incident was their fault. Adding a layer of guilt to an already highly emotionally challenging situation can be very harmful – and certainly is not helpful.

Conclusion

Organizations differ in the level of risk of aggression and violence occurring, but we have already noted – and it is worth re-emphasizing – that no organization is entirely free in terms of risks of aggression. We therefore have to be prepared for the possibility and aware of what we need to do: (i) to prevent aggression in the first place; (ii) to respond to it when it does occur; and (iii) to support the staff affected by it in the aftermath.

One of the most important elements of this is being aware of whether the organization concerned has a policy and related procedures, and, if so, making sure that we and our staff are familiar with it. If there is no policy in existence, then serious thought should be given to developing one, as there are significant risks involved in trying to deal with situations involving aggression where there are no guidelines in place. It leaves people ill-equipped to respond to the challenges involved, and the consequences of that could clearly be quite harmful. It may be a free-standing policy or a part of a wider policy (of workplace well-being, for example, or maybe health and safety).

Perhaps one of the most significant issues to consider in terms of handling aggression is the need to recognize that aggressive situations can produce a physical reaction (a release of adrenaline into our bloodstream) which can make us feel very tense, uncomfortable and unsettled. This reaction is not necessarily a problem in itself, but if we are not aware of it, it can have wider consequences (for example, in terms of having difficulty in concentrating). We therefore have to be reasonably well informed when it comes to tackling situations relating to aggression. This chapter will have taken you some way towards having that knowledge base, but it is not sufficient on its own.

Points to ponder
1. What are the main causes of aggression?
2. What would you see as warning signs of potential aggression or violence?
3. Why is it important to have a policy on aggression?

Exercise 26
Does the organization you are working (or studying) in have a policy on aggression and violence? If so, how helpful is it? If not, what would need to be included to make it a worthwhile document?

CHAPTER 27: LOSS, GRIEF AND TRAUMA

In this chapter you will learn how to respond to situations involving loss, grief and trauma.

Introduction

Of course, everyone will face a bereavement in their life sooner or later. This means that no workplace is immune from the impact of loss following a bereavement. Indeed, in large organizations it can be quite common for one or more employees to be grieving after a bereavement at any one Time. However, we also need to recognize that loss and grief apply in a wide range of situations where no-one has died – for example: divorce or other relationship breakdown; moving house; becoming disabled; or a new manager taking over a team after a much-loved manager moves on. There can even be a grief reaction after a positive change, such as becoming a parent.

Bereavement is therefore not the only cause of grief. Grief is a much more common and significant feature of people's lives than is generally recognized (Thompson, 2022). It would therefore be both naïve and unhelpful for organizations to fail to recognize the potential impact of grief. When we also consider that some forms of loss can be traumatic – that is, they are not only painful, but also wound us in a psychological sense – then it becomes even more pressing that employing organizations develop an understanding of what is involved in supporting their staff through a major transition in their life.

And, of course, staff do not leave their grief at home when they come to work. Consequently, as people managers, we need to be tuned in to such matters, as they can have very serious and wide-ranging effects in the workplace. As with issues relating to aggression (discussed in Chapter 26), it is dangerous to assume that the matter will not arise and therefore leave ourselves ill-prepared to deal with it when it does.
This chapter therefore tries to present a basic understanding of the significance of loss and change in people's lives and how these can produce a strong and significant grief reaction. The chapter also considers trauma which is a particular type of grief, and one which can have even more of an impact than grief itself. We begin by considering the significance of loss and change in people's lives.

Loss and change

If we consider that bereavement is not the only way in which someone can experience a grief reaction, we start to see that grief is a much broader concept than is generally appreciated. It is important to recognize that any significant change or transition in somebody's life (whether in work or outside it) can produce a grief reaction which has a range of implications that we will discuss below. As already mentioned, a good example of the type of situation that can produce grief without death being involved is divorce or the breakdown of a well-established relationship. The impact of such a situation can be just as devastating as a loss of a person through death. In fact, in some circumstances it can be even more of a powerful force in someone's life which can leave them ill-equipped to cope with the demands of their work at that particular time.

But, there are also changes within the workplace that can bring about a grief reaction. This could be, for example, where there is a reorganization which could mean that a team is disbanded, or an individual could be relocated because of the requirements of the organization. Either of these situations can mean that a person's sense of stability and security has been lost, leaving them feeling very vulnerable and unsettled and, possibly because of this, not in a fit state to carry out their duties to anything approaching their normal level of competence.

In some circumstances, the departure of a colleague can also produce a grief reaction. If there has been someone who has been particularly important or influential (a particularly skilful and charismatic team leader for example), then the result can be another grief reaction.

I mentioned earlier that divorce or a relationship breakdown can be a major loss issue in people's lives outside of the workplace, but, of course, it is not the only one. For example, a child or children leaving home can also produce a significant grief reaction. The departure of a child from a family, even in happy circumstances, can leave a big hole in people's lives and the psychological reaction can be quite powerful as a result of that. Even positive changes like promotion can provoke a grief reaction leaving the person concerned vulnerable temporarily. It is therefore important that, as people managers, we are aware of such issues and conscious of the fact that, when someone is grieving, they may not be able to concentrate as fully as they normally do and may not be as competent as would otherwise be the case. They may also have particular needs for support which, if not met, could lead to other problems connected with workplace well-being.

Overall, then, we can see that grief is a very broad phenomenon that can have a major impact on people's lives. What we also have to bear in mind is that these wider losses are in addition to death-related losses. In a large organization it will not belong before someone experiences the death of an important person in their lives. We should also not forget pet losses. Despite the common tendency to trivialize such losses ('It was only a dog'), the death of a much-loved pet can produce a very strong grief reaction indeed.

Practice focus 27.1
Jim was a very popular figure. He was always smiling, always encouraging people and being supportive wherever he could. He seemed to know everyone and everything. As well as being a valued colleague because he was such a mine of information, he was also much loved because he was such a pleasant and amiable character. When he retired there was much sadness. He left a huge hole not only in the workplace, but also in people's affection. The sense of grief at his departure was almost palpable, such was the extent of the affection and respect people had for him. Colleagues hoped that he would keep his promise and pop in from time to time to see them and to let them know how he was doing. Hi first visit was about a month after he had left. He called in for a cup of coffee and a chat one day, and everyone was delighted to see him. However, it tragically turned out that this was his last visit too, as a few weeks later – less than two months after retiring, Jim had a heart attack and died. Even though he was no longer officially a member of staff anymore, the effect on the staff group was immense. Still experiencing a strong sense of grief because of his retirement, they were now hit by an even stronger sense of grief on receiving the news of his death. Everyone knew it was going to be a major challenge to keep things going while also feeling so bereft at the loss of such an important figure.

Trauma

In its literal sense, a trauma is a wound, and the term is often used in this sense in medical settings to refer to direct physical injuries. However, it is also used in a more metaphorical sense to refer to a psychological wound (or more accurately, a psychosocial wound, as the impact relates to more than the individual concerned and therefore has social as well as psychological consequences). Trauma can devastate a person, leaving them very ill-equipped to deal with further life challenges. For example, someone who has been traumatized by rape may find it extremely difficult to go out alone.

Trauma generally arises as a result of extreme experiences of loss. These can include, but are not limited to, the areas we will explore below. Trauma needs to be recognized as a very serious matter. The reality of trauma is very far removed from the common tendency to trivialize it by using the term very loosely ('They asked me lots of difficult questions at the interview; it was quite a traumatic experience'). A real trauma is not something we simply get over – it can potentially have an adverse effect on us for the rest of our lives, not least in terms of low confidence and high anxiety.

Being a victim of crime or violence
It is not automatically the case that somebody will be traumatized by such a situation, but it is not uncommon for people to have a very strong emotional reaction to being

made to feel so vulnerable as a result of such an incident. Such experiences can leave people very wary indeed (to the point of paranoia at times) about risks of future violence. It is partly for this reason that the importance of preventing aggression and violence was emphasized so strongly in Chapter 26.

Being abused
Whether this is child abuse, domestic abuse or the abuse of a vulnerable adult (a person with a learning disability, for example) the consequences can be the same: a traumatic reaction. It is as if being abused leaves the person concerned feeling so vulnerable and insecure that they are not prepared to be in any situation that could lead to further abuse. This extreme wariness can be very limiting in both working life and personal life. We are now aware that, unfortunately, a significant number of adults were abused as children (Wilkins *et al*, 2019) and others are abused as adults (through domestic violence, for example – Harne and Radford, 2008), and so abuse is not as unusual as people tend to believe. If we also add bullying and harassment to our list of sources of abuse, we can see that the dangers of trauma are something we need to take very seriously.

Multiple losses
This refers to a situation where a number of losses occur simultaneously. This can be multiple deaths, for example (perhaps as a result of a road traffic accident) or a combination of losses that occur at the same time. It is quite possible for a number of losses to occur more or less simultaneously solely by chance, purely by misfortune and coincidence. However, sometimes multiple losses occur as a result of the same underlying cause. For example, somebody experiencing mental health problems and therefore going through a mental health crisis can experience several losses at the same time (breakdown of a relationship, loss of home, loss of job and so on). Interestingly, multiple losses can also be the cause of a mental health crisis as a result of the trauma involved.

Cumulative losses
Whereas 'multiple losses' is a term used to refer to losses occurring at more or less the same time, the idea of cumulative loss is that people can become traumatized because they undergo one major loss and, before they have had time to recover from that and find their equilibrium, they are hit by another major loss and, once again, before they have had time to recover from that, they then experience a further major loss, and so on. This cumulative effect can also be a significant source of trauma, leaving people's coping methods not only overwhelmed, but actually devastated.

These are just some of the main ways in which trauma can arise and are certainly not the only ones (see, for example, Practice focus 27.2). What I have presented should, though, be enough to show how prevalent potential causes of trauma are. This then places an onus on us as people managers to do whatever we reasonably can to prevent staff from being traumatized and, whenever we do encounter a staff member who has been traumatized, to be as supportive as we reasonably can.

It is therefore very important indeed that we are aware of trauma. We are not expected to be mental health professionals in being able to deal with these in any great depth, but we leave ourselves very ill-equipped to be effective people managers if we have little or no understanding of the significance of trauma in some people's lives.

The effects of grief and trauma
In some respects, grief is a fundamental part of human existence. It is the way we try to recover from a loss; it is the healing or rebuilding of our lives after part of that life has been destroyed in some way by one or more significant losses. Trauma, as we have already noted, is a more extreme form of loss, but is none the less part of the grief reactions that we experience. If we are to have an understanding of grief and trauma, so that we are better equipped to respond to situations involving these difficult phenomena, then we need to have some understanding of what impact grief has on people.
The effects of grief and trauma will vary from individual to individual (and context to context), but there are certain common themes that can be identified. These can be divided into four categories (based on Thompson, 2012b). It is worth exploring each of these in turn.

Physical
A grief response is a form of stress reaction, and so there will be similar physical responses in terms of, for example, potential headaches, stomach aches, weariness, loss of appetite (or even increased appetite through comfort eating). We can also, because of the effect on our immune system, be more open to infection at this vulnerable Time, and there is also the significance of existing health conditions to be taken into consideration. There are various conditions (heart disease, for example) where stress, including grief-related stress, can be a significant factor. These physical reactions can make quite a significant difference to an employee's ability to carry out their duties to their normal level of achievement.

Cognitive
This refers to processes of thinking and memory. When someone is grieving, particularly if the grief is quite intense because the loss was quite a significant one, the net result can be a reduced level of concentration and reduced memory capacity. This can mean that, in

some circumstances, people are not able to carry out their duties safely. This is therefore something that needs to be assessed fairly carefully in terms of a health and safety risk assessment. By the same token, however, it should not be automatically assumed that somebody who is grieving is not capable of doing their job. In fact, retaining as much of a sense of normality as possible can be very therapeutic for someone who is going through the very difficult and painful process of grieving a major loss.

Emotional

It is understandable that, at such a significant time in our lives as a major loss, our emotional reactions may be affected. Different people will be affected in different ways. For example, some people will become very quiet and withdrawn and will keep their emotions apparently under close control (although the reality may be very different on the inside for that person). Other people may become more open in their emotional expression – for example, crying or talking in an emotional way about their experiences and their feelings. This again means that, in certain jobs, the person concerned may not be suitably equipped at that time to carry out their work to a safe or adequate level. Clearly, considerable sensitivity is called for in responding to such situations.

Spiritual

We have already seen the importance of spirituality in people's lives in general as well as in the workplace. Spirituality is very much about meaning making and having a sense of purpose and direction, together with a sense of connectedness. All of these can be adversely affected, if not actually shattered, by a significant loss. People who are grieving – and particularly people who are traumatized – can feel that their life has little meaning at present, that they have lost any sense of who they are, and they feel somehow disconnected from the wider world, with no sense of purpose or direction, and sometimes little feeling of connection to other people. It is as if they are in a world of their own, disconnected (and perhaps alienated) from other people. This reflects both the C, for Connection, of *Staying CALM* and the M, for Meaning.

Of course, these different categories do not operate in isolation. They can influence each other and interrelate in significant ways. The aim of this chapter is, realistically, not to try and make you into an expert in loss, grief and trauma, but, rather, to alert you to the significant impact of loss and trauma on employees.

We should also be aware that, in trying to help others cope with their grief, we are not immune from our own experiences of loss. Helping people deal with their losses may well open up wounds of our own and, indeed, we may actually be actively grieving in our own right when we are trying to help others address their own grief-related needs. We therefore need to be wise enough to recognize that we may need support at times (perhaps in the form of time out), and so we should not be afraid to ask for it at such times. We cannot create genuinely people-oriented organizations if we do not take account of our own human needs.

> *Practice focus 27.2*
> Aoife came into work as usual but sat at her desk not saying or doing anything for quite some time. When a colleague asked her if she was all right, she burst into tears and ran out of the room. This pattern continued for the rest of the day and the following day. On the third day, Mina, the team manager, who had been informed of the situation the previous evening, called her into her office and tried to get her to talk about what was troubling her. This produced no positive results, as Aoife was too upset to talk about what had happened. In fact, it was ten days before Aoife was able to explain that her house, where she lived with her husband and two children, had been broken into and ransacked while the family were staying with her sister for a weekend break. Aoife had been devastated by this, and explained to Mina that she had not been sleeping because she was too nervous to go to sleep for fear of someone breaking in. She no longer felt secure at home, as her personal space had been violated. It was now creating tensions with her husband, who had been very supportive to begin with, but who was now becoming impatient and telling Aoife to 'get over it', something she felt that she could not do. Mina suspected that Aoife had been traumatized by the event, and so she referred her to occupational health for an assessment of her support needs. She wanted to be supportive, but she also recognized the need for specialist help.

The implications for people management
Given the significant issues discussed so far, we clearly need to be alert to the fact that grief is not something that *may* occur, but something that *will* occur, sooner or later. We therefore need to consider the implications of this for our role as people managers. The implications are quite wide ranging, and the following are some of the major ones.

Be 'grief aware'
It is very easy to miss the significance of grief in people's lives, especially where no death is involved. We therefore have to be fully aware that any major change or transition can result in a grief reaction, sometimes a more powerful grief reaction than when someone has died.

Be aware of relevant policies
Organizations that are not geared up to dealing with loss, grief and trauma place themselves in a very difficult situation, as staff and managers are likely to be ill-equipped to deal with the situations when they arise – and once again it is a matter of when, not if. It is therefore important to be aware of any policies relating to such matters. Few

organizations have a policy directly relating to loss, grief and trauma, but the issues may be covered in other policies (a workplace well-being policy, for example). Where there is no policy provision in existence, it would be very wise to begin the process of developing a clear policy or addition to an existing relevant policy.

Offer appropriate support
Very often there is little we can do to help in a direct practical sense somebody who is grieving, but the fact that we are making an offer of help, the fact that we are showing a degree of human warmth, can make a very positive difference to somebody who is grieving. This reflects the C, for Connection, of *Staying CALM*, the value of human connection, especially at Times of difficulty or challenge.

Refer for specialist support where necessary
This could be a referral to occupational health and/or confidential counselling services where available, but there are also potentially specialist support resources outside of the organization. However, it is important that we do not assume that a grieving person automatically needs support and, where they do need support, we should not assume that the actual support they need is counselling. Some people need counselling; others need other forms of support, and many will not need any support at all, other than the human warmth of connectedness I mentioned above, as they will have plenty of informal support to help them through this difficult time in their lives.

Listen and be empathic
This is not the first time that I have emphasized the importance of being effective listeners and being empathic. A good people manager is a good listener and somebody who is able to be empathic, to be able to see the situation from the other person's point of view (that is, being tuned in to people's feelings without necessarily sharing those feelings ourselves), so that they feel validated and affirmed by the fact that we are doing so. This is very important in general in terms of our workplace interactions and in establishing ourselves as effective people managers, but it is especially important in situations where people are grieving and are likely to be feeling very vulnerable.

Get support for yourself if you need to
The point was made earlier that no one is immune from grief. Helping people deal with their grief can remind us of our own losses. That is not necessarily a problem, and we may be able to handle this very effectively. However, as I emphasized above, we should not be afraid to ask for support, whether formally from our own organization or informally through our own personal networks, if we find ourselves in a situation where we have our own grief issues to handle.

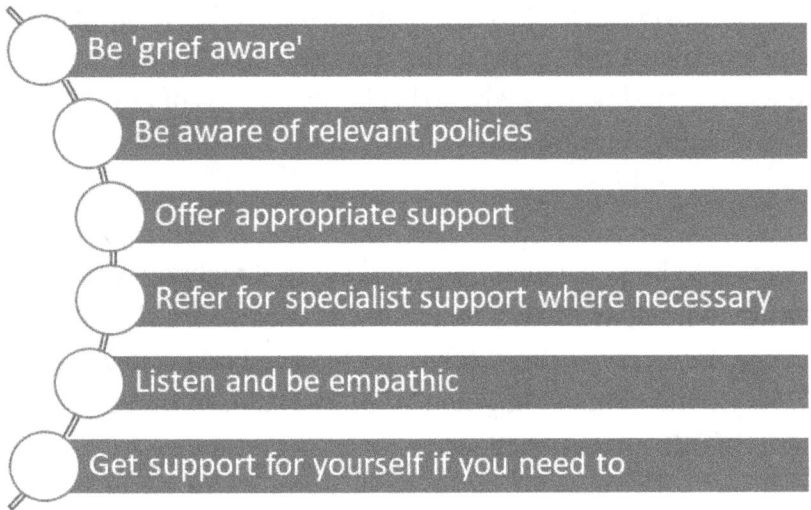

Figure 27.1 Responding to loss

 Different people react to losses in different way. Despite the widely accepted idea that people grieve in stages, the reality is that there is immense variation in how grief affects people and how they respond to it. So, be careful not to adopt a 'one size fits all' approach.

Conclusion

Loss, grief and trauma can be extremely difficult to deal with in life generally. When they arise in the workplace where there are other pressures (for example, to meet production deadlines and so on), then dealing with the challenges involved can be quite testing for all concerned. However, we should not focus purely on the negative side. What can be extremely helpful for people in their hour of need, as it were, is to know that there are important people in their life who are able to guide them and support them on a difficult journey. This notion of accompanying people on a journey is an important one when it comes to supporting people through loss, grief and trauma. If, as people managers, we are able to do this, we can make an immensely positive contribution to people, a contribution that can be greatly valued by the employees concerned over a long period of time. However, by contrast, organizations that are insensitive to issues of loss, grief and trauma and which leave their managers ill-equipped to understand, let alone address, the issues involved, then the result can be a total failure of leadership, with not only the grieving person, but also his or her colleagues, feeling dreadfully let down by an organization that has failed in its duty of care.

Points to ponder
1. Why is it important to remember that grief is our response to a major loss and not just to a death?
2. What is 'cumulative loss' and why do we need to be aware of it?
3. In what circumstances would you need to refer a grieving employee for specialist support?

Exercise 27
In what ways could you support someone who is grieving or who has been traumatized? What options would be available to you? What would you do if helping someone else deal with their losses reminded you of painful losses you have experienced?

CHAPTER 28: MENTAL HEALTH PROBLEMS

In this chapter you will learn how to respond to mental health challenges in the workplace.

Introduction

Mental health is a topic that can raise unnecessary fears, partly because of stereotypes that lead people to make too strong an association between mental health problems and violent crime, and partly because of the strong mystique traditionally associated with mental distress. However, many people with mental health problems are to be found operating successfully in employment, and many employees with no history of such problems can develop them while in our employment. From a people management perspective, it is therefore important that we have at least a basic awareness of mental health and its significance for the workplace.

Given our overall responsibility for trying to make sure that the people issues in the organization are handled as effectively as possible, it could be argued that to fail to tackle mental health problems with the understanding and commitment necessary is to fail in our duty to get the best out of people.

This chapter therefore offers a basic introduction to the topic of mental health problems in the workplace. It identifies some key issues relating to mental health and how people managers can be called upon to address some significant issues that arise in certain circumstances. We begin by focusing on some key issues relating to the complex topic of mental health problems. We then explore what is involved in rising to the challenges of mental health problems in the workplace.

Understanding mental health problems

When someone displays what are seemed to be mental health problems, it is traditionally seen that the person concerned is showing symptoms of some form of illness. The basic field of mental health is therefore perceived to be primarily biological in origin. However, there is now an increasing body of knowledge that challenges the idea that mental distress is simply a biologically based illness (Thompson, 2019c). We are now starting to recognize that the significance of social, psychological and spiritual factors, as well as biological ones, can be at play, influencing each other and interacting in complex ways with one another – starting to understand 'mental disorders' as particular ways of being, rather than as mental 'illnesses' in any direct sense. The finer detail of this need not concern us here, but it is important to recognize that we run the risk of getting things seriously wrong if we see mental health problems as purely symptoms of an illness and therefore making the misguided assumption that the way to address these problems is through medication or some other form of medical treatment. If we do not see the broader picture, we are likely to miss opportunities to be helpful and supportive and/or to relieve pressure on people who are wrestling with mental health difficulties. We may also fail to notice key factors that may be contributing to the problems – for example, unacknowledged grief or trauma; bullying or harassment; and stress. It would therefore be a significant – and potentially costly – mistake to see our role as people managers as being one of simply referring people experiencing mental health problems to a medical service (whether occupational health within the organization or psychiatric services outside of it).

Mental health problems can range from relatively minor neurotic (or 'nervous') disorders (which can none the less be quite debilitating for those so affected) to major psychotic disorders where people are behaving in what appear to be entirely bizarre, irrational ways. However, it is important to recognize that, across this spectrum, there is considerable variation and we need to guard against stereotypes that assume that anyone who is understood to have a mental health problem is necessarily at the most severe end of that continuum. Such assumptions can lead to problems of discrimination, with the extent and impact of people's mental health problems being significantly exaggerated. Mental health problems come in many forms and many degrees of severity, but the following conditions are broadly representative of the most common ways in which people can be affected by mental disorders:

- *Anxiety.* A degree of anxiety is, of course, a normal part of everyday life and nothing in itself to be concerned about. However, for some people, anxiety can reach debilitating levels, preventing them from functioning as fully as they would like (both within and outside the workplace). High levels of anxiety can be very distressing in their own right, but can also place great strain on relationships, make parenting very difficult, significantly reduce a person's enjoyment of life and cut off a wide range of opportunities that require a calmer outlook and approach. In some cases, people with an unduly high level of anxiety may find it impossible to hold down a job, because they find that worrying about so many minor details leads to their failing to make adequate progress with their duties. An additional problem is that people who have difficulties with high levels of anxiety may find relief in sedative medication and can become addicted to the use of these substances.
- *Obsessive compulsive disorder.* This term describes a condition in which people who are so affected translate their anxiety into a specific concern with keeping things in precise order – a concern that reaches the level of an obsession. This often takes the form of an obsession with cleanliness and/or personal hygiene.

For example, in some extreme cases, people can wash their hands so often that they become very sore. A feeling of comfort from feeling that things are clean, well ordered and under control is, of course, a perfectly normal part of everyday life for a significant proportion of people. However, obsessive compulsive disorder (or OCD for short) refers to situations where the person concerned has gone far beyond this. This is why the word 'compulsive' is included in the term – people feel compelled to clean things that are already perfectly clean or to place in order things that are already fairly well ordered. The condition can lead to considerable distress for the person concerned, and can also place immense pressure on family, friends and colleagues.

- *Eating disorders.* 'Anorexia nervosa' refers to a condition in which the person concerned eats far less than they need nutritionally, resulting in significant weight loss and, if not resolved in time, can result in death. It involves a distortion of perception whereby an individual sees him- or herself as fat and overweight, even though this is not the case. 'Bulimia nervosa' refers to a condition characterized by 'binge eating' – that is, eating far too much food in one sitting to the point of making themselves vomit. Once again, these conditions can be seen as distortions of perfectly normal behaviour (dieting and overeating respectively), everyday activities taken to harmful extremes.

- *Depression.* Everyone can have a low mood from time to time, but, for many people, this can become their normal state of mind for much of the time. Many people experience depression relentlessly over an extended period of time, while others are prone to intermittent depression – that is, they can be free of depression for some time and then become depressed again. The condition tends to involve a very negative mindset, very low motivation and energy levels and a general sense of foreboding. As well as being very debilitating for the individual concerned, depression can place great pressure on family, friends and colleagues. It can make it very difficult for the person concerned to hold down a job, although many people with depression do manage to do so, with appropriate support. It can also lead to suicide attempts.

- *Post-traumatic stress disorder.* We noted in Chapter 27 that certain life experiences involving severe loss can result in a psychological wound or 'trauma'. People can often recover from such trauma without professional help. However, in some situations, people may be so adversely affected by their experience that they require intensive professional help to be able to deal with the problems presented by the trauma. They can find the condition very debilitating and are likely to struggle to pursue their everyday life, including work.

- *Bipolar disorder.* This is a condition which involves extremes of behaviour. At times, people with bipolar disorder (previously referred to as 'manic-depressive psychosis') will feel very depressed (or 'low'), while at others they will feel quite manic (or 'high') – that is, highly energized and hyperactive. Either extreme can be highly problematic, as can the tendency to swing between the two. People with this condition can therefore find this very difficult to handle, although there are drugs available that can help to avoid these extremes.

- *Schizophrenia.* This is a highly contested condition (or set of conditions). The commonsense understanding of schizophrenia as the state of having a split personality is very inaccurate. A more accurate understanding is that it involves having a shattered personality, in the sense that someone with this condition will tend to find it very difficult to maintain a coherent sense of self. It can result in highly 'psychotic' behaviour – that is, very bizarre actions and reactions that seem to defy rationality. This sometimes highly disturbed state of mind can be frightening for all concerned. It was once thought that it was not possible to recover from schizophrenia, and so it was assumed to be a permanent condition. However, there is now a much stronger emphasis on recovery and the steps that can be taken to help people avoid the very damaging behaviours and cognitive and emotional reactions associated with this very debilitating condition.

KEY POINT

We should also recognize that mental health problems can be exacerbated – or, in some cases, precipitated – by alcohol and/or drugs problems (see Chapter 29). Where we encounter both sets of problems together (substance abuse and mental health problems), we can find ourselves on very challenging territory and will almost certainly require specialist help in dealing with such matters.

Mental health problems	Anxiety
	Obsessive compulsive disorder
	Eating disorders
	Depression
	Post-traumatic stress disorder
	Bipolar disorder
	Schizophrenia

Figure 28.1 Main mental health conditions

One thing we are now beginning to understand more fully is the idea that stress can exacerbate mental health problems considerably (if not be the *primary* reason for them developing in the first place). It is therefore important, when it comes to addressing mental health concerns in the workplace, to make sure that we are keeping pressures within manageable limits and not allowing stress to be a feature of the workplace (as discussed in Chapter 21). Stress can exacerbate any health problem, but it can be seen to be particularly detrimental in relation to mental health problems, and so the question of stress is very much one that needs to be given sufficient attention.

It is also important to learn more about the complexities of mental health. This is because it is important to get beyond the common and misleading stereotypes about mental health – for example, the romanticized, but dangerous notion of 'the mad axe murderer' who is a threat to the community. The reality of the mental health field is far removed from what most people assume it to be. An uninformed people manager will therefore not only be ill-equipped to deal with mental health issues as and when they arise, but could also potentially make the situation worse, with very unfortunate results for the member of staff concerned (as well as for the wider team and, indeed, the whole organization). Of course, it is not expected that people managers should become experts in mental health issues, but there is certainly much to be gained by going beyond the stereotypes and distorted understandings of mental health that are common in the popular consciousness. The better our level of understanding, the better equipped we will be for responding to the challenges involved, and the more confident we will be.

> *Practice focus 28.1*
> Keith was delighted to be appointed as the new team manager, as he knew it was a very hardworking and committed team. However, he was a little anxious about Lorraine, who was known to have mental health problems. He was unsure how he would respond to her, as he had had no previous experience of people with mental health problems in his work or private life. He had to admit that this situation made him feel quite anxious and unconfident – not a good way to be approaching his new job. However, he was very pleasantly surprised that Lorraine was fine for most of the time and, when she did start to get unduly anxious or to show any sign of becoming depressed, her colleagues would rally round and be very supportive of her. Keith was much reassured by this and could see that his concerns had been misplaced. He spoke to his supervisor about the situation, and she reinforced the important message that mental health issues in the workplace can be very challenging at Times, but there is certainly nothing to panic about and much that can be done to prevent difficult situations from arising and helping staff with mental health needs to get the benefits of being actively involved in the workplace.

Meeting the challenge

Mental health problems can be quite frightening at times, not only for the people experiencing them directly, but also for others around them. There can be times when people's behaviour can seem very irrational and can therefore be quite unsettling. It can take us outside our comfort zone and encourage us to get away from the situation at the earliest opportunity. When such feelings arise, it is important that we do not panic and overreact. There are ways in which such situations can be managed effectively, but it is important to remain calm and continue to be reasonable at all Times. It can be quite dangerous for people to respond to what they perceive as irrational behaviour on someone else's part by behaving irrationally in their own right.

There is, of course, a need to keep these matters in proportion. We should not assume that all manifestations of mental health problems are difficult and demanding or in some way extreme. It is true that mental health problems can be extreme at times, but the same argument could be made about aggression and violence – that is, although violence can take extreme forms at times, we need to keep incidences of aggression in proportion and recognize that the majority of them will not result in violence (see Chapter 26).

 I have already made the point that it is important to keep pressures manageable and therefore keep stress at bay. This is a sufficiently important point to merit being re-emphasized. We need to be fully aware that there is a strong relationship between stress and mental health problems, in so far as each can exacerbate the other, creating a potentially very destructive vicious circle.

It is also wise to make sure that we are protecting any staff who have mental health problems from discrimination, and particularly from bullying and harassment. It is unfortunately the case that many people regard someone with a mental health problem as an easy target for unfair, undignified treatment. There can therefore often be overt discrimination which can at times amount to bullying or harassment. However, there are also the more subtle forms of discrimination to take into consideration. Very often it is not deliberate, overt discrimination, but, rather, more subtle, institutionalized forms of discrimination where, for example, people are making unwarranted assumptions about a person with mental health problems or, indeed, about people with mental health problems as a category (again we return to the significance of stereotypes.)

A key aspect of meeting the challenge is being prepared to offer support where needed. Unfortunately, what many people do when they encounter somebody with a mental health problem is to back away from them, as if they are trying to protect themselves from some unknown danger. It is as if they have allowed themselves to be unduly influenced by the fantasies and mystique that have come to be associated with mental health problems. It is therefore particularly important that people managers do not allow this to happen, that we are sufficiently tuned in to the dangers of allowing such distortions to shape our thinking and our reactions. We have to get past the stereotypical images and the misinformation about mental health. It is indeed the case that some people with mental health problems can be violent and can even commit murder. However, this applies to only a tiny proportion of the number of people with mental health problems, and so we have to guard against any sort of disproportionate reaction to a person with mental health problems. We need to be able to offer support where it is needed and not make the significant mistake of backing away from someone.

> *Practice focus 28.2*
> Carla attended a course on mental health problems in the workplace because she was quite interested in the subject as her father had suffered from bipolar disorder for many years. She was surprised to learn how unfamiliar other participants were with mental health issues. They had been part of her experience of growing up, and she had not realized how anxiety provoking the subject could be for people who had had no direct experience. She was therefore able to make a very positive and helpful contribution to the course by talking about how she and her mother had coped over the years. She explained that, what had been quite difficult was the tendency for people to 'back off' whenever her father started to get manic (becoming overenthusiastic and highly charged) or to start being down (becoming depressed). These were the times when he needed support most, when he needed to understand his condition and help him deal with it, rather than leave him feeling abandoned and uncared for. Carla emphasized that her father's condition was nothing to be worried about, provided that his extremes of mood could be kept under control, but he could be quite demanding if he was given no help. She was therefore keen to make it clear that trying to turn our backs on the realities of mental health problems was likely to make the situation significantly worse.

It is also vitally important to make sure that we are familiar with the appropriate policies in the organization concerned or, where they do not exist, to be prepared to set in motion a process that will enable them to be developed. Some organizations have policies specifically relating to mental health issues, others include mental health issues under the general heading of disability, while yet others incorporate mental health issues into health and safety and/or diversity policies. Unfortunately, though, many organizations have no policy or strategy whatsoever, and individual people managers are therefore left to fend for themselves in what can at times be very difficult and unsettling circumstances.

Last but not least, in terms of rising to the challenges involved, it is essential that we seek specialist help where appropriate. Mental health problems are best dealt with by people who have a good understanding of the issues involved, a good knowledge base on which to develop their skills. Over time, people managers can develop their own good knowledge base and the skills to go with it. But, until such a Time as that knowledge base, and the associated skills, are available to draw upon, it may well be necessary to enlist the support of specialist help – for example, through occupational health, through an employee assistance programme where one is available, or through engaging a consultant who specializes in workplace well-being issues, including mental health concerns. As with the discussion of mediation in Chapter 25, this last option is likely to incur expense, but, given that this could prevent one or more people from leaving, that could be a very wise investment of money in the medium to long term.

Conclusion

The prevalence of mental health problems in society at large and in the workplace in particular is generally far higher than most people tend to realize. The common perception of people with mental health problems is that they are a small, but dangerous minority who should ideally be kept away from the community under lock and key where necessary. The reality, by contrast, is that significant numbers of people experience mental health problems, and the vast majority of those people present no threat to others. We therefore have to make sure that we are not basing our reaction to colleagues with mental health problems on distortions and stereotypical assumptions that were perhaps fed to us as part of our upbringing – through the media, for example. To equate mental health problems with the risk of, for example, serious violence is the equivalent of assuming that anyone who supports a football club is a football hooligan.

Once again, it has to be recognized that the very nature of mental health problems can mean that the presence of such difficulties can be very unsettling when they do arise. It is therefore important to emphasize the need not to panic, as that can escalate the situation and produce far higher levels of tension. Somebody who is experiencing mental health difficulties is likely to benefit from understanding and appropriate support. This again is an aspect of the employer's duty of care, and therefore something to be given serious attention.

Points to ponder

1. How might stress cause or exacerbate mental health problems?
2. Why is it important not to stereotype people who are experiencing mental health problems?
3. People will often back away from someone having mental health problems. In what ways is this dangerous and unhelpful?

Exercise 28

Why is it important not to rely on stereotypes of mental health problems? How can you ensure that staff are not causing problems by making stereotypical assumptions about one or more colleagues with mental health problems.

CHAPTER 29: DRUG AND ALCOHOL ABUSE

In this chapter you will learn how to respond to drug and alcohol problems.

Introduction

We have known for some time now that the misuse of drugs and alcohol presents a range of major problems in society at large and is often a cause, or aggravating factor, in many others (crime, violence and abuse, homelessness, and so on). We therefore have to be aware that the problems associated with drugs and alcohol can be of major proportions. We also have to recognize that the workplace is not exempt from alcohol- and drug-related problems. Indeed, if we bear in mind that a large organization can have a workforce similar in size to the population of a small town, then we should not be surprised that a certain proportion of employees will be struggling with problems associated with alcohol and/or drugs.

The Health and Social Care Information Centre (2011) gives an indication of the size of the problem in pointing out that, in relation to alcohol use in England:

> In 2003, the Cabinet Office report *Alcohol misuse: how much does it cost?* estimated that alcohol misuse costs the health service £1.7 billion per year (in 2001 prices), while the costs associated with alcohol-related crime and anti-social behaviour was estimated to be £7.3 billion each year. It also estimated that workplace costs of alcohol misuse are £6.4 billion per year through loss in productivity. (p. 63)

In addition, there will be major problems caused by the use of illegal drugs and the misuse of prescription drugs. It is therefore important that, as people managers, we are able to have at least a basic appreciation of the significance of drugs and alcohol and how they can be potentially highly problematic in the workplace for all concerned.
This chapter therefore lays the foundations for developing a fuller understanding of what we need to know and what we need to do in order to be on top of any situations that include an element of drug and/or alcohol abuse. We begin by considering the effects of alcohol and drugs problems before moving on to examine the range of responsibilities we have in trying to make sure that such problems are kept to a minimum.

The effects of alcohol and drugs problems

There is a great deal of literature available which documents just how harmful alcohol and drugs can be (see, for example, Ghodse, 2017). They can ruin people's lives. This includes, of course, the people who become addicted to the alcohol or other drugs, but is not limited to them. There can also be devastating effects for the partners, parents and children of people with drugs or alcohol problems. There can also be an adverse effect on colleagues and the organization in general. There is therefore a lot to be gained from taking seriously the problems associated with the misuse of alcohol and drugs.

The range of effects of alcohol and drugs problems is quite broad. It includes, but is not limited to, the following areas.

Reductions in quality and quantity of work
This can apply in two senses: the person who has the problem can experience a lowering of their capacity, thereby producing a lower quality and/or quantity of work, whether this is while they are directly under the influence of such substances or as a result of the overall negative effect that having such an addiction can have on someone. But, there is also a wider issue to consider, in so far as the presence of a person with such problems can produce a reduction in the quality and quantity of work on the part of other workers – other team members for example. This can be for a variety of reasons. For example, it may be that, if the person with the problem is not doing their work to a high enough standard, or is not completing their tasks fast enough, this then has a knock-on effect for a colleague who relies on good quality or Timely work from them to be able to do their own job properly.

Increased error rates
Of course, it is inevitable that there will be errors in the workplace. No person and no workplace is entirely free of errors, but the impact of alcohol and drugs can be such that the error rate increases significantly. That is, there can be more wastage of time, resources and possibly money as a result of such errors. This can have a negative effect in terms of the reputation not only of the individual concerned, but also of the team and, indeed, the organization. This in itself can have the effect of producing quite negative outcomes, something that can result in significant costs. However, there can also be increased error rates on the part of others who may, for example, be distracted by a person with drug or alcohol-related problems, or otherwise prevented from concentrating on what they are doing – for example, if they fear that somebody under the influence of alcohol or drugs may become aggressive.

KEY POINT

It is also important to recognize that it is not simply a matter that the error rate may increase, but also the significance of errors may increase, in the sense that the actual errors may become more serious. For example, an error that could have potentially catastrophic results is unlikely to occur when staff members are giving the job their full attention and are fully aware of the potentially disastrous consequences of getting something wrong. However, where drugs or alcohol are preventing the person concerned from fully focusing on the work, then the net result may well be an error that produces devastating consequences.

Tensions and conflicts
These can arise directly because of the behaviour of someone who has lost a degree of control as a result of the influence of whichever substance(s) they are using. It may also be the case that tensions and conflicts arise because different team members have different reactions to the presence of somebody with a drink or a drug-related problem. For example, it is not uncommon for teams to be split to the extent that some colleagues will be wanting to be supportive of somebody with a problem and seeking to be tolerant of any difficulties that may arise, while another group of colleagues may feel that it is dangerous to allow somebody with such problems to continue to be part of the workforce and will therefore want them to be removed.

Other staff becoming disaffected
This is an extension of the previous point in a sense. If people are aware that someone has a substance misuse-related problem, and they feel that nothing is being done about it, then the net result is that they may become disaffected. They may feel alienated, not valued by the organization. Because they do not have a sense of security, they lack the trust and the confidence in their people managers that are necessary for effective leadership. The net result of this can be that good staff leave, and take with them their experience, their competence and the learning that they have developed during their Time with the organization (see Chapter 16 for a discussion of the significant costs of staff leaving prematurely).

Potential law breaking
In some circumstances, a person with drug-related problems may be breaking the law while actually on works premises (for example, by smoking marijuana or taking some other illegal drug during a break). This clearly has significant implications for the organization concerned as a whole and specifically for people managers who are charged with ensuring that the organization and its employees are not in a position where the law is being broken.

This is not an exhaustive list, but it should be clear that there are many ways in which alcohol- and drug-related problems can be highly problematic in the workplace. What can be just as problematic, if not more so, is that these issues can interrelate and reinforce one another, producing a potentially explosive combination.

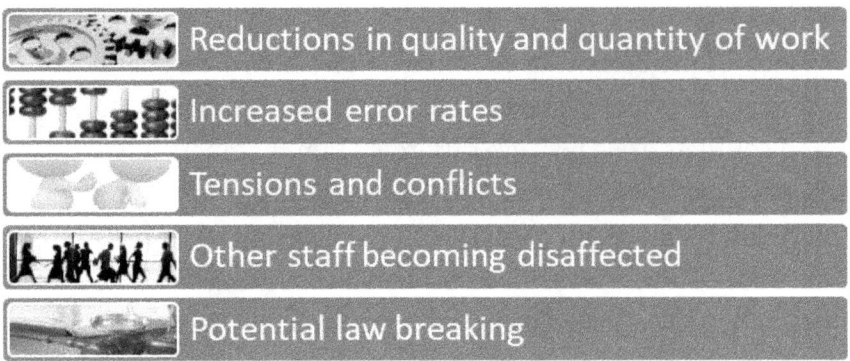

Figure 29.1 Problems associated with alcohol and drugs

It should be quite clear, then, that a head in the sand approach to alcohol and drugs problems in the workplace is a very unwise approach indeed. A much more sensible way of addressing these concerns is to develop our knowledge and understanding of what is involved and to be clear about how we need to respond to any issues that arise. With this in mind, we will now move on to look at what our responsibilities are as people managers.

> *Practice focus 29.1*
> Gavin had worked in the finance section for several years and was a highly respected and trusted employee. He did not have a single blemish on his performance record and had always been a pleasure to work with because of his cheerful and supportive manger. However, when his wife, Iris, died as a result of complications following an operation, his life changed drastically. Even months after his wife's death he showed no signs of his former cheerfulness and supportiveness. He just kept himself to himself and unsmilingly got on with his job. A few months later he started to show signs that he was 'losing it'. He was constantly making mistakes and, when gently challenged about them, he became very defensive. Steadily he went from bad to worse, and it became apparent that he was drinking heavily. Hi manager tried to talk to him about the situation in a supportive way, but Gavin again became defensive and denied that there was a problem – even though he smelled strongly of drink when he was saying this. It soon reached the point where he was making so many mistakes that he had to be suspended from duty while his manager, in conjunction with an HR adviser, decided how best to deal with the situation.

What are our responsibilities?

Fundamentally, we can see that drug and alcohol abuse issues are part of our commitment to health and safety in the workplace and the overall duty of care that goes with it. However, there is much more to it than this, in the sense that it is not simply a matter of ensuring legal compliance. There is a lot at stake in terms of how we respond to drug and alcohol abuse in terms of, for example, not wanting to lose a valuable employee (whether the person with the problems directly or someone who leaves because they are dissatisfied with the fact that someone in the workplace has such problems).

One basic, but very important, step that we can take is to make sure that we have a sufficient understanding of alcohol and drugs problems to be able to recognize problems in the early stages. Prompt early intervention can save not only a great deal of wasted Time and money, but also significant heartache. This involves being able to recognize any indicators of drink- or drug-related problems. An overall guideline that can be very useful would be: if you are at all suspicious, seek advice, specialist advice if necessary. If there is anything that is happening that leads us to believe that alcohol or drugs are at the root of the problem, then it would be very unwise to ignore any feelings of discomfort that we may have about the situation and thereby fail to take appropriate action. If you do not know what sources of advice are open to you in your particular organization, then it would be wise to find out now, rather than wait until such a problem arises and you are under pressure to do something about it.

In some ways, problems arising from drug and alcohol misuse can be very visible – for example, when somebody is obviously drunk or appears to be under the influence of a mind-altering substance. However, sometimes the indicators are more subtle than this, and it becomes a case of tuning in to people's behaviours and emotional responses to see what they tell us. What can be particularly important, though, in terms of recognizing early signs, is the wider issue of leadership, the L of *Staying CALM*. If you have managed to play an important role in developing a culture of support for one another within a team, if you have managed to encourage open communication, then it is likely that one or more members of the team will come to you if they have concerns about a colleague, not in a spirit of 'grassing them up', but, rather, in a constructive spirit of trying to make sure that they get help before the situation gets out of hand and potentially becomes a disciplinary matter.

It is also important to undertake a risk assessment in order to develop a clearer picture of the hazards involved. While we would not want to overreact and immediately think about dismissing somebody with a substance misuse problem, we also have to make sure that we are not complacent about such matters and thereby fail to recognize that there are significant risks involved (consider the list of effects of alcohol and drugs problems highlighted above). This risk assessment could take the form of a conventional health and safety risk assessment, or it may be something that is geared more narrowly towards the specifics of substance misuse. Again, you should consider seeking (specialist) advice if you are unsure about how best to proceed.

Once problems emerge it is important that we are supportive as part of our duty of care, but it is also important to make it clear that we (and our organization) will not be able to tolerate alcohol or drug misuse because of the dangerous consequences that can arise. In a sense, it is a case of getting a balance of the carrot and the stick. It is vitally important that there is clarity about: (a) the fact that we and our wider organization are willing to be supportive up to a point; but (b) there is also an important line, in the sense that, if it is crossed, then it may no longer be possible for that person to remain in employment. This can be linked to the risk assessment mentioned above.

The following guidelines can be drawn upon to help establish some clarity about what steps can be helpful in rising to the challenges involved.

Do not panic
Such situations can be very challenging and difficult to deal with in a variety of ways. It is therefore wise to seek support at an early stage. No reasonable supervisor is going to assume that you are incapable simply because you are asking for support in dealing with such a potentially fraught situation as tackling problems associated with drug and alcohol misuse. There is therefore nothing to fear in terms of losing face in seeking such support.

Panicking can create a vicious circle, in that the higher level of tension caused by such panic can lead to additional pressures, while the loss of trust, respect and credibility on our part as a result of 'losing our cool' can seriously undermine our ability to influence such situations. We can therefore be increasing pressures while also reducing our ability to deal with them effectively, clearly a dangerous undertaking. We therefore need to take the utmost care to ensure that we remain calm in responding to such difficult situations.

One step that can be useful in this regard is to consider what precisely we are afraid of. What exactly is it that we fear will happen if we are not careful? That can then provide us with a platform from which we can develop our strategies for making sure that things do not go awry, so that we are better equipped to remain calm and in control.

Refer to occupational health where necessary
Alcohol and drugs problems generally have a strong health component to them, in so far as the misuse of such substances can be very detrimental to health. Indeed, they can have devastating consequences for health, and can even be fatal at times. It is to be hoped that the occupational health service that the organization uses (whether in house or on a 'buying in' basis) will have sufficient knowledge and understanding of the particular

challenges associated with alcohol and drugs problems. If they do not, then it may at times be necessary to seek help from a specialist organization that deals with the complex challenges of drug- and alcohol-related problems.

Confidential counselling services, whether part of occupational health provision or separate from them, can also be of considerable benefit in the right circumstances, but once again it is important not to see counselling as a panacea for all problems. For example, somebody who is drinking heavily may be totally unwilling to engage with counselling services or may do so only in a tokenistic way (for example to avoid disciplinary proceedings).

Take note of policies and procedures

Once again, it is important to be aware of the policies and procedures of the organization concerned. One aspect in particular that it is important to be aware of is whether or not there is a policy and related procedure in relation to testing. This is a very contentious issue. One school of thought is that it can be very helpful for organizations to use random testing for the presence of alcohol or other drugs in employees' bloodstreams. However, another school of thought argues that this creates a culture of mistrust and can therefore be difficult to justify in the context of a commitment to human resources and the value of people as a key element of organizational success. However, whichever school of thought you subscribe to, it is none the less important that we are clear about what the policy of the organization is, to make sure that we do not potentially face difficulties ourselves for failing to adhere to appropriate policies and procedures.

Make sure you are aware of your organization's policy provisions in relation to drug and alcohol use For example, some organizations have zero tolerance of alcohol and will be prepared to discipline anyone who consumes alcohol at work or turns up for work under the influence of alcohol. Other organizations will allow a certain amount of social drinking, while others will have no guidelines at all. It is wise to be aware of what the boundaries are in relation to such matters *before* you get involved in what can be difficult situations, rather than wait until something happens and then find yourself having to deal with some complex matters without a full grasp of the organization's approach to such circumstances. Of course, you can always attempt to find out once the situation arises, but this is a far from ideal way of responding to such concerns.

It should be clear by now that there are various responsibilities that people managers face when it comes to addressing drug and alcohol problems. There is no simple or magic answer, but it is to be hoped that what we have discussed can lead to a fuller understanding and a firmer basis, therefore, for addressing the concerns presented by this aspect of working life.

Practice focus 29.2
Jenny was a well-liked and very competent member of the team. She dressed in a way that led many people to see her as something of a hippy character. Over Time her manager, Lisa, became suspicious that Jenny was using cannabis quite heavily. Lisa had no moral qualms about this, as she felt that small-scale personal use was nothing to worry about. What Lisa did worry about was that Jenny was becoming increasingly vague and unfocused, finding it increasingly difficult to concentrate. Lisa was aware of the dangers of stereotyping and assuming that, because of her dress style, Jenny was a cannabis smoker. She therefore sought advice from HR, as she did not want to confront Jenny about her concerns and then find herself being accused of stereotyping. She found the advice very helpful, namely that if she had concerns about performance, she had every right to raise the issue with Jenny in supervision and, while it was legitimate to explore the possibility of the problem owing much to long-term cannabis use, she should not jump to the conclusion that this was the case. Lisa therefore decided to put the issue on the agenda for Jenny's next supervision session.

Conclusion

Many organizations seem fortunate enough to be able to function for a long period of Time without alcohol- or drugs-related problem appearing. By contrast, many other organizations can face significant and recurring difficulties. Either way, it is important that, as people managers, we have a clear understanding of the nature of the types of problems we are likely to encounter and feel reasonably confident that we know what to do in order to tackle the complex and sensitive issues involved. These problems can be very challenging, in the sense that they can really put us to the test in terms of how calm we are able to remain in difficult circumstances, how clearly we can think in potentially fraught situations, and how well we can continue to be effective leaders in times that can be characterized by high levels of tension and potentially conflict. The positive side to this is that a people manager who is able to address drug and alcohol problems skilfully, constructively and sensitively is likely to not only win a lot of friends, but also, more importantly, establish a firm basis of respect, trust and credibility, the value of which I have already emphasized quite considerably. There is therefore much to be gained from building on the foundations of knowledge and understanding laid in this chapter.

Points to ponder

1. What adverse effects can drugs and alcohol have on the workplace?
2. Why is it important not to panic?
3. Why is it important to have alcohol and drugs issues covered by a relevant policy?

Exercise 29

How might you recognize that a member of staff was having problems with drugs or drink? What sources of help might you be able to access to support them?

CHAPTER 30: INCLUSION

In this chapter you will learn how to make your workplace as fair and inclusive as possible.

Introduction

This chapter reinforces the importance of issues discussed in Chapter 1 in relation to equality and diversity. The question of valuing everyone for what they bring and not excluding people because they are different in some way is an important part of not only the idea of valuing diversity, but also of inclusion. It has been known for some considerable time that there is a propensity for in-groups and out-groups to form in any collective setting, including work organizations. There are therefore various means by which some people who are perceived to be different in one or more ways can be assigned to the out-group category, and, whether deliberately or unwittingly, end up in a subordinate position where they are not fully included in what is happening. Clearly, this is not in keeping with the idea of valuing diversity, but nor is it in keeping with the idea of having a people management approach that is genuinely people oriented and not dehumanizing (as so much of the existing literature has been over the decades).

Not respecting diversity is one way in which certain individuals or groups of people can be excluded, but it is not the only one. For example, if we are not careful, we can unwittingly reinforce the process of exclusion (assigning people to out-groups, rather than in-groups) by writing people off as a by-product of trying to groom the high flyers for reaching the top (Hytner and Turnock, 2005). This is, in effect, a process of elitism that I am questioning. If the emphasis is on producing a small number of exceptional performers (as indeed many organizations do), then what is happening is that we are gearing ourselves up towards failure, by what amounts to defining those people who are not part of the elite few as, in some respect, failures or non-runners. We will return to this point below. If we are genuinely committed to helping people to achieve their best, then we have to make sure that we are as fully inclusive as we reasonably can be.

This chapter is therefore concerned with exploring the processes that can lead to certain people being systematically excluded from full participation in the organization and therefore blocked from achieving their best and making an optimal contribution to the success of the enterprise (and to their own growth and development). We begin by exploring patterns of exclusion and then move on to consider what is involved in having a genuine commitment to inclusion. The word 'genuine' is a key one here, as there has to be real commitment to exclusion, as tokenistic attempts will ultimately fail (and will also, in all likelihood, alienate people who become aware that there is no sincerity involved). This is a further example of the importance of the A, for Authenticity, of *Staying CALM*.

Patterns of exclusion

There are various ways in which people can come to be excluded and thereby assigned to what can be seen as a secondary or subordinate status. The following is not an exhaustive list, but it does cover some of the main areas in which there is a potential for certain people to be excluded. It should provide a good platform for us to develop our understanding of the complex and subtle ways in which exclusion generally works. That understanding, in turn should stand us in good stead when it comes to promoting inclusion, a topic to which we will return below.

Gender

'The boys' club' is a well-recognized phenomenon whereby people in positions of power are predominantly, if not exclusively, men and often from the same social background. This can leave women in an organization feeling that, at best, they can only ever play a secondary role, because they have no real access to what can be seen as important in an organization – in terms of their own career path, for example. These problems can often be reinforced by forms of language that are male oriented – for example, the common tendency to use 'he' to refer to individuals of unknown gender, thereby reinforcing the idea that it is a man's world. A related example would be the use of the term 'manpower' instead of gender-neutral terms like human resources or workforce.

Women can also be excluded by, for example, important decisions being made in the pub after work when many of the women have gone home to attend to domestic matters. In addition, there is the well-documented idea of the 'glass ceiling', the combination of subtle processes by which women can find it extremely difficult to break into management, especially senior management (Hayward, 2005). Linked to this is the idea of the 'sticky floor' which refers to the difficulties women and minority groups can have in moving away from the lowest-paid jobs in an organization. As Miller and Katz (2002) comment: 'White women may express concern about their organization's glass ceiling, while remaining oblivious to the plight of women of color who are stuck to its sticky floor' (p. 101).

Such processes of exclusion are generally very subtle, and so, if we are not alert to the dangers associated with them, we can easily miss them and then unwittingly reinforce their very unfair and destructive effects.

Race/ethnicity

Overt racism can exclude members of minority ethnic communities, but so too can institutionalized racism – that is, racial inequalities that are built in to systems, organizational cultures, stereotypes and taken-for-granted assumptions. This can be reflected in language use. It is often the case that subtle patterns of language and behaviour can give a clear (but not necessarily intentional) message: you do not belong here. If there is an atmosphere or a culture which supports the idea that this is a white environment and that black people are 'tolerated', rather than fully integrated into a multicultural, multi-ethnic, diverse work environment, then we should not be surprised if this stands in the way of members of ethnic minorities fulfilling their potential in such a setting.

KEY POINT

We need to make sure that we are not complacent about exclusion on racial or ethnic grounds. It is very easy to assume that, because we may have no racial prejudices ourselves, there is no problem to address. The reality, however, is very far removed from this simplistic idea, and so we need to take whatever reasonable steps we can to ensure that we do not lose sight of the dangers of exclusion. If *we do, we not only fail in our duty to get the best out of people, but also could face a backlash of subsequent claims of racial discrimination and the considerable ill feeling that can accompany them.

Disability

A failure to take disability issues seriously can lead to physical, social, developmental and psychological exclusion:

- *Physical.* Certain parts of buildings may be inaccessible to people with mobility or visual difficulties if appropriate facilities are not provided (in some cases whole buildings may be entirely inaccessible to some people). Similarly, some disabled people may not be able to use particular equipment if the necessary adjustments have not been made.
- *Social.* Anxieties on the part of some non-disabled people can mean that they may be reluctant to involved people with disabilities in social activities. In addition, in some cases, sadly, the tendency to exclude disabled people may be based on overt prejudice.
- *Developmental.* Some disabled people will be denied opportunities to learn and develop because insufficient thought was given to their needs. For example, I have come across situations where some training courses were not available to people with certain disabilities due to the unsuitability of the venue.
- *Psychological.* Partly as a result of the combination of the above three sets of factors, people with disabilities can feel isolated and alienated because they are made to feel that they are awkward and difficult – generally due to the lack of planning on the part of the organization as to how they would ensure that people with disabilities were not disadvantaged more than necessary.

These problems could simply be down to practical matters, such as failing to make the necessary adjustments to allow people with disabilities to make a full contribution to the organization, or, in some cases, there may be a more sinister underlying failure to recognize the importance of disability as part of a commitment to valuing diversity.

Age

Many organizations can be youth orientated, giving older staff the message that their experience is not valued, while, on the other hand, other organizations can have an older, more established group of staff who may make it difficult for the interests of younger people to feature as part of the wider organization. Younger people can therefore feel it is difficult to establish themselves, and may not feel that they are welcome in that particular team or organization. Age is potentially a significant source of discrimination and therefore, quite possibly, of exclusion. A genuinely authentic approach to inclusion therefore needs to take account of age factors too.

Once again, the processes of exclusion can be very subtle – for example, in terms of the language that is used, language that may imply that older people are past their best or that younger people have little to offer because of their lack of life experience.

> *Practice focus 30.1*
> Mark, the section manager, was asked by his boss, Sylvia, to draw up the text for an advertisement for the appointment of a new member of the team, following Sunil's departure, and to pass this on to the human resources team. He had never done this before and was a little apprehensive. He discussed the issue with a couple of the team members and then, after a number of false starts, he produced a draft that he was reasonably happy with – not bad for a first attempt, he thought. However, when he passed it on to the HR team, he was taken aback when Sheila, an HR adviser, told him they could not accept it. She explained that he could not use the term, 'Young and dynamic', due to age discrimination legislation. It was also explained to him that it was a discriminatory assumption to imply that you have to be young to be dynamic. Sheila went on to say that there are an awful lot of older people around who are very dynamic and a great deal of younger people who are anything but. Mark had never thought about this before, but Sheila's helpful explanation had helped him realize that he had indeed been making an ageist assumption. What they wanted, he now appreciated, was someone dynamic and the age of the person was actually irrelevant.

Sexual identity

Many workplace cultures reflect overt or subtle homophobic tendencies, leaving gay, lesbian, bisexual and trans people feeling at best unwelcome or even unsafe. It is important to note, therefore, that a commitment to valuing diversity does not limit itself to the major 'isms' of racism and sexism, but also recognizes how damaging it can be for the organization, and especially for the individuals concerned, if subtle patterns of exclusion lead to people whose sexual orientation is not that of the majority from feeling that they are not fully part of the team.

Again, the exclusion can be overt and fuelled by prejudice or more subtle and rooted in institutionalized discrimination (for example, the stereotypes, derogatory language and irrational fears associated with same-sex relationships). Either way, the result can be that certain members of the organization experience exclusion and are therefore prevented from achieving their best.

Job category

There are various ways in which hierarchies can be established, leaving certain groups who are at the lower end of the pecking order feeling excluded, not listened to and therefore not valued. For example, an emphasis on the needs and interests of professional staff can mean that administrative staff feel that they are not taken seriously, that they are just an 'add on', rather than an essential part of an effective organization.

Similarly, manual staff may feel that their needs are not a priority within the organization, because they are seen as in some way second-class citizens. It is therefore important that a commitment to inclusion recognizes the potential difficulties associated with cultures that can be quite divisive by attaching more kudos and prestige to certain groups and thereby assigning a lower status to others, without recognizing that everybody within an organization has an important role to play in terms of making it a successful organization.

It is therefore important that we give a strong, clear message that there are no unimportant people in our organization

New staff

Miller and Katz (2002) make the important point that: 'If an organization brings in new people but doesn't enable them to contribute, those new people are bound to fail, no matter how talented they are. *Diversity without inclusion does not work*' (p. 17). If there is a long-standing staff group who have formed a clique (an 'in-group'), then they may make it difficult for new staff to feel welcome and involved if they do not make the effort to make them feel at home in their new environment. In some cases, new staff can feel so unwelcome that they soon leave (see Chapter 16 for a discussion of the significance of this).

Not being a high flyer
The point was made earlier that the majority of staff can be excluded to a certain extent if the focus of the organization is on helping a small elite to achieve excellence, rather than helping everybody to achieve their best. Hyter and Turnock (2005) emphasize the significance of this: 'We propose a culture of development that will unlock everyone's potential, and replace the current business reality of wasted talent and lost productivity' (p. 9).

While there is no reason why 'high flyers' cannot be helped to achieve excellence, we have to make sure that this is not at the expense of promoting the learning and development of all staff and thereby helping them to fulfil their potential. Hyter and Turnock (2005) again make apt comment:

> Through an inclusive approach to development that provides all employees with the opportunities usually reserved for a select few, organizations would maximize potential and productivity.
>
> (p. 4)

As people managers we should therefore be asking ourselves whether the organization we work for has an inclusive approach to development or an elitist, exclusionary one. If the latter, we would be wise to consider how we can change things in the direction of the former.

This overview should give a picture of just how many different ways there can be potentially for individuals or groups of people to be excluded. If we come back to the idea that a key part of people management is to get the best out of people by helping them get the best out of themselves, then clearly inclusion is something we have to give our full attention to if we are not to allow certain people to function at a level way below their potential because they feel excluded and undervalued.

Promoting inclusion
Given the importance of inclusion and the damage that can be done by exclusionary tendencies, there is clearly an onus on people managers to do whatever we reasonably can to make sure that inclusion is high on the agenda and is given genuine attention. There are various ways in which this can happen, and it is important to give careful consideration to these. What they all have in common is a reliance on the L, for Leadership, of *Staying CALM,* in the sense that what we need to do establish an overview, to see the big picture, and develop a clear vision of where we are trying to get to and what path we need to follow to get there.

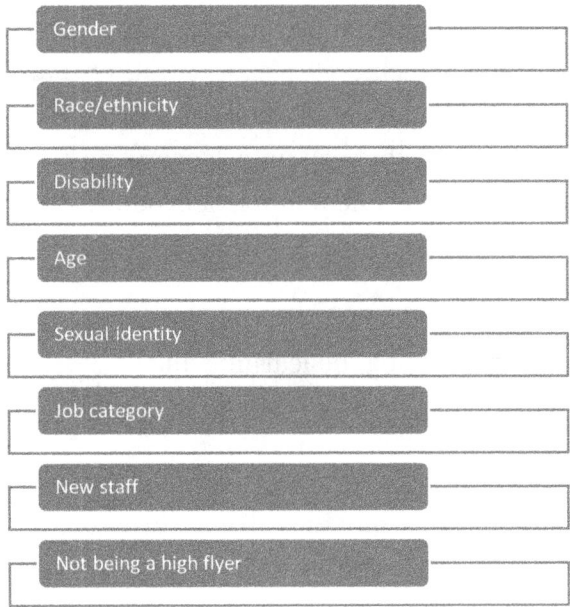

Figure 30.1 Common forms of exclusion

One important way is to make sure that we are taking seriously the matter of equality and diversity, as discussed in Chapter 1. If we have a tokenistic approach to such matters, then we are highly unlikely to get it right when it comes to inclusion. They are, in effect, two sides of the same coin.

It is also important to make sure that no groups of staff are being systematically excluded (whether deliberately or not). In Chapter 11 I made the point that a key characteristic of leadership is the ability to understand how organizations work and to be able to influence the culture within our own particular leadership domain. This is particularly the case here in terms of inclusion, in so far as a leader should be aware of what is going on and should be able to identify fairly easily any exclusionary processes and take whatever steps are necessary to halt them.

In some circumstances it is necessary to regard the exclusion of individuals as potentially an instance of bullying or harassment. If, as a result of this exclusion, a person is being treated in a way that falls below acceptable standards of dignity at work, then of course this is likely to constitute an incidence of bullying or harassment, and needs to be dealt with accordingly, as discussed in Chapter 24.

 When it comes to promoting inclusion, it is important to forge a culture in which the value of inclusion is recognized. There is a degree of irony here, in the sense that, if the culture we work in is itself a divisive and exclusionary, one then we are going to face major challenges in terms of how to get people to value inclusion and to work towards it as an important goal. It is therefore very important that we get this right as far as possible, that we are able to do what we reasonably can – especially by drawing on our leadership skills – to move forward in our efforts to put inclusion high on the agenda for our own domain of leadership.

> *Practice focus 30.2*
> Mike was surprised when he became the new centre manager just how divided the place was. He could detect no sense of common purpose or feeling of 'we are all in this together'. The vacancy for a manager had arisen because his predecessor had died, so he did not want to speak ill of the dead, but he did find himself doubting the leadership capabilities of the previous postholder. What soon became very clear to Mike was that there were various subgroups of staff, cliques that were more interested in their own little corner than they were in making the centre and its activities a success. He did not want to come across as the new broom that was trying to sweep clean, as he knew that would alienate a lot of people. However, he did know that he would need to find some ways of breaking up the current cliques and develop a more inclusive culture. He recognized that it could be a long, hard struggle to do that, but he was fully aware that he would have to, as the present set up, with such significant exclusionary practices, was certainly not acceptable to him and would not lead to a well-run centre that achieved its aims.

Conclusion

It was a deliberate decision on my part to begin the manual with a chapter on equality and diversity because I regard these issues as crucial to the success of any people management endeavour. It was similarly a deliberate decision on my part to end with a chapter on inclusion which, to a certain extent, echoes the concerns around discrimination that lead us to take equality and diversity seriously. We can therefore see a close connection between the opening and closing chapters, encasing, as it were, the other chapters in an overall commitment to treating people fairly (which is, after all, what equality is all about).

There are, as we have seen, various ways in which exclusion can occur, and so we have to be equally varied in our attempts to promote inclusion. However, each of the chapters in the three parts of the manual can make at least a small contribution towards developing inclusion. This is because, at the end of the day, organizations will only be effective if their people are effective, and their people will only be effective if there are effective people managers. The repetition of that word 'effective' is crucial here, because being effective means that we have to have clear goals, clear plans for achieving those goals and proper measures in place to ensure that people are empowered to achieve the goals that are likely to motivate them to move forward. People who are not feeling included or valued, who feel they are not being treated fairly, are highly unlikely to feel empowered, and are therefore going to be at a significant disadvantage when it comes to achieving their best. Hyter and Turnock (2005): 'inclusion and a culture of development, where all employees are encouraged to maximize their potential, will result in a company maximizing its productivity' (p. 112). A commitment to inclusion is therefore a key part of a broader commitment to effective people management.

Points to ponder
1. In what ways might sexism lead to a lack of inclusiveness?
2. In what ways might racism lead to a lack of inclusiveness?
3. How might organizational culture contribute to a lack of inclusiveness?

Exercise 30
What harm might the various forms of exclusion do in the workplace? What can you do to ensure that exclusionary practices are eliminated as far as possible?

References

ACAS (2015) *Code of Practice 1: Disciplinary and Grievance Procedures*, London, The Stationery Office. https://www.acas.org.uk/acas-code-of-practice-for-disciplinary-and-grievance-procedures/html

ACAS (2019) *Stress and Anxiety at Work*. https://www.acas.org.uk/stress-and-anxiety-at-work.

Adair, J. (2009) *Effective Motivation: How to Get the Best Results from Everyone*, 2nd edn, London, Pan.

Adams, J. (2007) *Managing People in Organizations: Contemporary Theory and Practice*, Basingstoke, Palgrave Macmillan.

Afshar, H. (ed.) (1998) *Women and Empowerment: Illustrations from the Third World*, Basingstoke, Macmillan.

Allcorn, S. (2009) *Organizational Dynamics and Intervention: Tools for Changing the Workplace*, Armonk, NY, M. E. Sharpe.

Argyris, C. (1999) *On Organizational Learning*, 2nd edn, Oxford, Blackwell.

Armstrong, M. (2020) *Armstrong's Handbook of Human Resource Management Practice*, 15th edn, London, Kogan Page.

Armstrong, M. (2021) *Armstrong's Handbook of Strategic Human Resource Management*, 7th edn, London, Kogan Page.

Arroba, T. and James, K. (1992) *Pressure at Work: A Survival Guide for Managers*, 2nd edn, London, McGraw-Hill.

Back, K. and Back, K. (2005) *Assertiveness at Work: A Practical Guide to Handling Awkward Situations*, 3rd edn, Maidenhead, McGraw-Hill.

Barnes, C. and Mercer, G. (2010) *Exploring Disability*, 2nd edn, Cambridge, Polity.

Barry, B. (2005) *Why Social Justice Matters*, Cambridge, Polity.

Bartel, C. A. and Garud, R. (2005) 'Narrative Knowledge in Action: Adaptive Abduction as a Mechanism for Knowledge Creation and Exchange in Organizations', in Easterby-Smith and Lyles (2005).

Bauman, Z. (2005) *Work, Consumerism and the New Poor*, Maidenhead, Open University Press.

Baumeister, R. F. (2001) *Evil: Inside Human Violence and Cruelty*, New York, Owl Books.

Becker, B. E., Huselid, M. A. and Ulrich, D. (2001) *The HR Score Card: Linking People, Strategy and Performance*, Boston, MA, Harvard Business School Press.

Belbin, R. M. (2010) *Team Roles at Work*, London, Butterworth-Heinemann.

Bennett, T., Saundry, R. and Fisher, V. (2020) *Managing Employment Relations*, 7th edn, London, Kogan Page.

Berger, L, and Berger, D. (eds) (2018) *The Talent Management Handbook: Making Culture a Competitive Advantage by Acquiring, Identifying, Developing, and Promoting the Best People*, 3rd edn, Maidenhead, McGraw-Hill.

Bevan, S. and Cooper, C. L. (2022) *The Healthy Workforce: Enhancing Wellbeing and Productivity in the Workers of the Future*, Bingley, Emerald Publishing.

Bolton, S. C. (ed.) (2007) *Dimensions of Dignity at Work*, Oxford, Butterworth-Heinemann.

Bolton, S. C. and Houlihan, M. (2007a) 'Beginning the Search for the HRM', in Bolton and Houlihan (2007b).

Bolton, S. C. and Houlihan, M. (eds) (2007b) *Searching for the Human in Human Resource Management: Theory, Practice and Workplace Contexts*, Basingstoke, Palgrave Macmillan.

Boorman, S. (2008) 'Employee Support Strategies in Large Organisations', in Kinder, Hughes and Cooper (2008a).

Braithwaite, R. (2001) *Handling Aggression*, London, Routledge.

Brewis, J. and Linstead, S. (2009) 'Gender and Management', in Linstead, Fulop and Lilley (2009).

Brown, W. (2010) 'Negotiation and Collective Bargaining', in Colling and Terry (2010b).

Buber, M. (1958) *I and Thou*, 2nd edn, London, Continuum.

Burnes, B. (2017) *Managing Change*, 7th edn, Harlow, Pearson Education.

Butt, T. (2004) *Understanding People*, Basingstoke, Palgrave Macmillan.

Cameron, D. (ed.) (1998) *The Feminist Critique of Language: A Reader*, 2nd edn, London, Routledge.

Carroll, J. S., Rudolph, J. W. and Hatakenaka, S. (2005) 'Learning from Organizational Experience', in Easterby-Smith and Lyles (2005).

Cheese, P. (2021) *The New World of Work: Shaping a Future that Helps People, Organizations and Our Societies to Thrive*, London, Kogan Page.

Clarke, J., Gewirtz, S. and McLaughlin, E. (eds) (2000) *New Managerialism, New Welfare*, London, Sage.

Clutterbuck, D. (1998) *Learning Alliances: Tapping into Talent*, London, Chartered Institute of Personnel and Development.

Clutterbuck, D. (2020) *Coaching the Team at Work: The Definitive Guide to Team Coaching*, 2nd edn, London, Nicholas Brealey.

Colling, T. and Terry, M. (eds) (2010a) *Industrial Relations: Theory and Practice*, 3rd edn, Chichester, John Wiley & Sons.

Colling, T. and Terry, M. (2010b) 'Work, The Employment Relationship and the Field of Industrial Relations', in Colling and Terry (2010a).

Cottrell, S. (2015) *Skills for Success: Personal Development and Employability*, 3rd edn, London, Red Globe Press.

Covey, S. M. R. (2008) *The Speed of Trust*, London, Simon & Schuster.

Covey, S. R., Merrill, A. R. and Merrill, R. R. (1999) *First Things First: Coping with the Ever-Increasing Demands of the Workplace*, London, Simon & Schuster.

Coyte, M. E., Gilbert, P. and Nicholls, V. (eds) (2007) *Spirituality, Values and Mental Health*, London, Jessica Kingsley.

Crane, A., McWilliams, A., Matten, D., Moon, J. and Siegel, D. S. (eds) (2009) *The Oxford Handbook of Corporate Social Responsibility*, Oxford, Oxford University Press.

Cranwell-Ward, J. and Abbey, A. (2005) *Organizational Stress*, Basingstoke, Palgrave Macmillan.

Daniels, K. (2006) *Employee Relations in an Organisational Context*, London, Chartered Institute of Personnel and Development.

Dean, D. and Liff, S. (2010) 'Equality and Diversity: The Ultimate Industrial Relations Concern', in Colling and Terry (2010a).

DeFillippi, R. and Ornstein, S. (2005) 'Psychological Perspectives Underlying Theories of Organizational Learning', in Easterby-Smith and Lyles (2005).

Dewe, P. (2008) 'Positive Coping Strategies at Work', in Kinder, Hughes and Cooper (2008a).

Dibben, P., Klerck, G. and Wood, G. (2011) *Employment Relations: A Critical and International Approach*, London, Chartered Institute of Personnel and Development, Chapter 13.

Doherty, N. and Guyler, M. (2008) *The Essential Guide to Workplace Mediation and Conflict Resolution: Rebuilding Working Relationships*, London, Kogan Page.

Doka, K. J. and Martin, T. L. (2010) *Grieving Beyond Gender: Understanding the Ways Men and Women Mourn*, London, Routledge.

Easterby-Smith, M. and Lyles, M. A. (eds) (2005) *The Blackwell Handbook of Organizational Learning and Knowledge Management*, Oxford, Blackwell.

Ehrenreich, B. (2005) *Bait and Switch: The (Futile) Pursuit of the American Dream*, New York, Metropolitan Books.

Einarsen, S. and Hoel, H. (2008) 'Bullying and Mistreatment at Work: How Managers May Prevent and Manage Such Problems', in Kinder, Hughes and Cooper (2008a).

Elkjaer, B. (2005) 'Social Learning Theory: Learning as Participation in Social Processes', in Easterby-Smith and Lyles (2005).

Fineman, S. (ed.) (2000) *Emotion in Organizations*, 2nd edn, London, Sage.

Fletcher, C. (2008) *Appraisal, Feedback and Development: Making Performance Review Work*, 4th edn, London, Routledge.

Fulop, L. and Linstead, S. (2009a) 'Power and Politics in Organizations', in Linstead, Fulop and Lilley (2009).

Fulop, L. and Linstead, S. (2009b) 'Motivation and Meaning', in Linstead, Fulop and Lilley (2009).

Fulop, L. and Linstead, S. (with Maréchal, G.) (2009) 'Introduction: A Critical Approach to Management and Organization', in Linstead, Fulop and Lilley (2009).

Furnham, A. and Taylor, J. (2004) *The Dark Side of Behaviour at Work: Understanding and Avoiding Employees Leaving, Thieving and Deceiving*, Basingstoke, Palgrave Macmillan.

Gallos, J. V. (ed.) (2006) *Organizational Development: A Jossey-Bass Reader*, San Francisco, CA, Jossey-Bass.

Ghodse, H. (ed.) (2017) *Addiction at Work: Tackling Drug Use and Misuse in the Workplace*, London, Routledge.

Gilbert, P. (2005) *Leadership: Being Effective and Remaining Human*, Lyme Regis, Russell House Publishing.

Gill, R. (2011) *Theory and Practice of Leadership*, 2nd edn, London, Sage.

Graham, P. (ed.) (1995) *Mary Parker Follett: Prophet of Management*, Frederick, MD, Beard Books.

Green, H. (2004) *Staff Recruitment and Retention: A Good Practice Guide*, Coventry, Chartered Institute of Housing.

Hall, D. T. (1976) *Careers in Organizations*, Glenview, IL, Scott Foresman. See https://smile.amazon.co.uk/Careers-Organizations-Foundations-Organizational-Science/dp/0761915478/ref=sr_1_1?dchild=1&keywords=Careers+in+Organizations&qid=1613389931&s=books&sr=1-1

Hargie, O. (ed.) (2019) *The Handbook of Communication Skills*, 4th edn, London, Routledge.

Harne, L. and Radford, J. (2008) *Tackling Domestic Violence: Theories, Policies and Practice*, Maidenhead, Open University Press.

Harvard Business Review (2007) *Managing Your Career*, Boston, MA, Harvard Business School Press.

Harvard Business Review (2009) *Performance Appraisal: Expert Solutions to Everyday Challenges*, Boston, MA, Harvard Business School Press.

Hawkins, P. (2008) 'Foreword', in Shohet (2008).

Hayes, N. and Walsham, G. (2005) 'Knowledge Sharing and ICTs: A Relational Perspective', in Easterby-Smith and Lyles (2005).

Hayward, S. (2005) *Women Leading*, Basingstoke, Palgrave Macmillan.

Health and Safety Executive (2004) Managing Sickness Absence and Return to Work: An Employers' and Managers' Guide, London, HSE Books.

The Health and Social Care Information Centre (2011) *Statistics on Alcohol in 2011*, http://www.ic.nhs.uk/webfiles/publications/003_Health_Lifestyles/Alcohol_2011/NHSIC_Statistics_on_Alcohol_England_2011.pdf

Henmans Freeth LLP (2015) *Health and Safety at Work Essentials*, 9th edn, London, Lawpack.

Howe, D. (2008) *The Emotionally Intelligent Social Worker*, Basingstoke, Palgrave Macmillan.

Hughes, M. (2019) *Managing Change: A Critical Perspective*, 2nd edn, London, Chartered Institute of Personnel and Development.

Hughes, P. and Ferrett, E. (2021) *Introduction to Health and Safety at Work*, 7th edn, Abingdon, Routledge.

Huq, R. (2016) *The Psychology of Employee Empowerment. Concepts, Critical Themes and a Framework for Implementation.* London, Routledge.

Hyter, M. C. and Turnock, J. L. (2005) *The Power of Inclusion: Unlock the Potential and Productivity of Your Workforce*, Mississauga, Ontario, John Wiley & Sons, Canada.

Jackson, D. (2000) *Becoming Dynamic: Creating and Sustaining the Dynamic Organisation*, Basingstoke, Palgrave Macmillan.

Jaffe, S. (2021). *Work Won't Love You Back: How Devotion to Our Jobs Keeps Us Exploited, Exhausted and Alone*, London, Hurst.

Jandt, F. E. (2015) *An Introduction to Intercultural Communication*, 8th edn, London, Sage.

Johnson, M. (2004) *The New Rules of Engagement: Life-Work Balance and Employee Commitment*, London, Chartered Institute of Personnel and Development.

June, A. A. (2011) *Examining Self-Disclosure of Workers through the Exit Interview Process*, Milton Keynes, Lightning Source UK.

Kahn, J. P. and Langlieb, A. M. (2002) *Mental Health and Productivity in the Workplace: A Handbook for Organizations and Clinicians*, Chichester, Wiley.

Kahn, W. A. (2005) *Holding Fast: The Struggle to Create Resilient Caregiving Organizations*, Hove, Brunner-Routledge.

Kallen, E. (2004) *Social Inequality and Social Injustice: A Human Rights Perspective*, Basingstoke, Palgrave Macmillan.

Kandola, R. and Fullerton, J. (2000) *Diversity in Action: Managing the Mosaic*, London, Chartered Institute of Personnel and Development.

Kelloway, E. K., Teed, M. and Prosser, M. (2008) 'Leading to a Healthy Workplace', in Kinder, Hughes and Cooper (2008).

Kinder, A., Hughes, R. and Cooper, C. L. (eds) (2008a) *Employee Well-Being Support: A Workplace Resource*, Chichester, John Wiley & Sons.

Kinder, A., Hughes, R. and Cooper, C. L. (2008b) 'Introduction: Adapting to Change', in Kinder, Hughes and Cooper (2008a).

Kotter, J. P. (2006) 'Leading Change: Why Transformation Efforts Fail', in Gallos (2006).

Kouzes, J. and Posner. B (2017) *The Leadership Challenge*, 6th edn, San Francisco, CA, Jossey-Bass.

Lancer, N., Clutterbuck, D. and Megginson, D. (2016) *Techniques for Coaching and Mentoring*, 2nd edn, London, Routledge.

Lewis, C. (2009) *The Definitive Guide to Workplace Mediation and Managing Conflict at Work*, Weybridge, Roper Benberthy Publishing.

Linstead, S., Fulop, L. and Lilley, S. (eds) (2009) *Management and Organization: A Critical Text*, 2nd edn, Basingstoke, Palgrave Macmillan.

Malik, K. (2008) *Strange Fruit: Why Both Sides are Wrong in the Race Debate*, Oxford, Oneworld.

Macdonald, L. A. C. (2005) *Wellness at Work: Protecting and Promoting Employee Wellbeing*, London, Chartered Institute of Personnel and Development.

Marchington, M. and Wilkinson, A. (2008) *Human Resource Management at Work: People Management and Development*, 4th edn, London, Chartered Institute of Personnel and Development.

Marris, P. H. (2006) 'Revolutions in OD: The New and the New, New Things', in Gallos (2006).

Mayon-White, B. (ed.) (1996) *Planning and Managing Change*, London, Harper & Row.

Michaels, W. B. (2016) *The Trouble with Diversity: How we Learned to Love Identity and Ignore Equality*, New York, Picador.

Micklethwait, J. and Wooldridge, A. (1997) *The Witch Doctors: What the Management Gurus are Saying, Why It Matters and How to Make Sense of It*, London, Mandarin.

Miller, F. A. and Katz, J. H. (2002) *The Inclusion Breakthrough: Unleashing the Real Power of Diversity*, San Francisco, CA, Berrett-Koehler Publishers.

Miller, W. R. and Rollnick, S. (2012) *Motivational Interviewing: Helping People Change*, 3rd edn, New York, Guilford.

Miller, D. M., Lipsedge, M. and Litchfield, P. (eds) (2002) *Work and Mental Health: An Employers' Guide*, London, Gaskell.

Morrison, T. (2006) *Supervision in Social Care*, 3rd edn, Brighton, Pavilion.

Moss, B. and Thompson, N. (2019) *Responding to Loss: A Learning and Development Manual*, 2nd edn, Brighton, Pavilion.

Moss, B. and Thompson, N. (2020) *The Values-based Practice Manual*, Wrexham, Avenue Media solutions.

Murphy, T. and Oberlin, L. H. (2016) *Overcoming Passive-Aggression: How to Stop Hidden Anger from Spoiling Your Relationships, Career and Happiness*, Boston, MA, Da Capo Lifelong Books.

Navarro, J. (2008) *What Everybody is Saying*, New York, HarperCollins.

Newell, S. and Shackleton, V. (2017) 'Selection and Assessment in an Interactive Decision-Action Process', in Redman and Wilkinson (2017).

Northouse, P. G. (2022) *Leadership: Theory and Practice*, 9th edn, London, Sage.

Oliver, M. (2009) *Understanding Disability: From Theory to Practice*, 2nd edn, Basingstoke, Palgrave Macmillan.

Orford, J., Natera, G., Copello, A. *et al.* (2014) *Coping with Alcohol and Drug Problems: The Experiences of Family Members in Three Contrasting Cultures*, London, Routledge.

Osborn-Jones, T. (2004) 'The Way People are Managed', in Rees and McBain (2004).

Parekh, B. (2006) *Rethinking Multiculturalism: Cultural Diversity and Political Theory*, 2nd edn, Basingstoke, Palgrave Macmillan.

Parker, G. M. (2008) *Team Players and Teamwork: New Strategies for Developing Successful Collaboration*, San Francisco, CA, Jossey-Bass.

Pedler, M., Burgoyne, J. and Boydell, T. (2013) *A Manager's Guide to Self-Development*, 6th edn, Maidenhead, McGraw-Hill.

Perlmutter, F. D., Bailey, D. and Netting, F. E. (2001) *Managing Human Resources in the Human Services: Supervisory Challenges*, Oxford, Oxford University Press.

Peter, L. J. (1993) *The Peter Principle*, Cutchogue, NY, Buccaneer Books.

Pink, D. (2018) *Drive*, Edinburgh, Canongate Books.

Porter, M. E. (2004) *The Competitive Strategy: Techniques for Analyzing Industries and Competitors*, New York, First Free Press Export Edition.

Procter, S., Fulop, L., Linstead, S., Mueller, F. and Sewell, G. (2009) 'Managing Teams', in Linstead, Fulop and Lilley (2009).

Pugh, D. (1986) 'Understanding and Managing Organizational Change', in Mayon-White (1996).

Redman, T. and Wilkinson, A. (eds) (2017) *Contemporary Human Resource Management: Text and Cases*, 5th edn, Harlow, Pearson Education.

Rees, D. and McBain, R. (eds) (2004) *People Management: Challenges and Opportunities*, Basingstoke, Palgrave Macmillan.

Revans, R. (1980) *Action Learning: New Techniques for Management*, London, Blond & Briggs.

Roberts, G. (2005) *Recruitment and Selection*, 2nd edn, London, Chartered Institute of Personnel and Development.

Robertson, I. and Cooper, C. (2011) *Well-Being: Productivity and Happiness at Work*, Basingstoke, Palgrave Macmillan.

Robertson, I. and Tinline, G. (2008) 'Understanding and Improving Psychological Well-Being for Individual and Organisational Effectiveness', in Kinder, Hughes and Cooper (2008a).

Robson, F. (2009) *Effective Inductions*, London, Chartered Institute of Personnel and Development (toolkit).

Rowlands, J. (1998) 'A Word of the Times, but What Does it Mean? Empowerment in the Discourse and Practice of Development', in Afshar (1998).

Russell, K. (2008) *Off the Sick List! How to Turn Employee Absence into Attendance*, London, MX Publishing.

Schnall, P. L., Dobson, M. and Rosskam, E. (eds) (2017) *Unhealthy Work: Causes, Consequences, Cures*, London, Routledge.

Schwarz, R. (2006) 'The Facilitator and Other Facilitative Roles', in Gallos (2006).

Senge, P. M. (2006) *The Fifth Discipline: The Art and Practice of the Learning Organization*, 2nd edn, London, Random House.

Shohet, R. (ed.) (2008) *Passionate Supervision*, London, Jessica Kingsley Publishers.

Simms, M. and Charlwood, D. (2010) 'Trade Unions: Power and Influence in a Changed Context', in Colling and Terry (2010a).

Smith, H. and Smith, M. K. (2008) *The Art of Helping Others: Being Around, Being There, Being Wise*, London, Jessica Kingsley Publishers.

Stein, H. F. (2007) *Insight and Imagination: A Study in Knowing and Not-Knowing in Organizational Life*, Plymouth, University Press of America.

Stephens, T. and Hallas, J. (2006) *Bullying and Sexual Harassment: A Practical Handbook*, Oxford, Chandos.

Stewart, M. (2009) *The Management Myth: Why the Experts Keep Getting it Wrong*, New York, W. W. Norton.

Tannen, D. (2001) *Talking from 9 to 5: Women and Men at Work*, 2nd edn, New York: Harper.

Taylor, F. (2003) *Principles of Scientific Management*, Mineola, NY, Dover Publications (originally published in 1911).

Tehan, M. (2007) 'The Compassionate Workplace: Leading with the Heart', *Illness, Crisis & Loss* 15(3).

Thompson, N. (2007) *Power and Empowerment*, Lyme Regis, Russell House Publishing.

Thompson, N. (2009) *Loss, Grief and Trauma in the Workplace*, New York, Routledge.

Thompson, N. (2016a) *The Authentic Leader*, London, Palgrave Macmillan.

Thompson, N. (2016b) *The Professional Social Worker: Meeting the Challenge*, 2nd edn, London, Bloomsbury.

Thompson, N. (2018a) *Effective Communication*, 3rd edn, London, Bloomsbury.

Thompson, N. (2018b) *Promoting Equality: Working with Diversity and Difference*, 4th edn, London, Bloomsbury.

Thompson, N. (2019a) *Promoting Equality, Valuing Diversity: A Learning and Development Manual*, 2nd edn, Brighton, Pavilion.

Thompson, N. (2019b) *The Managing Stress Practice Manual*, Wrexham, Avenue Media Solutions.

Thompson, N. (2019c) *Mental Health and Well-being: Alternatives to the Medical Model*, New York, Routledge.

Thompson, N. (2020) *The Problem Solver's Practice Manual*, Wrexham, Avenue Media Solutions.

Thompson, N. (2021a) *Anti-discriminatory Practice*, 7th edn, London, Bloomsbury.

Thompson, N. (2021b) *People Skills*, 5th edn, London, Bloomsbury.

Thompson, N. (2022) *The Loss and Grief Practice Manual*, Wrexham, Avenue Media Solutions.

Thompson, N. and Gilbert, P. (2019) *Reflective Supervision: A Learning and Development Manual*, 2nd edn, Brighton, Pavilion.

Thompson, S. and Thompson, N. (2023) *The Critically Reflective Practitioner*, 3rd edn, London, Bloomsbury.

Turner, P. (2002) *HR Forecasting and Planning*, London, Chartered Institute of Personnel and Development.

Uchitelle, L. (2007) *The Disposable American: Layoffs and their Consequences*, New York, Vintage.

Vigoda, E. (2003) *Developments in Organizational Politics: How Political Dynamics Affect Employee Performance in Modern Work Sites*, Cheltenham, Edward Elgar.

Walton, M. (2008) 'In Consideration of a Toxic Workplace: A Suitable Place for Treatment', in Kinder, Hughes and Cooper (2008b).

Whittington, R., Regner, P., Angwin, D., Johnson, G. and Scholes, K. (2020) *Exploring Strategy: Text and Cases*, 12th edn, London, Prentice-Hall.

Wilkins, D., Shemmings, D. and Pascoe, C. (2019) *Child Abuse: An Evidence Base for Confident Practice*, 5th edn, London, Open University Press.